Beachcomber's
Handbook

Also by Euell Gibbons

STALKING THE WILD ASPARAGUS

STALKING THE BLUE-EYED SCALLOP

STALKING THE HEALTHFUL HERBS

EUELL GIBBONS'

Beachcomber's Handbook

with drawings by ROBERT MOWRY

DAVID McKAY COMPANY, INC.

New York

BEACHCOMBER'S HANDBOOK

Library of Congress Catalog Card Number: 67-24913

MANUFACTURED IN THE UNITED STATES OF AMERICA

VAN REES PRESS • NEW YORK

To my favorite beachcombers,
Colleen, Kelly Jo, Mike, and Johnny,
who are also my grandchildren.

Contents

Beachcomber's
Handbook

1. So You Want to Go Native

DO you ever dream of a little South Sea isle where life is easy because it has been reduced to its simplest terms? Do you sometimes think that you would gladly trade your suburban split-level for a grass shack if only it were located in a climate so pleasant that it would make both central heating and air-conditioning redundant? Do you often feel that you are becoming enslaved to alarm clocks, train schedules, office schedules, starting time, quitting time, mealtime and bedtime?

Are you occasionally tempted to blow it all away, catch a boat for some tropical paradise where food and drink can be plucked from the nearest tree, where the only timepiece needed is the warm sun in a tropical sky and even that need not be heeded unless you choose to do so, where social and economic pressures cannot press you, and no man can order your coming and going?

If you experience such urges, feel neither proud nor guilty. The South Sea dream is almost universal in our culture, as you can easily discover if you pry into the private thoughts of your friends and neighbors. Man probably originated in a tropical environment where life was easy, so perhaps this widespread fantasy has a logical basis in our development.

I don't know when the South Sea dream first sprang up in me, for it has been there as long as I can remember. Early on, I learned to appreciate the gifts and beauty of every facet of nature in temperate regions. But always a part of me yearned quietly for coral reefs and coconuts and a climate that never grew cold.

In some ways all my early life was a preparation for the day I would land on a tropical isle. I developed skills in hunting, fishing, botany, boatbuilding, cooking, and carpentry, always with half an eye on how such accomplishments would be useful to a beachcomber. I very early discovered the voluminous literature on this subject and read my way through everything written about the areas toward which I was drawn. In common with many other children of my generation I read and reread *Robinson Crusoe, Masterman Ready, Swiss Family Robinson,* and *Coral Island,* among others. One of the amazing aspects of these books is that not one of the four authors ever set foot on a tropical island. They all made glaring errors in natural history, but out of their imaginations were able to create classics that fed the fantasies of many generations.

Later additions to the tropical island literature seemed to become more accurate. I worked my way through Melville, Stevenson, London, O'Brian, and, as they appeared, Frisbee, Nordhoff and Hall, and many less well-known authors. I read the journals of the early explorers, such as Captain Cook and George Vancouver, with the same avidity with which I consumed the finer novels with settings in this area. I soaked up the works of the naturalists of the tropical Pacific, from Darwin and Wallace to Degener and Abbot. I devoured hula novels and textbooks on tropical agriculture with complete impartiality. I was not seeking literary excellence, and even the dullest government report, encyclopedia entry, or treatise on the ethnology of island dwellers could interest me.

I was past thirty years old when I made my first tropical landfall, not on some primitive isle, but at the modern city of Honolulu, on Oahu, in the Hawaiian Islands. An opportunity to spend a year in Hawaii had been offered, and I jumped at the chance. My first coconut palm with its crown of feathery leaves and its large load of smooth, green coconuts sent a thrill through me reminiscent of my first adolescent kiss. A ripe mango, plucked from a wayside tree, tasted like a dream fulfilled.

At that time I had not the slightest intention of making any place in the Hawaiian Islands the site of my venture. I thought of my year there as a postgraduate course in beachcombing, with the Bishop Museum, the University of Hawaii, and the Library of Hawaii furnishing dozens of texts that I had never seen before, and the whole island to use as a laboratory of tropical living. I intended to soak up knowledge for a year, then move on to a more isolated and primitive island.

I was not disappointed in the island of Oahu. I had expected it to be badly infested with tourists, and it was, but I was pleasantly surprised to find that their addiction to super-service hotels, bars, taxicabs, and spectator entertainment kept the tourists fairly well confined to certain limited areas. Honolulu is an overcivilized American city with traffic jams, slums, high society, and industry. Yet only a few miles from the center of this populous city you can find wild isolated mountain valleys where untamed tropical fruits of many kinds go untouched. Waikiki Beach is small, crowded, and hemmed in by luxurious tourist hotels, but across the island there are miles of unspoiled beach and rugged but wonderful shoreline.

As a graduate school in beachcombing Oahu was superb. As the year wore on I discovered that all the elements of the kind of life I wanted to live could be found there. Coconut palms were plentiful, and best of all, most of the nuts went unclaimed, so I could have all the coconuts I could use for the taking. In the mountains, and even by rural roadsides, I found wild bananas, breadfruit, citrus fruits, avocados, macadamia nuts, passionfruit, mangoes, guavas, and other species of wild tropical fruit in greater quantities than I could ever use. The surrounding sea was filled with tasty fish of many varieties, as well as crabs, spiny lobsters, and many other kinds of seafood just waiting for someone with interest and skill enough to take them. Wild pigs and wild goats could be hunted in the mountains, and on nearby islands there were wild cattle and deer, and wild sheep.

My year of apprenticeship ended. I secretly awarded myself an advanced degree in beachcombing and prepared to set off in search of the ideal South Sea isle. I did not plan to devote the rest of my life to beachcombing. Life holds too many interests for me to want to devote all of it to any one thing. But I did want to cut myself a large slice of this kind of life and savor it slowly, so as to relish its flavor and texture to the utmost.

Then I met Jim, a bona-fide beachcomber and a kindred spirit. Appropriately enough, we met in a coconut grove. I was driving my secondhand Jeep along a sandy road where someone had recently chopped down a dozen heavily fruited coconut palms to make room for a house foundation. I couldn't resist such a windfall. I set to work loading my Jeep with ripe eating nuts and drinking nuts, and then started hacking at the leafy crowns of the trees with my machete. At the very top of the trunk of each coconut palm, buried down at the center of that crown of leaves, there is a snow-white, tender, crisp and tasty palm heart that is the finest salad material in all nature. I refuse to destroy a living palm in order to get this delicacy, but when "progress" decrees that a coconut palm be destroyed, I would never hesitate to show up with my machete to salvage that delicious heart.

One time, when I was busy cutting out palm hearts, an old car pulled up behind my Jeep and a big, red-faced man got out carrying a cane knife. He limped to the nearest felled palm and started hacking out the heart. Up until then, I'd often wondered if I were the only person on the island interested in such wild produce, so this was like meeting a relative in Timbuctoo. He, too, recognized our brotherhood. We soon were seated on a palm trunk with opened drinking nuts in deepest fraternity, talking away the whole tropical afternoon.

As a young man, Jim had sailed on tramp steamers, blackbirding (or labor-recruiting) vessels, and trading schooners, all over the Pacific. At one time or another he had been stranded in every so-called beachcomber's paradise in the South Seas. His seagoing career had abruptly ended some twenty years before when his right leg was badly crushed in a shipboard accident, and he was awarded a lifetime pension as compensation. Permanently beached, with a small but steady income, Jim soon married a native girl from a community of Samoans that had immigrated to Hawaii. They acquired a cottage by the sea and had been doing a pretty efficient job of beachcombing ever since, right on Oahu.

When the sun touched the mountain behind us, Jim suggested that we move the conversation indoors. We drove to his place near the beach, an unpretentious, square, tropical bungalow. It had boxed-and-stripped walls and a low-pitched sheet-iron roof with wide, overhang-ing eaves, and was set in a tangle of tropical fruit trees and colorful ornamentals. The outside walls had been painted green years before, but time had mellowed the color until it blended beautifully with the riotous growth around it.

We dined simply but exceedingly well on broiled butterfish, palm heart salad and bowls of poi served with onions, red peppers, and small dishes of reddish Hawaiian salt, all graciously served by Jim's enormous Samoan wife, Falani. She had been a typical South Sea beauty in her youth, but, like many women in the tropics, had put on weight very easily as she grew older. She carried all that poundage with a gracefulness, however, that only Polynesian women seem to possess. Their two children, a girl 18, and a boy 20, came in sepa-rately and briefly to grab a bite to eat before going out for the eve-ning, rather bluntly refusing to tell their parents where they were headed. The genes of white men and Polynesian women blend beau-tifully, and Jim's two offspring were as handsome a pair of rebellious adolescents as I ever met.

When the table was cleared, Falani opened one of the drinking nuts for herself, and made Jim and me a pot of fragrant Kona coffee to sip while the three of us sat around the kitchen table and talked. I liked this hospitable couple from the very first, and when I told them of my plans to do nothing for a time but live off the land on some tropical island, they backed me up with enthusiasm and advice.

Jim chewed awhile on my problem, then said, "Look, mate, in this last year of playing around at survival on this island, didn't it occur to you that you are already in the best possible place to live the kind of life you want? There isn't a thing on those more isolated islands you keep talking about that can't be found where you're sit-ting right now. The wild fruits, the edible wild plants, the fish and the wild game, are all here in any quantity you want, and there's less competition for it than there was when this was one of those primi-tive islands. The trouble with the real South Seas is that the people are poor, and every palm and every fruit tree has an owner who will claim its produce. Do you think you could just walk up and help yourself to drinking nuts and palm heart down there as we did here this afternoon? The man who cut the trees and the owner of the land would probably be squabbling over them, because both of them would need the food. The people here are so rich by comparison that they wouldn't be seen dead hacking out a palm heart. They'd be afraid their neighbors might think they couldn't afford to buy their food at the supermarket. Most of them never tasted either drinking nuts or palm heart, and don't want to. I'll tell you, if there's a beachcomber's paradise anywhere in the Pacific, it's right here on good old civilized Oahu."

I protested that trying to live a beachcomber's existence around sophisticated Honolulu would rob the experience of meaning.

"Meaning!" Jim snorted. Suddenly his face cleared and brightened. He said, "Let's look at something else for a minute. When Thoreau wanted to live the simple life in a primitive manner, did he pack up and go to the Maine woods or out to the Western wilderness? He did not. He built a shack on the shore of Walden Pond just a half-hour's walk from Concord, and only a good day's walk from the big city of Boston. If he had gone out to the frontier, he would have been living just like everybody else lived out there, not because they wanted to, but because they had to, and the experience would have had very little meaning. If there was anything to prove by living that way out in the backwoods, the people there had already proved it. To show that living close to nature had meaning and value he had to do it where nobody else was living that way. Do you think that his experience at Walden Pond had no meaning because it was only twenty miles from Boston? That's what gave it meaning. The only way he could prove that such existence was worthwhile, and even enjoyable, was to live it where he could walk out on it any time he wanted to. That's the only way he could convince himself, and everybody else, that he was really living such a life from free choice, and not just because that's all there was out there."

The very next day I stopped studying how to become a beachcomber and started being one.

The job I had on a newspaper was coming to a finish, and I had made no future commitments, so there was nothing to hold me back. I had a little money in the bank, but not enough to live even one year in the style in which I was then living. My small, but expensive, apartment in Honolulu simply wouldn't do as a beachcomber's headquarters. Only a day or two before, an acquaintance had told me that he would like to find someone willing to exchange a bit of yard work for the rent on a little cottage that stood on his place, out beyond Diamond Head. I was at his door before he sat down to breakfast. He owned two acres, lying between the road and a small tidal creek, with a very satisfactory rural and tropical atmosphere about it. His was a modern house, near the road, but behind it were obviously neglected grounds, overrun by a jungle of tropical trees and palms, with no cottage in sight. He was surprised to find me interested in his proposition, and led me on a path through many kinds of trees and shrubs, then along the creek bank, past a huge clump of bamboo. There, under a mighty kamani-nut tree, stood my beachcomber's shack. It was just a tiny cottage of single-wall construction, with a flat, tar-paper-covered roof, piled high with leaves and nuts that had fallen from the kamani tree. But I could already see, in my mind's eye, how it would look when I had finished with it. We made a deal, and before nightfall I had moved into my new home.

The next morning, when I explored the grounds, I knew I had found my tropical paradise. There were twenty-two coconut palms, most of the dwarf or Samoan variety, but there is nothing "dwarf" about such palms except their height. The leaves are often longer and the nuts larger than on the tall varieties. A hedge that separated the place from the next property was of carissa, or Natal plum, and the thorny shrubs bore fragrant white blossoms, green and ripe fruit, all at the same time. Up near the road were three large mango trees, all bearing heavy crops of fruit, which at this time, in early March, were still green and hard. Along the driveway there were half a dozen carambolas, or starfruit trees. There was neither bloom nor fruit on these trees now, but I knew there would be an abundance of delicious starfruit come next November. Just behind the landlord's house were three tall breadfruit trees that cast a beautiful pattern of shadows with their lacy leaves. Their fruit was not yet ripe, but they seemed to be setting a good crop.

Opposite the main house there was a long row of papaya trees that had been topped at some time in the past, causing them to branch. They were most exotic and ancient-looking, like something out of the coal age. Each branch terminated in a tiny, palm-like top bearing a few ripe fruits, some green ones, some blossoms and buds, for the papaya is a true tropical plant and knows no season.

Near the stream I found a clump of bananas, growing too thickly to do well, but there was one bunch that had ripened on the stalk, and the ripe bananas were beginning to fall off on the ground. Here also I found four fig trees, one with a few ripe figs on it, which I immediately appropriated. I also picked a few Surinam cherries from some bushes that overhung the stream. Near my shack there were three lime trees, head-high, that characteristically were bearing blooms, young limes, and fully grown fruit, all at the same time. Finally, there was a spreading litchi tree that would bear this favorite fruit of the Chinese when ripe.

I gloried in a beachcomber breakfast of fresh figs, bananas, sweet ripe papaya with a wedge of lime, and a green coconut, all picked right from the grounds. I not only drank the refreshing water from the green coconut, but also split it open and ate the custard-like spoon-meat from the inside, to top off my meal. And then to work. For the next few weeks, my life had little resemblance to the popular picture of a beachcomber loafing in the shade while some half-dressed beauty fans his brow. My landlord was highly pleased at the speed with which I brought the unruly grounds into subjection. Then I started working twelve hours a day remodeling the hut under the kamani tree.

In my daydreams I had always seen myself beachcombing from a pretty little thatched hut that blended perfectly with its tropical background, and I determined that in this respect, at least, reality would be faithful to the dream. I bought a load of secondhand two-by-fours and framed a steeply pitched roof right over the flat roof that was already on the cottage. As I cleaned the grounds, I had saved every huge leaf that I could pull from the palms, and I had a mighty pile of them, though it turned out to be not nearly enough. I split strips from each side of the heavy leaf midribs with all the leaflets still attached to the strip, and thatched the roof by laying the strips of leaflets on the rafters as one would lay shingles. When I tacked the first strip right on the eaves, the long leaflets hung down and almost touched the ground. The next strip, laid just above and touching the first one, drooped its leaflets nearly as low, and as I worked upward I soon had a dense curtain of thatch hanging from the eaves that almost hid the house.

I had visitors. The Hawaiians who lived in the neighborhood gathered around to see this strange operation. Few of them had ever seen a thatched roof, and this crazy *haole* with his primitive building methods excited their curiosity. When it became apparent that my pile of coconut leaves would never finish the job, their natural friendliness sent them scouting for more thatch. When one reported a new source of coconut leaves, we would jump into my Jeep and go after them. While gathering the leaves we helped ourselves to Jeep-loads of drinking nuts to refresh our local sidewalk superintendents. When these nuts were opened, ukuleles made their appearance, songs were started, and the house raising always turned into a party.

The onlookers and merrymakers became helpers, some splitting off the strips of leaflets, some passing them up, and others tacking and tying them into place. Everybody wanted to get into the act, and I could have played Tom Sawyer and levied a fee for the privilege. The thatch was soon laid to the ridge and then was capped with the heavy base sections of the coconut leaf midribs, laid concave side down and spiked into place with long nails into the ridge pole. Then we took the hedge shears and trimmed the untidy, overhanging leaves into a neat line at the eaves, and with this haircut my thatched roof took on a surprisingly well-groomed and businesslike appearance.

A thatched roof over conventional walls may be picturesque in Ireland, but for a tropical island it simply won't do. I decided to complete my exterior decoration by covering the outside walls with coconut leaf matting. The mats used were simple things, made by weaving the leaflets of two thatching strips together. My Hawaiian helpers all knew how to weave these "lover's mats," though they had never before used them as house siding. Most of the older Hawaiians there had, however, used them for other purposes in their younger days, and they made many broad jokes as they wove them for me. We tacked the long mats upright, edge to edge, right around the house, covering everything but the doors and windows. One of the Hawaiian women, with an artistic bent, painted the entrance door a sand color, then decorated it with a Hawaiian *tapa* design in dark brown. At one end I built a thatched lean-to to shelter my wood-lathe, for I intended to earn some of the cash I would need by turning decorative bowls from the beautiful tropical hardwoods available in the Islands.

The exterior appearance of my beachcomber's shack was now deeply satisfying to me, for it was an almost exact replica of the house of my daydreams. The lover's mats with which it was sided had been woven of green leaves, so my house changed color daily as the leaves ripened into patterns of greens, golds, and browns. This everchanging mosaic of soft colors and blending patterns was a source of delight to me for several weeks before my unusual siding settled permanently into a soft shade of brown that seemed perfectly at home in its exotic setting.

The interior of my cottage was an improvement over anything I had ever dared to dream. Not only was it spacious, homey, and comfortable, but there was a kitchen with electrical appliances and a bathroom with a shower and a flush toilet. The rest of the house was one big bed-sitting-dining room where a sense of spaciousness was achieved by holding to Spartan simplicity in the furnishings. A happy Hawaiian combination, the *punee*, was a help, for it is a sofa by day and a bed by night. The floor was covered with lauhala matting, wall to wall, which felt good to the soles of my bare feet, for I had acquired the Japanese habit of leaving my shoes at the door, if I happened to be wearing those abominable articles of civilized dress, which was as little as possible. I never felt cramped in my little house, for in Hawaii's glorious year-round summer my living space didn't stop at the front door, but extended out under the kamani tree, around the clump of bamboo, through the coconut grove, and to wherever I might choose to spend my day or night on the island.

I lived in my thatched hut for almost three years, and during that time over ninety percent of all my food came from hunting, fishing, and foraging for the wild fruits and plants that grow so bountifully on that island. At no other period of my life have I enjoyed a better diet, either nutritionally or gastronomically. My goal was not merely to prove that one could survive on foraged fare; I had no desire to demonstrate how little I could get by on and survive. I wanted to live the good life on nature's generosity, and in the matter of food I succeeded very well. I enjoyed such toothsome morsels as crayfish cocktails, crab salads, and broiled spiny lobsters. I ate Portuguese sausage made of wild goat and wild pig meat, and *teriyaki* steaks of venison and wild beef. I had some of the tastiest fish that swam, prepared in many appetizing ways. I waxed healthy and happy over salads of tender palm heart, rich avocados, and crisp *limu*, or edible seaweed. My taste buds were thrilled by sliced mangoes covered with whipped coconut cream, guava chiffon pie, and passionfruit sherbets. For beverages I had coconut water and many kinds of fruit juices and punches. If I wanted more potent potables, there were palm wine, panini swipes, arrack, and *okolehau*, all prepared in my kitchen of native materials. My meals were often simple, by choice, but with the wide variety of delicacies that were available for the taking, they were never monotonous.

I made no attempt to live entirely without money, but I found, as time went on, that I was living higher on less, as I perfected the fine art of freeloading on Mother Nature. The little cash that I found necessary was earned by selling fish, wood-turning, selling or bartering wild produce, and (in minute amounts) from writing. Sometimes my bank account became precariously low, but at the end of the three years it was back almost exactly to where it started.

I believe it is the duty of every man who treads a little-known path to make it easier for the next person who might come that way.

Whenever I discovered a technique that worked, or developed a recipe that I thought especially good, I made a note of it, and these I now pass on to you in this book. Outside of those few jottings, I made no attempt to write about the life as I lived it, for I feared that this would inject a note of artificiality into my actions. At that time I wanted any talent I may possess to be applied to living, not writing. I believe that one can only write about such an experience after time and distance have given the perspective needed to evaluate it properly.

Don't think that the information in this book is applicable only to Hawaii. The same plants that are found in Hawaii grow around the world on tropical islands. An outrigger canoe will sail as well on Chesapeake Bay or Lake Okechobee as it will on the Pacific. The coconut palms of Florida and the Bahamas stand ready to yield toddy to the first person who approaches them armed with the correct techniques and the right spirit. The breadfruit of the West Indies is the same valuable food that is the staff of life in the Marquesas, even if you find the West Indian natives ignoring it.

Do not be stopped from trying the things you learn here because you don't find them practiced by local residents in other tropical areas. The techniques, recipes, and methods you will find in this book were collected from many sources, and many of them had never, to my knowledge, been practiced in Hawaii until I introduced them into my own domestic economy. I have caught squillas along the New Jersey shore and crabs in Maine using techniques I learned in Hawaii. I have used methods learned on the Red River to catch fish in Honolulu Harbor. Don't be timid about transferring practices from one area to another, even though the local residents never heard about them. The natives just might learn something they never knew before. It has been done.

It is not necessary to become a full-time beachcomber in order to use the information in this book. Any resident or visitor of almost any tropical area will find things here to make his life richer or his visit more memorable. A man who travels to a tropical country and then tries to live exactly as he did at home has wasted his passage money. However, even those who stay home and only travel to tropical islands from an armchair will find here the technical direction necessary in order to create a really first-class daydream.

Are you tempted? Would you like to shake off the shackles of conventional society and live the carefree life of a beachcomber? Could it actually be done in this modern age? Well, the fruit, fish, and game are all still there. The physical requisites of a well-founded life of beachcombing actually exist in many areas. However, making a success of it depends a great deal more on the attitudes, attributes, and skills of the man who is doing it than it does on the place he is in. The big question is whether you are the beachcomber type. Are your talents and temperament such that you could actually make your living outside our commercial-industrial complex and enjoy doing it? I won't try to devise an aptitude test for potential beachcombers, but I've often asked some questions that can help decide whether or not you are geared to this life.

First: Are you lazy? Contrary to popular opinion a lazy man makes a poor beachcomber. Hunting, hiking, fishing, food gathering, and tree climbing are all strenuous activities, so if you hate to move a muscle, then this life is not for you. On the other hand there are people who hate work but put unbelievable amounts of energy into hobbies, recreation, or fun, and these people make excellent beachcombers. Artistic beachcombing is a strenuous sport, but that's what it is, a sport. I probably put forth more effort during my beachcombing years than I ever did on a paid job, but since no one was telling me what to do, and no one was paying me for it, I never considered it work. I was merely playing hard and enjoying every minute of it.

Second: Are you *really* interested? Are you certain that you would enjoy gathering nature's bounty and converting it to your own use? Do you engage in any beachcomber-like activities right now? Do you ever go fishing, hunting, crabbing, or clam-digging, and even more important, do you enjoy cleaning and cooking your own catch? Have you ever picked mulberries, blackberries, blueberries, or wild strawberries? Do you know how to find, identify, and cook any of the many delicious varieties of wild mushroom that grow throughout our country? Do you ever gather and eat any of the many kinds of wild greens, salads, and vegetables that grow all around us? Did you ever collect a hoard of black walnuts, hickory nuts, hazelnuts, or any of the many other kinds of excellent wild food that can be found along any country roadside? If you have done none of these things, what makes you think you will change merely by going to a tropical island?

If you have not actually practiced any of these things, but still find the subject fascinating, why not try a little beachcombing right where you are? I have continued to be a beachcomber wherever I have gone, and find the pursuit scarcely less fascinating in mainland United States than it is on a tropical island. If you will investigate, you will find that I have tried to make that path easier, too, by writing several manuals on how to glean food from our own fields, forests, roadsides, and shores, and have a lot of fun and good eating while doing it. If you find joy in such foraging, you would make a fine beachcomber, and the experience gained during your home-town novitiate will serve you well on a tropical island.

Third: How set are your food prejudices? Some people find it a real trial to eat any food with which they are not already familiar. I have seen foreigners here, and Americans abroad, who actually suffered because familiar food wasn't available. If a man can eat only the kinds of food that Mother used to make, he had better stay pretty close to Mother.

Fourth: Are you security conscious? There is no future in beachcombing. There are no pension plans or fringe benefits. Beachcombing is for those adventurous souls who believe in life in the present and the bounty it offers in all its aspects. On the other hand, a dedicated application of the basic principles of beachcombing can make a tiny income stretch miraculously.

Fifth: Are you a status seeker? Films and TV have glamorized the beachcomber, but in the tropics he is still considered a bum. If it takes social recognition, prestige, and status symbols to keep you contented, you would make a most unhappy beachcomber. Don't imagine that you can escape the social stigma by posing as a writer who is gathering material for a book. Half the beachcombers in the tropics have tried this gambit, and it long ago has lost any usefulness it may once have had. General opinion remains that the beachcomber is a bum and that a beachcomber who poses as a writer is both a bum *and* a fraud.

Now, perhaps, you want to ask me some questions. One image of a beachcomber is that of a dissolute character living in a sort of tropical harem. I'm afraid this leads us into a field where I am far from being an expert. I never had to elude the pursuit of women before

going to the Islands, and things did not change very much when I
got there. True, my Hawaiian friends considered my celibate life a
grave hardship and tried to remedy it, but the women they shoved
my way were mostly spinsters and widows about my own age, and
this is hardly the most desirable segment of Island femininity. I was
advancing into my thirties when I went there, and this may be a
bit late to exploit this side of life to its fullest. A Hawaiian friend of
mine who was visiting the mainland was asked what was the best
time to visit the Islands and he replied, "The best time is between
the ages of twenty and thirty."

I don't usually think of women as an asset to a beachcomber, but
rather as one of the hazards he will face. I have known several promising young beachcombers who seemed to be developing real art in
this way of life, only to have their careers wrecked by women. These
handsome youngsters thought that being a beachcomber included leaving a trail of ravished maidens and broken hearts among the female
population of the Islands. Such predatory thinking fails to take into
account the counter-predatory skills possessed by women of all races
and nations. Most of these men are now married, working at steady
jobs and raising housefuls of beautiful little *hapa-haoles,* and have
long since lost their identities as beachcombers.

Alcohol can be a major hazard to the beachcomber. I have nothing
against liquor when it is used in moderation by a man who can
handle it, and later I'll even tell you how you can make your own
potent beverages from tropical ingredients, but overindulgence in
drink has ruined many an otherwise promising beachcomber by rob-
bing him of energy and dulling the interest he must have in order
to get a real kick out of foraging his own living from the land and
sea. He is likely to find himself turning down opportunities to go
hunting, fishing, or foraging in order to nurse a hangover. Some
beachcombers obviously become wastrels and barflies. If that is what
you want to be, there is no need to go to a tropical island, for that
species seems to survive in all countries and climates.

Women and liquor are not, however, the greatest hazards the
beachcomber will have to hurdle. The biggest obstacle of all is the
constant and persistent temptation to reform and become respectable.
The beachcomber who has decided to abandon the rat-race will in-

evitably be offered chances to "better himself" more seductive than any that came along when he would have welcomed them. The conventional world must envy true insouciance, for society seems to conspire to destroy this happy state whenever it crops up.

Frequently, someone asks a question that goes something like this, "If life as a beachcomber is so all-fired pleasant, why did you ever leave it?" That's a good question and deserves a better answer than I am likely to give, but I'll try. Primarily, I wanted to learn what beachcombing had to teach me about nature and her stores and then go on to explore some other facet of the fascinating possibilities that life offers. In a sense, I didn't quit—I graduated. I have found other experiences to be lived and other joys to savor.

Maybe that sounds like a pretty good answer, but it doesn't happen to be the whole truth. The facts are that I succumbed to some of the very hazards against which I have warned others. During my last year of beachcombing I found it very easy to provide for my needs and had ample time for peripheral pursuits. I enrolled in some courses that were related to the life I was leading, such as botany, biology, and Pacific anthropology, at the University of Hawaii. I undertook these studies purely for pleasure, but they had a result that I had not foreseen. Suddenly, my social status bounded upward, and the image of a university student began to eclipse my identity as a beachcomber, even in my own mind. Ambition, the cardinal sin of the beachcomber's decalogue, began to stir.

Then, in one of my classes at the university, I met The Wahine, not an exotic island beauty, but a pretty schoolteacher, near my own age, who came from Philadelphia. One thing led to another, as things will, and I found myself a married man, holding down a respectable position with regular hours, responsibilities, and paychecks. This was far from being an unmitigated disaster, partly because The Wahine turned out to be a pretty good beachcomber in her own right.

We moved to the island of Maui and reveled in its rural atmosphere and ample opportunities to satisfy our beachcombing bent. We plucked a large part of our food from the woods, mountains, and sea, not from necessity, but because we infinitely preferred this fresh, natural food to the stale, imported stuff in the markets. Foraging, no longer a full-time vocation for me, became an interesting and pleasant avocation for us both. It not only brought us fresh and delicious food,

but furnished us with fun and recreation and taught us a new approach to nature, a new attitude toward life, and new methods of
adapting to our environment that have enriched our lives wherever
we have gone. This common interest and shared hobby have been
some of the finest fruits of the training I acquired during the three
years of intensive beachcombing that preceded our marriage.

What was accomplished, and what did I prove by those three years?
Very little in the eyes of some. An ex-friend of mine, who is a pro-
fessor of economics, once tried to argue that my beachcoming experience offered no solution to the frustrations and complications of
modern life, because it was not universally applicable. "What would
happen," he asked, "if everyone ran off and became a beachcomber?"
I couldn't resist observing that in that case, more of them would be
likely to survive than if everybody became professional economists.
As I say, he's an ex-friend.

I hope no way of life is ever discovered that is so universally applicable that it will reduce us all to dull uniformity. I want to live
in a world with as many different kinds of people in it as possible,
and I believe an individual sometimes contributes merely by being
different in a creative way. I do not advocate a general abandonment
of civilization and a return to the primitive, but for some individuals,
especially those who may be "heeding a distant drum," neither that
door nor any other should be completely closed.

I spent three years doing exactly as I wanted to do, and in my eyes
those years need no further justification. I also acquired a body of
knowledge that would be hard to come by in any other way, and I
learned a kind of self-reliance that is rare in this intricately inter-
dependent, industrial civilization. I lost the unhealthy urge to battle
with nature, and completely recovered from the idea that man should
be engaged in the conquest of nature. I found nature full of unexpected kindnesses, mercies, and joys. I learned to live intimately with
nature in a spirit of cooperation and love, bolstered by deep respect
for her ways.

I learned to recognize the plants and trees that could minister to
my needs, and developed new methods of utilizing them. I learned
the ways of the sea and its myriads of strange and beautiful inhabitants. I learned to stalk the wild animals of the mountains and discovered many of their secrets. My eyes developed new discrimination,

my hands new skills, and my body new strength and agility, while my mind acquired greater ingenuity and my soul learned to be at peace. I not only built a house and a boat, but also a way of life, and at the same time I was engaged in building a man. In those three short years was crowded an experience that is my most treasured memory. No other period of my life is so free of regrets. I had very little money, but I did have huge estates of time—time to fish, hunt, and forage, time to teach myself new skills and handicrafts, time to observe and ponder, time to study and read, time to write, time to think, and time to dream.

AVOCADO
Persea americana

In recent years the avocado has become a familiar item on the produce shelves of Northern supermarkets, and many Americans have learned to relish its buttery flesh and nut-like taste. It adds not only delicious flavor, but a touch of exotic luxury to party spreads, dips, hors d'oeuvres, or fancy salads. Thanks to the availability of avocados on the Islands, in this respect, as in many others, the penniless beachcomber can live as luxuriously as any millionaire. I have known Hawaiian families, living in shacks and so poor they couldn't raise the price of a pound of poi, who nevertheless gathered avocados by the bushelbasketful and fed them to their pigs.

The Aztecs cultivated this rich fruit in Mexico long before the coming of the Spaniards. They called it *ahaucatl* in their language, a name that the Spaniards corrupted to *aguacate*, and we in turn further corrupted to avocado, or even worse, alligator pear. Hawaiians usually just call them "pears," a very ambiguous and unsatisfactory term.

The avocado was unknown to the ancient Hawaiians, as it was only introduced into the Islands in the 19th century, but this fruit has found a congenial home there and often grows spontaneously in the forests and along moist, shady roadsides. It is a quick-growing tree, often producing fruit the fourth year after the seed is planted. Any beachcomber worth his salt can always find a source of wild avocados for his table, although he might have to search to get the very best varieties.

Like so many tropical fruits, the avocado is borne on a beautiful tree that is well worth planting as an ornamental. Due to seedling variation and accidental hybridization the avocado in Hawaii has already proliferated into dozens of varieties. These vary in size, shape, color, and quality of fruit, the ratio of edible flesh to seed, and the time of fruiting. The Hawaiians roughly divide these into "summer pears" and "winter pears," but there are numberless varieties of each, some of which have acquired local, common names, but these folk terms vary too widely to be of much use in identification.

The flesh of the ripe avocado is usually yellow about the seed, shading off to deep green near the rind. This flesh may be buttery or watery, fibrous or fiberless, according to variety. The cultivated kinds are selected seedlings of the best varieties, although many wild trees bear delicious fruit that would be well worth preserving and propagating. Besides the olive, no other commonly used fruit has as high a fat content as the avocado. The natives of Central America commonly use the avocado as a meat substitute, and calorie-wise, avocado flesh is more nutritious, pound for pound, than beefsteak. Even carnivorous animals, like the dog and cat, readily eat avocados when introduced to them at an early age, and pigs thrive and grow fat on this oily fruit. The practice of feeding avocados to these animals has been the source of some of the common names used for different varieties.

By keeping close watch on a dozen wild trees of several varieties I was able to keep myself well-supplied with avocados from about the middle of June until the following February. I fondly remember one tree of "winter pears" that bore bumper crops of almost perfectly spherical fruit, about the size and shape of a baseball, with a hard woody shell. The flesh of these fruits was entirely fiber-free, with a delicious nutty flavor. They ripened over a long period, and I was able to gather a pailful of ripe fruit, once per week, from this one tree, for over three months. I fairly reveled in avocados while this tree was in production, and even shared them with my neighbors.

I once presented some of these prime fruits to the minister of a nearby church, and a few evenings later, while I was visiting in their home, his wife asked me whether I liked avocados. When I assured her that I did, she brought the same avocados to me and said, "Someone, I forget who, gave us these a few days ago. We don't like avocados, but I never refuse a gift, for it does people so much good merely to give things away."

I thanked her profusely and did not enlighten her about the source of the fruit she was so graciously giving me, for, I reflected, the case in hand proved her contention. I had received the joy of making a generous gift, and she had experienced the same pleasure; I had also enjoyed receiving a gift and could still look forward to the pleasure of eating the avocados, which cost nothing in the first place. Despite the hard service these avocados had seen, they didn't taste the least bit shopworn.

The simplest way to eat an avocado is to slice it in half, remove the seed, pour some kind of dressing into the cavity, and serve it "on the half-shell." As to the proper dressing for an avocado, tastes differ widely. I once sat at a table where six of us were eating avocados. One merely salted his, another filled the cavity with mayonnaise, another used French dressing, one covered his with catsup, another ate his covered with finely minced onion, while the sixth one sprinkled sugar over the avocado. Sugar? Yes, gruesome as it may sound, avocado really combines well with sugar. Try it sometime. My own favorite dressings are guava catsup (see index) or French dressing flavored liberally with onion juice.

As a salad or fruit cocktail ingredient the avocado has no peer, as it combines well with almost any kind of fruit or vegetable. I have used it in tossed salads, arranged salads, fruit salads, and gelatin salads. To make one of my favorite lunches I used to peel half a wild avocado and fill the cavity heaping full of crab or lobster salad, made from freshly caught crustaceans that I had pulled from the water myself. Man! that was living, with a capital L, in the very lap of luxury.

To make a mouth-watering sandwich filling, canapé spread, or party dip, put the flesh of one avocado through a sieve to mash it thoroughly and to remove any fiber. To this sieved pulp add ¼ teaspoon salt, 1 teaspoon grated onion, a little lime juice, and a dash of Worcestershire sauce. If it is to be served as a dip, rub the serving bowl with a cut clove of garlic before putting the avocado mixture into it. This is really good with potato chips, corn chips, crackers, or bread.

To us the avocado is a salad fruit, but in Brazil its chief use is in the flavoring of ice creams and sherbets. The Brazilians know what they are about, and Avocado Ice Cream is something pretty special. To 2 cups of sieved avocado pulp add ¼ teaspoon salt, 2½ cups of sugar, 1 cup pineapple juice, the juice of 2 oranges, and the juice of 2 limes, and stir until the sugar has dissolved. Add 1 pint of milk gradually, stirring until you have a smooth mixture, then freeze in an ice-cream freezer using 8 parts of crushed ice to 1 part rock salt. Coconut milk can be substituted for the cow's milk if you are a purist, but the resulting ice cream will be a bit too fatty for some tastes. With cow's milk this ice cream freezes into a smooth, creamy dream of a dessert that is delicious, healthful, and very nutritious.

Avocado flesh contains a tannin that causes it to develop a very bitter principle if it is cooked for any length of time, so don't try to can any surplus for out-of-season use. However, diced avocados can be added to such hot dishes as soups, stews, or omelettes if you put them in just before serving, only. I have even placed avocado halves in the oven or under the broiler until they were just warmed through, then served them filled with creamed kippered salmon.

Finally, there is Avocado Chiffon Pie. Don't dismiss the avocado as a dessert fruit until you have tried this fluffy, delectable pastry. In a deep saucepan combine ¾ cup of raw sugar (palm sugar is even better), one envelope unflavored gelatin, ½ teaspoon salt, and ¼ teaspoon freshly grated nutmeg. Beat 3 egg yolks slightly, combine with ¾ cup of milk and stir the egg-milk mixture into the raw-sugar mixture. Cook and stir until the mixture just comes to a boil, remove from the heat, and stir until it has cooled slightly; then thoroughly mix in 1¼ cups of sieved avocado pulp. Set the saucepan into the refrigerator until the mixture mounds slightly when spooned. This will take the better part of an hour, so you have plenty of time to make the Graham-Cracker Crust. Crush 18 graham crackers into very fine crumbs; add ¼ cup white sugar, 1 teaspoon unflavored gelatin, and ½ cup melted butter or margarine. Press into shape in a 9-inch pie plate and bake in a 375° oven for only 8 minutes; then cool.

Now, if your avocado mixture is ready, beat the whites of 3 eggs until they stand in soft peaks, gradually add ¼ cup of white sugar, and beat until the egg whites look glossy and will stand up in stiff peaks. Fold the avocado mixture thoroughly into the egg whites and heap the whole into the graham-cracker crust. Chill until set, then serve it proudly, or keep it hidden away for your private consumption.

I'm now sure that everyone can see that the avocado can add to the amenities of life on a tropical island. Before you select the site for your own beachcombing adventure, consider whether the avocado grows there.

2. The Coconut Palm

(Cocos nucifera)

THE coconut palm with its graceful crown of feathery leaves and its burden of meaty fruit is an essential ingredient in the South Sea dream, sometimes vying with bare-breasted *wahines* dancing in its shade for the attention of the dreamer. These semi-nude beauties mainly exist in Northern imaginations, but the coconut palms are really there, on tropical seacoasts everywhere, offering beauty, shade, food, drink, and shelter to the beachcomber who will take the trouble to learn the poorly kept secrets of the coconut.

No one knows where the coconut originated, for this unique palm long ago developed a method of making ocean voyages and has spread itself around the tropical world. Coconuts were the original beachcombers, loving the coral sands of sun-drenched islands, sometimes bending their trunks out over the surf. The ripe nuts, with their buoyant husks and leathery outside skin, may drop from these seaside palms directly into the ocean to be carried by currents to some new land.

The many varieties of the coconut have never been classified botanically. They vary in denseness of crown, length of leaf, size and quality of fruit, and in height, some palms shooting slender trunks 60 to 80 feet in the air, twisting in strange curves and angles against the sky, while other, thicker, more stocky varieties produce huge, delicious coconuts that can be reached from the ground.

Tall or short, the coconut palm is one of the most ornamental objects in the whole plant kingdom. The trunk terminates in a feathery crown of pinnate leaves that wave about in every breeze, and clusters of huge, green triangular nuts hang invitingly beneath. Each leaf is composed of a large, woody midrib, from 6 to 20 feet long, edged with slender leaflets, longer near the base and tapering toward the apex, giving the whole leaf the appearance of a giant feather. As the lower leaves grow old they break from the trunk with a clean cleavage and fall to the ground, so the coconut never has a rat's nest of hanging dead leaves as do some palms. As the old leaves fall, new leaves sprout from the top, and so the tree grows taller, leaf by leaf, each fallen leaf leaving a permanent scar on the trunk which exactly fits the sole of a barefoot climber.

The bloom is produced within a woody spathe resembling a huge ear of green corn, 3 to 4 feet long. If the spathe is cut open, one finds the bloom proper, tightly folded inside. This strange blossom can be displayed in the canoe-shaped bottom half of the spathe, or it can be removed, if one does it carefully, for it is brittle and very easily broken. If one sets the bloom upright it will fall open to resemble an exotic, queerly jointed little tree of polished ivory. Arranged either way, it is a thing of rare beauty.

If the huge spathe is left on the tree, the bloom eventually expands it and breaks free, quickly turning from ivory to brown on exposure to the light. It goes on to produce a cluster of ten to twenty full-sized drinking nuts in about six months, and ripe, fully matured coconuts in less than a year. The coconut is a true tropical palm and knows no season, so one will find blooms, baby nuts, drinking nuts, and ripe nuts all on the same tree at the same time.

The uninitiated usually think only of the coconut as a source of ripe meat and "coconut milk," which is the name applied by the mainland American to the cloudy liquid in the cavity of the ripe nut. In the tropics, however, the liquid inside the ripe or green nuts is called coconut water, and the term milk is reserved exclusively for the creamy white liquid that can be pressed from the meat of the ripe nut.

Coconut water, the clear, cool liquid from the green coconut, is the natural, God-given beverage of the tropics, needing no processing or flavoring, or even a container in which to pour it, for it is best drunk directly from the huge green fruit that produces it. I have seen people add sugar, lemon juice, or even rum or gin to coconut water, but to my taste it was never improved by these additions. Those who have only tasted the cloudy, half-rancid residue of water left in the ripe husked coconuts one buys in Northern markets have no idea what coconut water is like at its best. We sometimes used the water from ripe coconuts in cooking, but one would hardly consider ripe coconut water as a beverage of preference when green "drinking nuts" are hanging on the palms outside one's door.

The perfect drinking nut is full-sized but immature, dark-green, without a trace of the yellow color that characterizes the ripening nut. The husk will be crisp and juicy at the stem end and can be sliced away with one stroke of a sharp machete. The finest drinking nuts are so tightly filled with liquid that one can hear no sloshing when the nut is shaken. If the husk is cut away from the soft eye on such a drinking nut, the membrane that closes the eye will be seen to be bulging outward from the pressure of the liquid within. The water in these perfect nuts has a "bite," as if it had been slightly carbonated, and this adds to its refreshing quality.

Coconuts in prime drinking stage never fall to the ground themselves, but must be plucked from the tree, and here's the rub. This is all very well if the coconuts are of the low-growing kind that can be reached from the ground or a stepladder, but how can you take securely fastened coconuts from the taller palms? The natives simply grasp the small trunk at arms' length, place their feet against the old leaf-scars, and "walk up" to the crown. This is not too hard to learn if you are young and athletic, but I find, as middle age overtakes me, that I can demonstrate my ability to "walk up" a palm only on very low trees that are leaning a long way over from the perpendicular.

Of course, the beachcomber who is also a professional "coconut defruiter" (see page 66) never lacks for coconuts in all stages, but the lineman's spurs he uses will badly scar the trunk if they are used on the same palm too often.

The best device for gathering coconuts, without having to climb the tree at all, is a small, completely recurved pruning hook mounted on the end of a long bamboo pole (see illustration). If you can't buy a suitable hook, any blacksmith will make one for you at a reasonable cost. Keep the inside edge razor-sharp, and all you have to do is poke the hook up behind a coconut, slip it over the stem, and give a slight tug. Or, you can slip it over the main stem and bring the whole cluster tumbling down. You'll never reach the nuts in the tallest palms this way, but I've found that there are always plenty within reach to keep one supplied with fresh drinking nuts.

The Hawaiians have a beautiful song in their language about the glorious feeling of cool coconut water rolling down a thirsty throat. It's a feeling worth singing about. Once The Wahine and I were attempting to walk along the beach from Paia to Kahului on the island of Maui, a distance of about 7 miles. The hot sun, beating down on us and reflecting from the white coral sand, soon dehydrated our bodies and made us dreadfully thirsty. Just when our thirst was becoming unbearable, I spied a low-growing palm of the kind called "Samoan coconut," loaded with huge drinking nuts that could be reached from the ground. Since we were in swimming clothes, we had no knives or tools with us, but I managed to twist several nuts from the trees and crack them on some rocks. The water ran out all along the crack, but by tipping our heads back and holding the cracked coconuts high over our mouths we managed to catch most of the cool liquid. How wonderfully refreshing it was! At that moment I thought this sweet, pleasant drink the most delicious beverage in the world. Never mind if the water we missed dribbled down over our bodies and almost instantly dried into a sticky film. It was worth it, and besides, at our feet was the largest ocean in the world in which to wash ourselves.

A prime drinking nut will contain nearly a quart of this ready-made beverage; the Northerner in the tropics who is living off the land refuses this free offering at the risk of his health. Coconut water has a definite acid reaction in the body, and since most of the food a competent forager will be eating leaves an alkaline residue, this acid is badly needed in the beachcomber's diet. I long have believed that the lethargy which traditionally overcomes the beachcombing white man is in part due to his failure to maintain a proper acid-alkaline balance in his diet.

There is no need to husk a coconut if it is to be used for drinking.

Just slice off a bit of the husk, without breaking into the interior of the nut, at the stem end with a machete or an ordinary carpenter's saw to make a flat surface on which the nut can sit without toppling over. Then, with a brace and bit, drill a hole near the pointed end, into the cavity. Set the coconut on a plate, put a soda-fountain straw into the hole, and serve it proudly. If you are a purist, and find the incongruously civilized plate and soda-fountain straw jarring notes, then by all means serve the drinking nut on a square of *ti* leaf and cut a drinking tube from a section of slender bamboo.

After your drinking nut is emptied, it can be split open with a single stroke of a sharp machete. Inside, next to the hardening shell, you will find a thin layer of soft, jelly-like meat that is nature's own custard. This is called spoon-meat in Hawaii, and it is one of the coconut's finest products, but unfortunately there is very little of it. It would take several coconuts to yield a cupful. Still, I hate to see anything so good go to waste, so I usually split my empty drinking nuts open and eat the sweet, translucent meat with a spoon or a small section of the coconut shell.

We do use ripe coconuts in the tropics, but we seldom just eat the ripe meat. In selecting ripe nuts either from the tree or from those that have fallen to the ground, or for that matter, from the supermarket, always give the nuts a shake and take only those in which you can hear a good quantity of juice sloshing around. Unless you buy your nuts from a market, they have to be husked, and this can be a terrible task. Take an ordinary pick, such as ditch-diggers use, and drive the flattened end firmly into the ground, leaving the pointed end sticking up. Grasp the coconut by the two ends and drive it down on the sharp point, then twist the nut toward you and pry off a section of the husk. Turn the nut over and repeat the process. An expert can remove the husk in less than half a minute, taking it off in three or four pieces. If you want the coconut water, pierce the soft eye with a narrow-bladed knife and drain it into a container. Now, tap the nut all over with a hammer to help loosen the meat from the shell, then strike it sharply around the "equator" until the shell breaks. Use a knife with a heavy blade and pry out the coconut meat in as large pieces as possible.

Unless you are going to eat your coconut meat "as is" it will have to be grated or shredded. The easiest way to do this is with one of the "salad-makers" or "Salad-chefs" that are now on the market, with interchangeable rotary, cone-shaped cutters. With this device you can, in a very few minutes and with little effort, shred more coconut than you can use in a week. If you are making coconut products only for yourself and an occasional guest, one of the flat hand-shredders that fit over a mixing bowl or pan will be good enough. With this simple gadget, which can be purchased for fifty cents or less, I have found that I can cut three to four cups of beautifully shredded meat from one coconut, in about fifteen minutes. A beachcomber who is making an art of existence will always have the time and patience to peel and shred a coconut.

The first coconut recipes I worked out were those that use freshly grated coconut directly. When you try them, don't forget to peel the brown outside skin from the coconut meat before grating it. The right tool for this job is a simple potato peeler.

The best Coconut Cookies are made by taking the shredded meat of 1 coconut and adding to it 2 beaten eggs. Mix well, and add 1 cup of sugar. Again mix well, then gradually add ½ cup of flour while stirring the mixture around so the flour will be evenly distributed through the other ingredients. Stir and knead until the mixture assumes a dough-like consistency, then form it into little balls about an inch in diameter and bake in a 350° oven for 30 minutes, or until lightly browned. This recipe makes from four to five dozen golden coconut balls that are moist and luscious inside. It also is an easy, inexpensive way to fill your cookie jar.

For an informal dessert, I recommend Coconut Turnovers. Make one recipe of plain pastry (see index) and roll it to about ⅛-inch thickness. Then, using a saucer for a pattern, cut 5-inch circles (as many as you can get) out of the dough. Mix the grated meat of 1 coconut with 1 cup of sugar and a few drops of almond flavoring. Put about 2 tablespoons of the coconut on each circle of pastry. Dampen the edges of the circles with a pastry brush dipped in water, fold the pastry over to form semicircles, and seal the edges with a fork. Bake in a 450° oven for about 30 minutes, or until nicely browned.

The Coconut Candy I like best is made by cooking 3 cups of sugar with 1 cup of water until it forms a soft ball when dropped into a glass of cold water. Quickly stir in the freshly shredded meat of 1 coconut and cook slowly for another 15 minutes, stirring often; then remove from the heat and stir hard until the candy stiffens somewhat and gets cool enough to handle. Now wet your hands and form the candy into little balls about the size of a marble and put them on waxed paper to dry. After standing in the open for an hour or so, these little snowballs are firm to the touch, but soft and creamy inside, and if made with freshly shredded coconut, they are utterly delicious. The only fault I can find with this confection is that you start out with 3 cups of sugar, 1 of water, and about 4 cups of shredded coconut, and you end up with less than 3 cups of finished candy.

Shredded coconut has, of course, many other uses. There are, obviously, whole families of coconut pies, cakes, and puddings. However, since you can find perfectly good recipes for them in any cookbook, let's pass on to the more exotic concoctions that you might have difficulty learning about elsewhere.

Making Coconut Chips is a long-drawn-out process, but since there is more time than work involved, they are well worth the effort. Pierce the soft eye of a coconut and drain out the water. Put the whole coconut into a 300° oven for 1 hour; then cool it quickly by running cold water over the outside of the shell. Tap the nut all over with a hammer to loosen the meat; then break the shell and remove the coconut in as large pieces as possible. A skilled hand can sometimes remove the whole meat, unbroken, after this kind of processing, but the chips will be just as good if the meat comes out in several pieces. There is no need to peel off the brown skin of the coconut for this dish. Just pare off the meat into very thin strips with a sharp potato peeler, or slice it in thin strips with a keen knife, spread the strips on cookie sheets, and place in a 200° oven for 2 hours, stirring occasionally so they will roast evenly. By this time they should be dry and brittle, lightly browned along the inside edges. While still warm, store the chips in fruit jars with tightly sealed lids and keep in a cool place until they are needed. These are crisply delicious as nibbles or party snacks, with or without a dip, or they can be used to replace nuts in cookies, candies, and cakes.

In tropical cookery, one of the most important products of the coconut is the real Coconut Milk or Coconut Cream. To make this rich, coconut-flavored liquid, extract the meat from 1 nut as described under shredded coconut (there is no need to peel off the brown skin). Shred the meat fine, then pour 2 cups of boiling water over it. Use coconut water for this, if you have it, but you can add boiling tap water to eke out a sufficient quantity. Using a perforated potato masher, press, mash, and work the coconut in the hot water. As soon as it becomes sufficiently cool, you can get your hands into it and knead, squeeze, and stir the shredded coconut to extract all the milk possible. Let it stay in the hot water at least 15 minutes; then strain through a double thickness of cheesecloth, and squeeze out as much milk as you can get.

This should give you about four cups of what looks like rich cow's milk, but it is far different nutritionally, being high in fat and low in protein. This milk is the basis for some of the finest foods that can be made from the versatile coconut. It is delicious on hot or cold breakfast cereal, and it makes superb milk shakes, malteds, and hot chocolate. The beachcomber should remember, however, that it does not furnish the protein, calcium, and phosphorus of cow's milk, and he should be careful to get enough of these nutritionally important foods elsewhere in his diet. Beachcombing is no fun unless you keep yourself vigorously healthy.

To make a simple and tasty Coconut Ice Cream, just add 1 cup of raw sugar to 4 cups of coconut milk and freeze in an ice-cream freezer, using 8 parts of crushed ice to 1 part rock salt. The Hawaiians sometimes add vanilla to this ice cream, but I think it masks the already delicious flavor of the coconut. If you must add something to this frosty richness, let it be mashed ripe bananas, sieved papaya pulp, strained ripe mangoes, or crushed pineapple. These will add fresh-fruit sprightliness, and they are flavors that combine well with coconut.

When I was beachcombing, I used to forage the ice to make this freeze. I discovered that the refrigeration plant at a brewery near my grass shack scraped frost from the pipes once a week. They were always willing to let me have a couple of buckets of frost with which to pack my freezer, so I planned coconut ice cream for those ice-scraping days.

Haupia is a smooth coconut-milk pudding that inevitably makes its appearance at every Hawaiian *luau*. During our sojourn in Hawaii,

The Wahine and I ate *haupia* so regularly that we began considering it a staple. Now that we are far from the tropics, we find ourselves hungering for this creamy pudding. I sometimes buy fresh coconuts at the market and make a batch of *haupia* as a special treat. Each time we sample its sweet goodness we wonder why we ever left the Islands (and it tasted even better there, made with coconut right off the trees).

All that is required to make this exotic pudding is 1 cup of sugar, 8 tablespoons of cornstarch, and 4 cups of coconut milk. Mix the sugar and cornstarch together, and moisten with enough coconut milk to make a smooth paste. Bring the remainder of the coconut milk to a boil, then stir in the sugar-starch mixture and keep stirring and cooking for about 5 minutes as the pudding thickens. Pour it quickly into a fancy mold or a square bake pan, let it cool, and then chill it in the refrigerator. Unmold on a pretty plate or a large square of banana leaf, or, if you use a bake pan, cut the pudding into 2-inch cubes and serve on squares of *ti* leaf.

Nothing beats Caramel-Coconut Syrup as a spread for hot pancakes, and since this rich syrup carries its own fat, there is no need to butter the cakes. To make this delicacy put 2 cups of dry sugar into a deep frying pan and place over high heat. The sugar will start melting on the bottom, and, as you stir, it will form into small lumps. When most of the sugar in the pan has lumped up in this way, pour in 2 cups of coconut milk to which ¼ teaspoon of cream of tartar has been added. The hot sugar will cause the coconut milk to boil up furiously at first, but it will soon settle down. Stir occasionally and boil until the lumps have all dissolved and the syrup is the right consistency. This can be determined by dropping a bit of the syrup onto a cold saucer, or, if you have a candy thermometer, you will find that it will be just right when removed from the heat as soon as it reaches 220°. Pour the hot syrup into jars or bottles, and cap tightly. When it is to be used, set the jar or bottle in a pan of hot water to warm the syrup slightly, then shake or stir, and pour it onto your pancakes. It's really good!

A beachcomber who is also a skillful cook will find many ways to use coconut milk for seasoning meats and vegetables. Chicken, quickly fried until it is golden brown on the outside, then covered with coconut milk and simmered for an hour, is delicious. Fresh fish of many kinds is very good boiled for about 20 minutes in coconut milk. Wrap the fish in cheesecloth before putting it into the coconut milk, to keep it from cooking apart. It may seem anachronistic to you, but I often use the coconut milk of the primitives to season modern frozen vegetables. Just dump the vegetables, still frozen, into coconut milk and simmer until done. The only other seasoning required is a dash of salt and about the same amount of monosodium glutamate.

If coconut milk is allowed to stand in a cool place, the "cream" will rise on it, just as it used to on cow's milk before the days of homogenization—remember? Coconut cream can be used just like cow's cream in coffee, over fruits or other desserts, or in cooking. You can even whip it.

Coconut Whipped Cream is smooth, puffy, sweet, and coconut-flavored, and on many foods I prefer it to real whipped cream. It is perfect on pineapple desserts. Thick, heavy coconut cream, thoroughly chilled, whips easily in an electric mixer. You can add powdered sugar to it as it whips, if you like, but I find its natural sweetness enough for most dishes. The only secret to making coconut whipped cream is to whip it ice-cold; at ordinary room temperatures, coconut cream doesn't whip—it churns.

Coconut Butter is easily churned from coconut cream when it is at about 65° to 70° temperature. You can use a regular butter churn, an electric mixer or blender, or you can make plenty for a lone beachcomber with a hand eggbeater. It churns much more easily than cream from cow's milk. Just beat coconut cream that is at room temperature for a few minutes, and the butter will come, that is, thick lumps of butter will appear in the cream and begin to clog the eggbeater. Gather these lumps together, and work the butter just as our grandmothers used to with home-churned butter, that is, knead the butter in a chilled dish until it is smooth and creamy, pouring off the water that worked out of it. Then it can be molded or hand-shaped into attractive butter-pats, and it's ready to use. Coconut butter can be used to replace butter both for table use and in cooking. Don't go telling people that I said it tastes just like butter, for it doesn't. It has a sweet coconut flavor and aroma, and it is very good on toast or hot biscuits. In cooking it can be used to replace the fat usually obtained by adding butter, and while it doesn't have a butter flavor, it has an even better taste all its own. At very high heats, coconut butter, like butter and margarine, has a tendency to scorch. This fault can be circumvented by clarifying it before using it for frying.

Clarified Coconut Butter is made by melting coconut butter at low heat and cooking it gently until it stops bubbling, then straining it through a bit of muslin or flannel. It still will impart a hint of coconut flavor to the food fried in it. This is not a fault, but a virtue, for the addition of a mild coconut flavor improves the taste of most fried foods. I am especially fond of fowl and fish fried in clarified coconut butter.

Coconut butter, clarified or unclarified, is one of the most completely digestible fats that exist. It contains a fair percentage of unsaturated fatty acids and seems to be as wholesome as a fat can be.

I have not referred to coconut butter as "coconut oil," for I want no one to confuse this excellent food with the rancid, ill-smelling substance that usually goes under the name of coconut oil. This commercial product is expressed, or removed with petroleum solvents, from *copra*, which is the dried meat of coconuts. It has little resemblance to the sweet, fragrant butter made from freshly shredded coconut.

Even for non-food uses, I much prefer fresh coconut butter to commercial coconut oil. Coconut butter is the natural cosmetic of the tropics and has probably contributed in no small measure to the far-famed beauty of South Sea Island maidens. Coconut butter is solid at ordinary room temperatures, but it melts instantly when applied to the skin. Used regularly on the face and hands, it keeps the skin soft, supple, and smooth. In South India, tender-skinned infants are rubbed with coconut butter before they are bathed, to keep their skins healthy and beautiful. As a suntan lotion it is unsurpassed, giving an even tan and preventing painful burning. These beauty hints are not put here solely for the benefit of possible female beachcombers, for coconut butter is also a manly cosmetic. I have seen rugged fishermen who used it regularly on their hands and faces to prevent chapping and windburn as they handled their nets in salty spray and inclement weather.

If a beachcomber is really a purist, and wants to provide as many of his needs as possible from natural sources, he can even make his own soap from coconut butter, and in many ways it will be superior to any soap he can buy. A trial batch can be made with one cup of clarified coconut butter. This means processing about four coconuts, but once the butter is made, the soapmaking is a comparatively simple process.

Just dissolve two level tablespoons of sodium hydroxide, commonly called "lye" or "caustic soda," in ⅓ cup of cold water. Use only glass, iron, enamelware, or stainless steel containers while making soap; *never* use aluminum. The lye will cause the water to heat up. Let it cool until it is lukewarm, but be sure you feel only the outside of the container, or you might end up wondering what became of your finger. Pour the lukewarm solution into 1 cup of lukewarm, clarified coconut butter, and stir for 20 minutes. Then pour into molds and set them in a warm place for 3 days. Coconut butter and lye turn into soap very easily and completely, but this chemical reaction takes time, so don't try to hurry it. Halves of coconut shells make excellent molds and give you man-sized bars of tropical beauty soap. The stearate of the coconut butter completely neutralizes the caustic principle of the lye as it turns to soap, and you are left with a mild, freely lathering, pure white soap faintly redolent of fresh coconut. Unlike other soaps, it lathers freely in saltwater, enabling the beachcomber to use the whole ocean as his bathtub.

A valuable by-product—the "butter" milk—is left over after you churn coconut cream for butter. In appearance it resembles sweet cow's milk, and since the high fat content has been reduced in churning, this now approaches fresh milk in constitution. Like fresh milk, coconut buttermilk is a complete food in that it contains fats, proteins and carbohydrates in well-proportioned amounts, but it must be remembered that the fats, proteins, and sugars are not precisely the same in the two products. This difference is not entirely to the disadvantage of the coconut. The protein in coconut buttermilk is a complete protein, furnishing all the amino acids essential to growth and health, and its fats, sugars, and proteins are all highly digestible, while the sometimes deleterious cholesterol found in cow's milk is entirely absent. Coconut buttermilk even contains significant amounts of calcium, iron, phosphorus, potassium, and some ascorbic acid

(Vitamin C). Among the potent B-vitamins it contains are thiamin, riboflavin, and niacin. It is not rich enough in these nutrients to furnish all our requirements, however, and obviously should be supplemented with other foods.

Although it might be possible, I am certainly not advocating that the beachcomber attempt to live on coconut alone. I have little patience with the single-food diets advocated by some faddists. Man is naturally an omnivorous animal, and I believe that modern man is best nourished when he eats as great a variety of foods as possible. Also, if you eat widely and adventurously, you will not go to your grave having missed some of the best things life has to offer.

Coconut buttermilk could advantageously replace milk for those on a low-cholesterol diet, and I sometimes suspect that all of us should be on a low-cholesterol diet by the time we reach middle age. Coconut buttermilk is not sour and coagulated like regular buttermilk, but is smooth and sweet. It is delicious as a beverage, and I have found that it can admirably replace milk in cooking. Radical vegetarians who eschew all foods of animal origin will find coconut butter and buttermilk welcome substitutes for dairy products.

When a coconut falls in a favorable spot, it soon sends out a sprout from the soft eye. One end of the sprout sends a sharp point into the ground to start a root system; then it sends a spear upward that starts about the business of growing into another palm. This doesn't mean that the usefulness of that particular nut is at an end, for it still has a contribution to make to those who know its secrets. As the sprout develops, a wonderful thing happens inside the nut. A little sphere of spongy tissue starts growing and gradually expands until it fills the cavity, and this organ has the ability to dissolve the coconut meat and transform it into food suitable for the developing sprout. This food is fed to the baby palm through a sort of vegetable umbilical cord which is connected to the sprout through the eye of the coconut. By the time the nutrients from inside the coconut are used up, the young palm has developed a root system so that it can feed itself. The plant placenta inside the coconut finally feeds itself to the young palm, then the connection withers away, and the palm is on its own. The empty coconut shell just lies there until it rots, its purpose served.

The feeding organ that develops inside the sprouting coconut not only is good food for a young palm, but can also feed a full-grown beachcomber. Split open a sprouted nut, and find this soft, yellow fruit that ranges from the size of an egg to that of a baseball, with a texture like moist sponge cake and a sweet, pleasant flavor, only slightly reminiscent of fresh coconut. When I was hiking along the shore, I would often look for sprouted coconuts and let their placental sponge cakes furnish my lunch. They are best eaten just as they are, or sliced into salads.

Speaking of salads, I consider the coconut palm the absolute monarch of salad plants. The salad material comes not from the fruit, but from the heart of the feathery crown of leaves. Each time it is gathered, a palm tree dies. You don't have to go out and destroy a palm tree to enjoy this salad, however. If the modern Jeep-borne beachcomber keeps his forager's eye open as he drives about, he will discover many coconut palms that have been felled in road-widening, housebuilding, and landscaping operations, and these will be his source of palm hearts.

To cut out the edible heart you will need an axe, machete, or cane knife, but any beachcomber worth his salt will have his Jeep permanently equipped with such tools. The heart will keep perfectly fresh inside a felled palm for several weeks, so one doesn't have to find a newly cut coconut palm. Chop the trunk in two just below the crown of leaves, then remove the leaves and outside layers of the palm-top, leaving only the tender, white center. In a large palm the crisp, white heart will be as large, and nearly as long, as your leg. This succulent vegetable is called "palm cabbage" in some localities, but the name utterly fails to describe its tender goodness.

Sliced into man-sized bites and covered with your favorite dressing, this is the "Millionaire's Salad" for which some tropical resort hotels charge outrageous prices. It is snow-white and tenderly crisp, with a sweet, mild, coconut flavor. I have sampled the hearts from many other species of palm, and they are nearly all edible, but none of them approach the coconut palm in flavor, tenderness, and texture.

Since a single palm will yield such a large quantity of this tasty food, the beachcomber will be pleased to learn that Palm Heart also makes an excellent cooked vegetable. Diced, boiled, and seasoned with butter and salt, or just slowly sautéed in peanut oil, it is liked by everyone who tries it. My own favorite way of preparing palm heart is to sauté it with bite-sized chunks of tender beef until the meat is done. The intermingling of the flavors of beef and palm heart makes a dish that is as near perfection as you'll ever get.

After all the uses we have discussed for the coconut palm's output, you might think that we have asked enough of a single species, but the coconut palm has another offering that is eminently worthy of our attention. This is the sweet juice that exudes from the half-grown bloom-spathe when it has been skillfully trained and tapped. This sweet liquid is called "tuba" in Guam and "neera" in India, and it is commonly called "palm-toddy" or "palm wine" in English. I call the fresh, unfermented juice "sweet toddy," and the fermented product, "palm wine."

Tapping the flower sheath of the coconut palm to obtain the maximum flow of juice requires skill that can be acquired only by experience. I will tell you my method of draining and tapping, however, and you can take it from there.

When the spathe-enclosed bud of the coconut first appears in the leaf-axil it is a slender spike which points upward. This is all wrong, for I want it to point downward, so that when I tap the outer end the juice will drip into a container instead of running back down the spathe. In the South Seas the natives run up the tree two or three times a day and push these blooms down by hand, but I'm lazy, so I cut a strip of rubber from an old inner tube, tie it to a lower leaf-midrib, pass it over the young spathe, and tie the other end below with enough tension so there is a gentle but steady pull downwards on the bloom that is undergoing training. Then I only have to go up about once a week and tighten the rubber, and in two or three weeks the neck of the bloom has grown into a curve that lets the point of the bloom come below the horizontal where I want it.

We must keep a watch over this spathe-with-a-crooked-neck. When a swelling that looks suspiciously like pregnancy appears near its base, the bloom is ready for binding and bruising.

The fluid we call toddy is not part of the normal circulation system of the palm, but is the coconut's reaction to a wound. To induce a copious flow we must mash and abuse the developing blossom while

it is still being tightly held within the spathe. But before we start
this torturing process we must tightly bind up the spathe, lest it burst
open in protest against our misuse of it. The best binding material
I have found is another long strip of rubber from that same old inner
tube. Keeping considerable tension on the rubber, wrap the spathe
tightly for two-thirds of its length, beginning at the butt, then secure
the running end of the rubber strip by passing it under the last turn.

Squeezing the bloom into production is best done with a pair of
home-made tongs such as those used in the Philippines. These are
nothing more than a pair of stout sticks about two feet long, linked
together near one end with two small eyebolts. With the spathe between the sticks near the eyebolt end, one can exert considerable
leverage with the long handles and mash the bloom just hard enough
so it is ready to bleed freely. Here is where skill and judgment enter
the picture; if a blossom is reduced to a pulp, it will be useless for
tapping, and if it is handled too gently, it will produce a meager flow.
In toddy-producing countries the bloom is given a daily bruising for
a week before the first tap is made.

The actual tapping is done by slicing off 6 to 8 inches of the pointed
end of the spathe. Don't be disappointed if the sap doesn't start gush-
ing forth, for ordinarily a bloom has to be pampered for several days
before it will give the first reluctant drop, and it is usually two or
three weeks before it comes into full flow. There are many things a
skillful tapper can do to coax a recalcitrant flower into early and
proper production. A thin slice is removed from the cut end each
morning and evening, and the cut face is bruised all over by tapping
it gently with back of the knife, and sometimes the face is pounded
with the knife handle. Further bruising by a judicious application of
the tongs may be helpful. All these operations are designed to in-
crease the area of the injured surface from which the juice will ooze.

After a few days of this treatment, the cut surface will appear damp
and the long-awaited toddy will start to drip. This may seem a labori-
ous and long-drawn-out process just to obtain a little sweet juice, but
remember, once it is flowing you will be training the second bloom
while milking the first, so each toddy-palm can be kept in continuous
production. Once under way each palm can be expected to yield from
one to four quarts of toddy per day. Naturally, blooms mangled and

cut away in this manner develop no fruit, so the toddy-palm never gives us any coconuts.

As a container to catch the dripping juice, a coconut shell is used in the South Seas; a section of bamboo serves in the Philippines; in India, where they do not train the blooms to point downward, they use a specially made clay pot of peculiar shape. In this respect I am afraid I have abandoned the old natural ways and gone modern, for I use plastic bags and find they have many advantages over the picturesque receptacles of yore. Plastic bags are handy to carry and easy to keep clean, and they fasten securely and quickly around the spathe with a stout rubber band. I always fasten a plastic bag over the cut end of the blossom immediately after tapping it, although it may be several days before I get any toddy, for the bag excludes the air and helps to prevent the cut surface from drying out and healing over.

In India, when sweet toddy is desired, the cut surface and the inside of the container are smeared with lime to retard fermentation; then the toddy is subjected to another process to remove the excess lime. I have found that by employing plastic bags instead of the porous containers that are traditionally used, I can substitute sanitation for chemicals and get perfectly sweet toddy that requires no extra processing. The ultraviolet rays of the sun, penetrating the transparent plastic, have a sterilizing effect on the toddy, which also helps to prevent spoilage.

The palm-top routine is to remove the plastic bag with its load of toddy from the spathe, fasten it securely to a light line and lower it gently to the ground, then cut another thin slice from the business end of the bloom, pound or hack the newly cut surface, and fit on a clean bag. Then attend to any training chores required by the developing blossoms, and you're through. The work in each treetop can be done in about two minutes, so once the toddy is dripping, the labor of collecting it is not excessive. All plastic bags, carrying pails, and other utensils that come in contact with the toddy should be washed in a solution of sal soda after each use. Scrupulous sanitation will guarantee fresh, clean toddy with its naturally high sugar content unaltered.

Toddy should be collected twice daily, so, unless there are some low-growing coconuts at your disposal, you are going to be doing a lot of tree-climbing. In Guam, the Chamorros select leaning palms as their toddy-trees and cut shallow steps or toeholds along the upper side of the trunk to aid them in their twice-daily climb. In the Philippines, where this kind of sap-collecting is a big business, two stout bamboos are tied from tree to tree, and the daring collector passes from palm to palm without coming to the ground, walking on the lower bamboo while holding on to the upper one. Since civilization has robbed us of much of the tree-climbing and bamboo-walking abilities of our more natural-living cousins, I would suggest that the modern beachcomber select as his toddy-trees those bearing blooms that can be reached from a light ladder.

Now that we have collected all this sticky juice, what are we to do with it? Sweet toddy is essentially a solution of sugar and water and contains only very small amounts of other substances, but these minor ingredients are not negligible, for it is these minute "impurities" that give palm-toddy and its products their unique and delightful flavor. The most obvious use of this nourishing nectar is to chill it in the refrigerator and drink it, sweet and fresh, on the day it is collected. In some of the Micronesian islands the fresh, sweet toddy is reserved for nursing mothers, babies, and small children, and it is believed to be the best substitute for mother's milk produced by nature. The analysis of toddy doesn't indicate that it is an adequate substitute for milk, but it is energy-giving and is certainly more wholesome than the tooth-destroying, carbonated beverages that are rapidly replacing palm-toddy in the South Seas.

The next most obvious use of palm-toddy is to allow it to ferment and become the Palm Wine that is consumed in large quantities all over the tropical East. Fermentation is usually complete in 24 hours, and, while palm wine can be kept in drinkable condition for several days in the refrigerator, it doesn't improve with age. It is about 7½ percent alcohol, so it must be classed with the light wines. I don't care for the bouquet of palm wine, but once you get past the aroma, the taste is not at all bad. Making and drinking palm wine is a perfectly legitimate use of this coconut-bloom water, as long as one doesn't drink it to excess. The beachcomber who wants to enjoy life to the fullest will use palm wine in moderation, for overindulgence in this beverage depresses the appetite, thus preventing the enjoyment of the delicious foods available in the tropics and possibly leading to malnutrition.

By rigging up a homemade and highly illegal still you can turn six quarts of palm wine into one quart of a highly potent and fiery liquor which, in common with some liquors from other sources, is called "arrack." The Chamorros of Guam call this liquid dynamite *aguardiente*, but the American servicemen stationed there usually refer to it as "firewater" or "sudden death," and these are descriptive terms indeed. I think this palm-wine distillate must be absorbed into the blood more rapidly than alcohol from other sources, for it goes to the head with a fierce suddenness.

Instead of allowing your palm-toddy to ferment, a much more constructive use of it would be to turn it into syrup, sugar, or "jaggery." Fresh, sweet toddy is about 16 percent sugar, which means that it is at least five times as concentrated as average maple sap. Palm Syrup is made by boiling the juice to evaporate the excess water until it reaches the right consistency, just as one makes maple syrup, except that the boiling operation is not nearly so long and tedious with palm-toddy. Four quarts of toddy will yield one quart of syrup. The proper consistency can be judged by dropping a bit of the syrup on a cold saucer, and seeing if the cooled concoction is as thick as syrup should be. Or, if you have a cooking thermometer, you will find that it is just right when removed from the fire as the temperature reaches 219° F. Palm syrup doesn't taste like maple syrup, but it is fully as good, and especially delicious on hot biscuits or pancakes.

If one allows the syrup to continue boiling until it reaches a temperature of 230° F., it will crystallize on cooling. After about 24 hours in a cool place, the crystallization is as complete as it's going to be, and you have Palm Sugar. It can be and often is used with no further processing. It is dark, damp, and delicious. It is also pretty sticky, because of its content of Palm Molasses, which refuses to crystallize. In India, the molasses is removed by centrifuging, just as it is in the manufacture of cane sugar. Strangely enough, this can be done at home, if you own one of the fruit and vegetable juicers so widely advertised by health-food suppliers. For refining your own palm sugar the best kind of juicer is one that does not eject the pulp, but retains it in the perforated basket from which the juice is thrown by centrifugal force. Just feed the sugar into the juicer while it is running;

the molasses will drip from the juice spout, and in a few minutes you will have a basketful of soft, dry, brown sugar.

Palm molasses is a rugged sweetener and doesn't taste at all like the palm syrup described above. In India it is sometimes used in the preparation of those carbonated drinks, or "aerated waters," with the strange flavors and flowery fragrances so well loved by Easterners. In Western cookery, it can be used in cookies, in gingerbread, or wherever the recipe calls for molasses. I suspect that most of the vitamins and minerals contained in toddy are retained by this molasses, so it should be a healthful product.

If palm syrup is allowed to boil until the temperature reaches 245° F., it can be poured into molds and will solidify on cooling. This is the Jaggery so much used in Eastern cookery. Again, halves of coconut shells make convenient and appropriate molds.

All of these products of boiled toddy are easily made on an ordinary cookstove. When toddy first starts boiling, a frothy foam forms on top of it, and this should be skimmed off with a perforated cooking spoon. As the syrup thickens, the heat should be carefully controlled to prevent scorching. A few drops of coconut cream or a small pat of coconut butter added to the syrup will help to prevent it from boiling over.

Palm sugar, jaggery, or even palm syrup can be substituted for the sugar called for in most of the recipes found in this book, and the final product will usually be improved in flavor. I have not specified palm sugar because I wanted to avoid the impression that it was an essential ingredient, which might prevent your enjoyment of some delicious tropical dishes because you might think they could not be made unless palm sugar were available.

The final product of palm-toddy that we will discuss is Palm Vinegar. Vinegar-making is a slow process, but there is little work involved. Just pour a crock three-fourths full of fresh toddy, cover it with a cloth, and forget it. The alcohol ferment proceeds very rapidly, quickly transforming the sugar into alcohol; then the vinegar ferment takes over and gradually transmutes the alcohol into acetic acid. Don't be dismayed by the unsightly masses of molds and yeasts you see floating in your developing vinegar. Those are the fermenting agents doing their work. After about 3 months, the vinegar will clear, the ferments will settle to the bottom, and your vinegar is ready. Decant it carefully into clean bottles, cork them tightly, and you will have a good-tasting vinegar as strong as any you can buy in the stores.

Lumber made of the trunk of the coconut is called "porcupine wood" in England, and it is very beautiful, being thickly speckled or "eyed" all over, but it is not very durable and is extremely difficult to season without its developing cracks. Once, on the beach, I found a salt-and-barnacle-encrusted section of coconut log that had dried out without cracking. I took it home, and on my wood-lathe turned it into a tall vase with a Grecian-urn shape. I didn't attempt to hollow out the inside but had a machinist friend drill a hole, 3 inches in diameter and 12 inches deep, down the center. A galvanized can was fitted into this hole to hold water, and I used the vase, standing on the floor, to display torch ginger, bird-of-paradise, coconut blossom, and other floral wonders of the tropics that were too tall to arrange on a tabletop. Yes, a beachcomber can decorate his grass shack with flowers and still be ruggedly masculine.

I took a hint from this piece of coconut driftwood and found that coconut trunks could be seasoned without cracking if they were first soaked in saltwater for a month or more. The floor vases I made from this wood sold well at good prices, but the seasoning process was too complicated and slow to allow me to make too much money and thus endanger my beachcombing status.

Coconut shells, roughly spherical in shape and capable of taking a high polish, readily lend themselves to many craft projects. I have seen useful objects made of this hard shell, which ranged from a beautiful, silver-inlaid sugar bowl from India down to the unfinished bottom of an opened shell that is serving me for an ashtray as I write. Coconut shells are easily made into many kinds of cups and bowls that would make a picturesque and appropriate service for the beachcomber's table.

In India some coconut shells are burned to make charcoal, which is highly valued as fuel and for industrial and medical uses. Some of this charcoal is finely powdered and sold as a dentifrice, and it is reputed to keep the teeth wonderfully white.

Don't expect to find the natives of just any tropical country to which you may travel practicing all the coconut arts I have outlined here. With the possible exception of South India, there is no one place in the world where the local people make the fullest possible use of this most useful of all plants. The coconut lore I have accumulated originated in many countries. Actually, there are many uses for this Tree of Heaven that I haven't mentioned here, as I sought to cover only those uses that might interest the practicing or prospective beachcomber.

3. The Beachcomber Afloat

AN ISLAND is a small body of land surrounded by the need for a boat. In the Islands one meets any number of merry tropical adventurers—half yachtsman, half beachcomber—who make their boats serve as dwellings, means of transportation, sources of recreation, and business enterprises. These are people enamored of the sea and sailing. They make their livings while having fun taking out parties for day-sailing, or fishing, or else chartering their craft with crew for more extended cruises. These are real little ships, large enough to equip with all the comforts of home and capable of making an ocean crossing. It's not a bad way to live, if you can afford the initial expense and the upkeep until you have established a clientele.

However, I wanted to live on a tropical island, not merely around its periphery. I love boats and the sea as well as anyone does, but I also love the jungles and mountains, so mine must be an amphibious existence. Besides, a boat large enough to live aboard is too large to go poking around over coral reefs and into shallow bays and inlets, and I find this kind of "gunkholing" one of the chief joys of boating. Then, too, I loved my little home under the kamani tree, but since I intended to call on the surrounding sea for much of my food, recreation, and cash income, some kind of boat was a necessity.

Having been a professional boatbuilder, I knew something about small craft, but this did not make my choice of a boat any easier. Any

boat is a compromise, and mine could not be an exception. I wanted
a craft light enough so I could beach or launch her alone, yet seaworthy enough to go out after the big ones in good weather. She
must have a shallow enough draft to get over mudbanks and coral
reefs, yet have lateral resistance enough to sail well. She must be able
to carry heavy nets and fish traps and a friend or two, and yet be
simple enough so that I could sail her single-handed. Of only one
thing was I sure. I detest the noise and smell of engines, and I glory
in foraging my own power from natural forces, so the motive power
of my boat could only be sails.

With all these contradictory qualities in mind, I was torn between
two totally different kinds of boats, the native outrigger canoe and
the codfish dory. Although as unlike one another as two boats can
be, either of these craft is light enough for one strong man to beach
or launch, both can carry a good load, and both have a well-deserved
reputation for seaworthiness.

The dory has proved its ability to ride out the vilest kind of weather
in some of the worst waters of the world, the North Sea, the Bering
Sea, the Newfoundland Banks, and the open Atlantic. In 1875, a
hardy fisherman by the name of Alfred Johnson single-handedly sailed
a dory all the way from Gloucester, Massachusetts, to Plymouth, England.

The outrigger canoe, which bore the Polynesians on their distant
migrations, has traversed the length and breadth of the Indian and
Pacific Oceans. This frail-looking, lopsided craft, although still strange
and unfamiliar to most Westerners, is today found from Madagascar
to Easter Island and from New Zealand to Hawaii. The original mod-
els from which present-day outriggers are copied arrived at these far-
flung destinations on their own bottoms.

Either of these boats would meet my needs, and since both are
fairly easy and economical to build, it was no easy matter to choose
between them. I finally settled this internal argument by building a
dory that I kept moored across the island near Jim's place, where he
could keep an eye on her and we could use her for fishing Kaneohe
Bay, and then building an outrigger canoe that I kept in a drainage
canal near my thatched cottage in Honolulu.

It is hard for one who has been accustomed to traditional naval
architecture to think straight about the outrigger canoe. We in the

West have always thought of a boat as bilaterally symmetrical along a fore-and-aft center line, that is, one side is supposed to be the mirror image of the other. The outrigger canoe, with its strange appendage jutting out to one side, supported on its outer end with a smaller hull or a float, plainly violates this principle. I have heard people who should know better speak of the outrigger as an asymmetrical craft, but it really isn't. The sailing outrigger canoe is just as symmetrical as our boats, *but the axis of symmetry has been rotated ninety degrees.* Stand on the outrigger side of one of these canoes that has been correctly built and you will see what I mean. It is the two *ends,* rather than the two sides, that are exactly alike.

These identical ends serve alternately as bow and stern, and the outrigger is always on the windward side when the boat is under sail. Not only are these boats symmetrical, but that symmetry has a certain relation to the direction of the wind, and what could be more logical in a sailing craft?

One almost never sees outriggers with this perfect double-ended symmetry in Hawaii nowadays, and most Hawaiians have forgotten how to sail them. Farther west in the Pacific, these graceful craft are still in use. In the Carolines, Marianas, and Marshalls, the natives have learned to construct their canoes of modern materials, but they have retained the old forms, rigs, and uses.

In Hawaii, present-day outriggers are of two kinds. There are the beautiful canoes made of hollowed *koa* logs, that are used to ride the unmatchable surf at Waikiki at express-train speeds, and there are the work-boat types used by some Hawaiian fishermen. The latter are narrow, straight-topsided, slender boats with an outrigger to give them stability. Most of them are propelled by outboard motors. I have seen only one of these under sail, and it had a conventional fore-and-aft rig. It made a most unsatisfactory sailboat for, with this unsuitable rig, it could only sail on one tack and had to be paddled on the other, since these canoes become clumsy and unmanageable if you try to sail with the outrigger to leeward.

Despite the problems involved in rigging and sailing the outrigger canoe, with its strange, sidewise symmetry, this was the craft I chose to build. Perhaps it was because of these problems that I chose this boat, for I think most of us like a challenge to our ingenuity. Then, too, I hated to see the ancient technique of sailing these strange craft become a lost art. Anyone who has ever seen a Micronesian sailing his outrigger across a lagoon at the speed of a motorboat will agree that this is a sailing thrill that should not be lost to mankind.

Although I studied many an ancient model and primitive design before commencing, I built my boat of the most modern materials. Topsides, deck, outrigger hull, and platform were all built of marine plywood, which I purchased at a surplus property sale. The main hull was 24 feet long overall, but she was still a tiny boat, for her greatest beam was only two feet, and she was much less than that on the waterline. The outrigger, 12 feet long, was built like a smaller canoe and was fastened 6 feet to one side of the main hull with stout timbers over which I built a platform. Both hulls were decked, and there were enough watertight compartments so that even if a wave broke right over me, the boat not only would not sink, but would rise up, shake off the water, and go right on sailing.

I find it very difficult to explain the rigging and sailing of these two-ended craft to those who have never seen them in operation. Strangely, it is even harder to explain these mysteries to a seasoned sailor than to a landlubber, partly because the nautical terms used to locate oneself aboard a conventional sailboat become useless on a sailing outrigger. "Bow" and "stern" are definite, findable, permanent locations on our boats, but these terms become meaningless when the bow becomes the stern and the stern becomes the bow every time the boat comes about and starts sailing on a new tack. "Port" and "starboard" switch in the same fashion, making these handy terms meaningless. On the other hand, when we speak of the leeward and windward sides of our boats, we are aware that these sides change as our conventional craft go from tack to tack, and on a sailing outrigger these are the very things that stay put, for the outrigger side of the boat is always the windward side.

Obviously, none of the conventional fore-and-aft rigs, which are designed to push the boat only in the direction of the permanent bow, will work on the outrigger canoe. What was needed was a reversible sail to push a reversible boat in either direction. The rig I chose was my own modification of the Micronesian lateen sail.

My sail was made of parachute cloth, all recut and resewn. It was triangular in shape, with a long, light bamboo spar permanently fastened along one edge of the sail. On a lateen rig this spar is called a yard, as it is on a squaresail. A stout bamboo mast was stepped in the very center of the main hull, right on the sidewise axis of symmetry, and stayed in place with clothesline wire and turnbuckles. The sail was hoisted up the mast by a halyard attached to the exact middle of the yard. The end of the yard that would be the forward end on the first tack was pulled down and fastened to what would be the forward deck on that tack, making the yard rise diagonally up and aft, the after end projecting behind and above the top of the comparatively short mast. The sheet, the line with which the sail is handled, was fastened to the corner of the triangle opposite the yard, and led through a block on the afterdeck. All fittings at one end of the boat were duplicated at the other end. On a beat to windward I planned to let the temporary bow of the boat fall off the wind in the direction opposite the outrigger until the sail filled. Then I planned to trim the sail with the sheet until it was pulling its best and the boat began moving through the water at that dazzling outrigger speed that always surprises sailors of conventional craft. It was a safe rig, for whenever the outrigger left the water and the boat threatened to capsize, all I had to do was to let the sheet run and spill some wind from the sail, let the outrigger drop back into the water, and retrim the sail to make her go her best, which was exceedingly good.

To come about and put such a boat on the other tack is not only hard to explain, but it is very hard to do properly, until one becomes practiced at this art. It requires great skill, good judgment, perfect timing, and the ability to move with speed and agility. Until I acquired these attributes by long practice I often, ignominiously, had to use a paddle to reposition my boat in relation to the direction of the wind, when I changed tacks.

When ready to come about, the outrigger canoe is first headed right into the teeth of the wind to slow her down. Then she is slowed until she has exactly enough steerage way left to complete the maneuver. The tiller is put, not hard alee as in most boats, but hard to windward, turning the boat right around with the small outrigger swinging across the wind. Quickly then, the line that held the forward end of the yard down to the deck is cast off its cleat, and the high end of the yard is hauled down and made fast to what was formerly the after end of the boat but will be the forward end on this tack. The sheet block is unsnapped from a ring in what was formerly the stern deck but

will now be the bow deck, and resnapped in an identical ring on
what was formerly the bow deck but will now be the stern deck. If
all this has been done with split-second timing and great speed, the
job will be completed just as the boat reaches the right position in
relation to wind direction for the sail to fill and will move off in the
new direction, with the former stern becoming the bow, and vice
versa.

At first I tried to hold my boat on the wind with a steering oar,
as I thought this would be easier than a rudder to carry from end to
end as I changed tacks. However, my sail arrangement threw the
center of effort too far aft, giving the boat a decided tendency to head
into the wind. To correct this I mounted a rudder, not on the stern
of the boat, but on the after end of the platform between the hulls.
This not only enabled me to steer, but since the rudder blade was of
considerable area and fairly deep, it had the effect of moving the center of lateral resistance farther aft, giving better balance with the

effort of my outlandish sail. I put two L-shaped pintles on the forward side of the rudder post and mounted two sets of eyebolts for these to drop into, one on either end of the platform. It took only a second or two to move the rudder from one end of the platform to the other as I changed tacks.

With this improvement my boat would beat to windward with the best of them, but she was still cranky on a reach or a run. I figured this could be corrected if I could find a way to get more sail area up forward when I had the wind abaft the beam. I cut out just one-third of an Army-surplus parachute to fly as a spinnaker. I left the parachute shroud lines intact and spliced them into a halyard at the head of the sail and into a sort of exterior boltrope around its foot. The first time I tried the almost ready-made sail, I rigged it in stops from the masthead to what would be the forward end of the canoe on the return run, and took along a bamboo whisker pole to help me spread her to the wind. I then beat upwind for what seemed like hours, until the land looked dim and misty. When I had my gear all in place for the homeward run, I gave the sheet of my new sail a hearty yank to break the weak yarn stops. The spinnaker filled with a noise like a cannon report and for a moment I thought it would lift the boat right out of the water. By the time I had rigged the whisker pole and had control of the sheet we were scampering for home like a runaway horse.

I soon found that by shifting my weight in and out on the platform I could balance the canoe on her main hull with the outrigger just clear of the water, and it was in this position that she made her best speed. And what speed it was! This was as near flying as a water-bound craft will ever get. For a week I neglected all other tasks and spent hours beating to windward for a few minutes' thrilling downwind run. By experiment I found other uses for my new sail. Rigged from masthead to the forward end of the main hull, she could be flown as a Genoa jib, overlapping the mainsail, and making a reach almost as thrilling as a run. I could even leave the mainsail ashore and sail my canoe with this new loose-footed sail alone. Upwind work was a bit difficult, but by sheeting this sail as flat as her spherical cut would allow, I could make my way to windward, after a fashion. I sailed this boat for several years, and my chief complaint was that she made ordinary sailing seem too tame to be any fun.

The dory I built was a conventional craft, although her rig was a bit nonconformist. I didn't design this boat, but built her from some plans I found in a boating magazine, changing these only enough to allow me to plank her with marine plywood. She was 16 feet long, 5 feet in the beam, had a folding centerboard and a 16-foot mast, and with the centerboard up and two men and their gear on board she drew less than 6 inches of water. As Jim expressed it, "She could sail on a heavy dew." I named her *Mokuiki*, which simply means "the little boat," and she was a tiny thing to entrust to the largest ocean in the world. However, I found her to be a stout, able, and seaworthy little craft, and I learned to love her.

To the horror of the boating fraternity, I rigged her with a spritsail that I made of an ordinary flat piece of light canvas. This sail was an unapologetic rectangle, 13 feet high and 11 feet wide, and was spread by a bamboo sprit that ran from the lower part of the mast diagonally across the sail to a pocket in the upper after corner. The sprit was fastened to the mast with a short line, called a "snotter," which was bent on the mast in such a way that I could tighten the sprit by sliding the knot up the mast or remove the sprit entirely in a second if I had to reduce sail in a hurry. The sail was loose-footed and controlled by a sheet from the lower after corner. Both the sail and its rigging appeared crude and clumsy to anyone accustomed to the high, trim rigs of modern sailing yachts.

The spritsail was once a popular rig on small vessels, but it has so fallen into disuse that many modern yachtsmen have never seen one in operation. To discover its secrets I had to dig into boating books published in the 19th century and earlier. Maybe modern boatmen are prudes and resent the spritsail's bastard origin, for she is half square-sail and half fore-and-after. Also, the diagonal sprit, running up only one side of the sail, is tampering with that sacred bilateral symmetry again.

Spritsail-rigged boats never sail the same on both tacks. On one tack the sprit will be on the weather side of the sail and the canvas will belly out from it, while on the other tack the sprit will cut into the sail, making a diagonal ridge across it from corner to corner. By experience I found that on a broad reach or a run she would sail better with the sprit on the windward side of the sail, and on a close reach to windward she would do better with the sprit to leeward.

I hear a thousand yachtsmen asking, "But how does this knowledge help on a beat to windward where it is necessary to go from tack to tack several times?"

This question only arises because we tend to think exclusively in terms of racing craft. In sailing races the course is always laid out so there will be one beat to windward, and it is on this leg of the course that races are won or lost. When sailing for fishing and fun, it is amazing how seldom a good seaman will get himself into a position where he must make a long beat to windward. In the dependable trade winds of the Islands I could usually position my fish traps and nets so I could sail a close reach going out and a broad reach returning, or vice versa, and I could rig my sprit on the side of the sail where it would be in the best sailing attitude both going and coming. When, on rare occasions, I had to sail dead to windward, I would make two long legs of it rather than making a number of short tacks. When I came about, it wasn't too much trouble to move the sprit to the other side of the sail and thus enjoy optimum performance on both tacks. The extra ten or fifteen minutes this procedure consumed would be vital to a racing yachtsman, but it was of no consequence whatever to a beachcomber.

When I was building and rigging the *Mokuiki,* my ears fairly ached from the din raised by the "scientific" boatmen who always cluster around any boatbuilding operation. One can get more free advice on boatbuilding than on any subject in the world, except possibly on cures for the common cold. I grew so tired of technical terms like "aerofoil form," "hydrodynamics," and "aerodynamic flow" that I couldn't say "aspect ratio" without gagging. Sure, those things are important in racing classes, where the rules limit the sail area, but I was working under no such restrictions. I already knew that my sprit rig wasn't the most efficient sail that could be made, but if I wanted a bit more push, there was nothing to prevent my adding a few more feet of sail area. On a racing sailboat, an extra 10 yards per hour can mean the difference between winning and losing, but I couldn't care less about such minute gains in efficiency and speed. I was free of all rules and determined to exercise my freedom. I wanted a rig that was cheap and easy to make, easy to handle, and safe, and my sprit-sail rig filled the bill in these particulars very nicely.

There were some who objected on aesthetic grounds, saying that this squat, square piece of canvas was ugly. Styles in beauty change, and after I grew familiar with my billowing square spritsail I thought it far prettier than the skinny, flimsy-appearing Marconi rigs about me. I sometimes sailed the *Mokuiki* with a small overlapping jib on the forestay, and I made her a little spinnaker by cutting a four-gore section from a parachute. Once I stood on shore and watched Jim bring her into harbor with the spinnaker out one side and the sprit-sail out the other, wing and wing, and I have seldom seen a lovelier sailing sight.

In a hard blow I would remove the sprit and allow the peak to fall down over the lower half of the sail. This is called "scandalizing" the sail, and it reduced the sail area by half. I could carry that little leg-o'-mutton trysail in a gale. With the sprit out, you can let the sheet run on this kind of sail and it becomes nothing but a harmless flag fluttering from the mast with no weight of wind to push you over. I consider this the safest possible rig for a small boat, and yet when it is properly set and handled the spritsail will pull like a mule.

The cost of building the two boats had left my bank account sadly depleted, and I felt that I must soon dream up some adventure that would help replenish the coffers. This enterprise must have something to do with the sea, for I was still enamored of my two new boats and determined to demonstrate that they could repay the labor, love, and expense I had invested in them. After looking over the possibilities, I decided the surest money-making scheme in sight was trapping fish for the market.

Fish trapping is a legal, recognized, and much practiced method of commercial fishing in the Islands, so this was no innovation. The law limits the size of fish traps to 10 feet long, 6 feet wide, and 6 feet high. I suspect the Hawaiians figure that since the law sets a maximum size of traps, this must mean that larger traps are better, for they always build them the maximum legal size. However, I had seen commercial fishermen of the lower Mississippi take a great many big fish in traps of much smaller size, and I wondered whether such a large and awkward trap was necessary. It seemed to me that one's chances were multiplied by having more and smaller traps instead of fewer and larger ones. Besides, the construction of those large traps is a big job, as they require a welded iron frame over which is stretched wire netting. Transportation of these tremendous traps was a problem beyond the capacity of my little dory.

I bought a roll of very heavy-gauge welded wire mesh, 6 feet wide and 100 feet long with openings 1-by-2 inches. This material was sturdy enough so that it required no frame, yet light enough so that it was easy to fabricate and handle. Jim and I finished two traps, 6 feet long, 3 feet wide, and 3 feet high, in one day, using no tools but

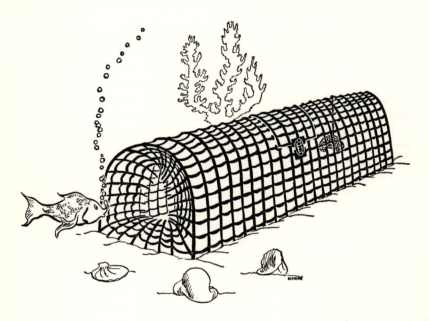

heavy electricians' pliers. Four days later we had eight traps in operation, and within a week they had caught enough fish to pay for the wire and labor we had put into them.

We soon discovered that we could handle more traps without overworking, so I obtained another roll of wire and we eventually had sixteen traps scattered about Kaneohe Bay. The dory could easily carry two of these little traps at one time, and they were so light and handy that we didn't mind moving them about if we found a location was returning poor yields.

The greatest secret of successful trap fishing is to find the right hole in which to set your trap. These good fishing places can only be located by searching out and trying any number of likely-looking spots. In this pursuit we came to know and recognize each individual coral head, cliff, channel, and cave along our underwater trapline. When we wanted to determine our position in the bay, we never lined up objects on shore, as one must do where the waters are turbid and murky. We grew so familiar with the topography of this under-sea land that we could find our way by observing the bottom features through the perfectly clear waters of Kaneohe Bay.

Most of our catch was of four or five common species, but one never knew what might be found in a trap, and strange and unusual specimens were occasionally caught. Once we captured an *ulua* that was actually too large to enter the funnel-shaped mouth of the trap. He had managed to poke his head in, and the projecting wires at the mouth of the funnel had slipped behind his gills and held him fast. He must have been caught only a short time before we arrived at the trap, for he was still thrashing around when we pulled him up.

If I told you how much we made from our line of fish traps, I'm sure you wouldn't believe me. Suffice it to say that I had no economic worries after we set out our traps, and it was not too uncommon for us to bring in fifty dollars' worth of fish after one run of the traps.

We sailed or rowed to and from our fishing grounds, so we had no expense of fuel and motor maintenance. Once the business was launched, we invested almost nothing but time and work, and since we found this work great fun, we felt that the fish we caught and sold were clear profit. There wasn't even any expense for bait, for strangely enough, these traps are not baited. One merely hangs some bright object like a piece of broken china, a metal shaving mirror or some colored plastic toy in the trap, and the curiosity of the fish does the rest. Once a fish is inside, others seem to want to come in and keep him company, so it is quite usual to find a trap either en-tirely empty or very well filled.

Since I was keeping the dory at Jim's place, and he was helping me attend the traps, I took him in as a full partner in this enterprise. Jim's affairs greatly improved about this time, and his huge Samoan wife, Falani, gave me all the credit, though much of it was none of my doing. When his son, Hugo, almost to his surprise, found him-self married to his steady girl friend, and about to be a father, he took a steady job in the Navy Yard and became an all-round "good Joe." He often went fishing with Jim and me, and he was a good companion, a good fisherman, and one of the best skin-divers I have ever seen in action. We became very good friends, and he often went with me on hunting and foraging trips up in the mountains where Jim was prevented from going by his game leg.

With one less mouth to feed and the increased income from the fish trapping, Jim's financial condition was in better shape than it had ever been. He even started raising his own fruit and vegetables in a garden behind his house, and these, with the fish and forageables that Jim and Hugo brought home, furnished them with better food than they had ever before enjoyed. Falani fairly blossomed under these conditions and put on another twenty-five pounds, which was hardly noticeable when fitted into her already ample bulk.

Sometimes, when Jim and I reached our last trap early in the day, we would spend an hour or two bottom-fishing before taking our catch in. With the boat anchored over a likely-looking reef or channel we would sit chewing dried shrimp and spitting the bits into the water to attract the fish and hold them in our neighborhood. With handlines, baited with shrimp or octopus tentacle, we would angle near the bottom while watching our hooks through glass-bottom boxes. There is nothing that increases the interest of line fishing like being able to watch just what is going on down there. The excitement is almost continuous as fish after fish approaches the bait, and even those that refuse it have at least given a momentary thrill of anticipation. No other kind of fishing furnishes so many good stories about the big ones that got away.

When Hugo was along, he and I sometimes donned our diving goggles and went spearfishing. This was before scuba gear was available, and we were limited to little over a minute underwater, but it is surprising how many shots one can get in with a sling gun in that time. I have seen Hugo return to the surface with three fish on his spear at once.

Underwater spearfishing where one pursues the fish in his own element amid the weird spookiness of coral cliffs and undersea caves is a totally different experience from any other kind of fishing. I'll never forget the day I was watching Hugo as he speared fish from out of a hole in a coral cliff. He looked up, saw my box, and motioned me to come down. I quickly slipped my goggles over my eyes and dived. As I came beside him, he pointed toward the hole in the coral, then swam for the surface and some badly needed air. I looked into the hole he had indicated and saw a school of *u'u,* or red squirrelfish, swimming rapidly about but afraid to come out past me. I tried a couple of shots at almost point-blank range, but these little fish were moving too fast for me to hit them. Just when I felt that I must return to the surface for air, Hugo came down beside me. When I reached the surface and started gasping in air, Jim told me I must get down again before Hugo came up, for by relieving each other in this way, we could hold the fish in the hole until we had speared every one of them.

Hugo was bringing up fish every time, but I couldn't seem to connect with these rapidly moving targets. About the third time down, I noticed that in their rapid movement to and fro, each fish seemed to have a certain spot in the hole where he stopped for a moment before turning back in the other direction. The next time down, instead of trying to watch the whole school, I kept my eyes on only one fish. When I located the exact place where he always stopped before turning back, I pointed my spear at this spot and on his next pause I got him. Now I had learned their secret, and we both began bringing up fish. It took a dozen more dives apiece to finish off the school, and we were richer by forty of the most delicious and highest-priced fish to be found in Hawaiian waters. It had been tremendous fun, but I was exhausted, although Hugo seemed fresh as ever and went swimming off in search of more fish-laden caves.

When diving we often saw large lobsters, and we sometimes found them in our fish traps, but the season on these crustaceans was closed during June, July, and August, so we had to release those we caught. These are not the large-clawed monsters that are found on our own Northeast Coast, but the pincerless spiny lobster of tropical waters. They make delicious eating, and a large one can weigh up to eight or ten pounds. They command a good price on the local market, so I was determined to get my share of them when the season opened.

Spiny lobsters are taken by spearing, by hook and line, or in fish traps, but to make it really worthwhile one must go after them with nets. A lobster net is only about 2 feet wide, has a very coarse mesh, and may be 1000 feet long. It is held against the ocean floor by a line of lead weights along the bottom and is kept stretched upward by a line of floats along the upper edge. Because of the large mesh, these nets are quickly and easily made at home, so we decided to produce our own. Falani's nimble fingers were very clever at netting, and she could turn out a hundred feet of stout new lobster net per day. Hugo collected junk lead and cast it into net weights while I sawed short pieces from a large redwood dowel and drilled holes through them for floats, and so we had a thousand-foot net ready to lay on September first.

A lobster net is best laid along the base of a coral cliff, or snaked around and between the numerous coral heads that stud Kaneohe Bay. Running these nets is not simply a matter of raising the net and taking out the lobsters, for after they are entangled, these huge crustaceans will often drag a section of the net into a cave or hole and get it hung up on the jagged coral that is everywhere on the bottom there. One must be almost continuously in the water, diving down and freeing the net where it has become entangled.

While diving to tend the net I often saw uncaught lobsters scurrying about the coral heads, and then there was a merry chase. When a lobster runs into a hole in the coral, it is better to think twice before reaching in after him. The *puhi uha*, or Pacific conger eel, often hides in such holes, and one could easily lose a finger to his sharp teeth, while a large one might take a whole hand. Hugo told me that when you see a lobster at the mouth of a hole with one antenna pointed forward and the other pointed back it is a sure sign that there is an eel in the hole behind him. Attached to my bathing trunks I carried a slender stick with some ribbons of cloth tied to one end. Shaking these ribbons in the hole would cause the lobster to come scuttling out where he could be grabbed with a gloved hand.

The eeriest method of catching lobsters is angling for them from some rocky ledge on dark nights. There are several little barren, rocky islets just off the windward shore of Oahu, and around these we found some good lobster-fishing holes. Sometimes Jim, Hugo, and I would sail out to one of these projecting rocks for an hour or so of fishing at night, but if the lobsters were biting well, we couldn't tear ourselves away and were often still there when the sudden tropical dawn sent the lobsters back into their cavern hideaways.

Before leaving home we would pound into small pieces the entrails of the fish we had caught that day and put this mess into a coarsely woven gunnysack. This bag of chum, or *palu*, as it is called by the Hawaiians, was lowered by a line from an overhanging ledge into waters where lobsters were apt to feed at night. Our tackle was long bamboo poles with stout lines and wire leaders to which were attached small triple hooks like those used on bass lures back home. A light sinker took it to the bottom, and the hook was baited with a piece of skinned octopus tentacle.

We would sit in silent companionship in the warm, tropical night, giving the line to the *palu* bag an occasional shake so the dispersing chum would attract our spiny game. Then, if the lobsters had decided to give us any business that night, one or another of us would detect a pull on his line and with a long sweep of the stout pole bring a scuttling, flapping monster ashore. Sometimes they came thick and fast, and sometimes it was hours between bites. If Hugo had to work next day, he would often roll himself in a blanket and catch a few hours' sleep on the sand; then Jim and I would carry on interminable conversations in low tones, occasionally punctuated by the excitement of landing a big one.

This lobster business often paid us handsome dividends, and it gave us still another excuse to be out on the sea, sailing and fishing, and these are sports I have never ceased to enjoy.

The excitement was multiplied when, instead of a lobster, a big conger or a brown eel would take our bait. These are vicious creatures with terribly sharp teeth, and they are extremely hard to kill. They were not, however, entirely unwelcome, for they have fat, tasty flesh and make very good eating. Often, after a night on a lone bit of rock, we would come ashore in the morning hungry as wolves. Then big fat Falani would cut one of our eels into small pieces, soak the meat a few minutes in shoyu sauce, and broil it over a charcoal brazier. I care little for most broiled fish, for their flesh is apt to be dry, but eel flesh contains enough oil to make this form of cooking more than satisfactory. A plateful of shoyu-flavored broiled eel, a big bowl of poi, and a hot cup of Kona coffee make an eminently satisfying meal for a hungry fisherman.

Falani was an excellent cook with a huge repertory of fish dishes. Like most Polynesians she considered fish and other seafood the primary source of protein and used meat only as an occasional treat or condiment. If an Islander is asked whether he ever grows tired of fish, he is likely to reply by asking what kind of fish you mean. There are probably greater differences in taste, texture, firmness, and quality among the various fish found in Island waters than there are among the meats we commonly eat, such as beef, pork, lamb, or fowl. While a Polynesian, like anyone else, may grow tired of one kind of fish, especially if it is continually prepared in only one way, this does not prevent his enjoyment of another kind of fish prepared in a different way, for he considers the eating of these two kinds of fish totally different experiences, and they actually are.

Certainly, eating *maiko* that has been dried in the sun for just two days and then broiled over a hibachi is a vastly different gastronomic experience from eating raw *aku* that has been cut into bite sizes and dipped in shoyu and hot mustard. Dozens of instances of these wide differences among the various elements of the rich seafood cuisine of the Islands could be cited, and if one broadens the term "fish" to include the various kinds of crabs, lobsters, octopuses, and shellfish, this difference is even more pronounced.

To hear a person say, "I don't like fish," would sound as strange to Hawaiian ears as it would to ours if we heard someone say, "I don't like food." The Polynesian may like or dislike specific kinds of fish, and he certainly has his preferences among them, but to lump everything that comes from the waters together as something to like or dislike would, to him, be unthinkable.

The Hawaiians were, and are, exceedingly skillful fishermen. Over the centuries they have studied the habits of each of the hundreds of species of fish that inhabit their waters. They have accumulated a tremendous amount of fishing lore, which the beachcomber would do well to study in detail. A Hawaiian seldom says, "I am going fishing," but will rather say, "I am going *aku* fishing," or "*maiko* fishing," or "*opelu* fishing," as the case may be, always naming the species he intends to catch. He will vary his methods, tackle, and techniques according to the breed of fish he is seeking, and he can usually "call his shots" and return with exactly the kind of fish he set out to catch.

Falani, with her Samoan background and her Hawaiian upbringing, had a double exposure to this treasury of island fishing lore, and Jim, through his long association with natives of many island groups, had picked up a thing or two himself, while I brought fishing skills acquired on mainland America, from the Gulf of Mexico to Puget Sound. We never slavishly followed the customs or methods of others, but it was on the solid base of this pooled knowledge that we improvised, and more often than not, our innovations brought good results.

Some of our fishing methods may resemble black magic more than science, but as long as a technique caught fish, we never quarreled with it because it was odd or unusual.

After our initial success with lobster nets, Falani started an even more ambitious netmaking project. Using thousands of yards of fine linen net twine, she worked through the winter months fabricating a net 150 feet long and 6 feet wide, with a 2-inch mesh, which was the minimum opening the law would allow. Again, Hugo cast the lead weights, and I sawed *hau* branches for the floats. When completed and tanned in a solution of *kukui* bark (see index), we had a wonderful net for gill-netting or *hukilau* fishing.

The Hawaiian word "hukilau" translates literally as "pull the leaves," and before we could practice this interesting kind of fishing, we had to make the *lau*. This was a 200-foot length of rope with a cluster of *ti* leaves tied onto it every 18 inches. We used two of these leaf-festooned ropes, one for each end of the net. In use, we laid the net in the water in a semicircle, some distance from the beach, using the dory or the canoe to carry it out. Then the two *laus* were attached to the ends of the net and extended out until the whole rig covered a total distance of several hundred feet, parallel to the beach. When the two ends of the laus were brought toward the shore, the hanging lines of *ti* leaves frightened the fish into the area immediately in front of the net. The laus and finally the net were pulled ashore, sometimes bringing in a tremendous haul of fish. It took at least three people to operate the hukilau, and more were better, for the net had to be worked in slowly with swimmers behind it to free it when it became entangled on the coral. According to Hawaiian custom, which we respected, anyone who happened by could join in the fun, and, as was customary, we gave everyone who so much as wet his feet in the operation a fish to carry home.

We used the net without the lau for gill-netting by just laying it across a channel or the mouth of a bay and next morning removing the fish that had become entangled in the meshes during the night. Besides several kinds of common food fishes we often found a number of small hammerhead sharks and some huge Samoan crabs when we took in the gill net.

Both Hugo and I caught the netting fever from Falani, and under her tutelage we made ourselves a throw-net apiece. These are circular nets, with a 1½- to 2-inch mesh and from 12 to 16 feet in diameter, with a ring of small lead weights about the circumference. In use, the throw-net is draped over the left arm in a certain manner, then, when a school of fish are seen near the shore, the net is cast by a powerful sweep of the right arm which imparts a twirling motion to it, causing the lead weights to open it up by centrifugal force. After the requisite skill is acquired through long and arduous practice, the net can be dropped over the school of fish, and a real artist at this sport can even make the net assume the shape of the hole in which the fish are hiding. The lead weights quickly carry the outside edges of the net to the bottom, entrapping the school, whereupon the fisherman leaps into the water and gathers up the open bottom end and secures the fish. Hugo, with his great strength and athletic skill, was a past master at this kind of fishing, and even I, after almost despairing of ever learning this art, finally became able to capture a few fish in this manner.

We also used our netting skills in making equipment to catch crabs. The four kinds of crabs we caught were the Kanaka crab, the white crab, the Samoan crab, and best of all, the Kona crab. The first three kinds inhabit shallow bays and inlets and are caught in circular nets about 2 feet across, baited with fish heads or other offal. A line from the net was attached to a float at the water's surface, and we found, on our crabbing expeditions, that we could tend up to two dozen nets, pulling them every 15 or 20 minutes. I'll never forget the evening that Jim pulled in a crab net containing the largest Samoan crab I ever saw; the legs of this huge crustacean were actually hanging over the edge of the 2-foot wire net-rim all the way around. As Jim brought the net over the boat the crab fell off onto one of the seats and immediately began climbing over the side of the boat, headed for his watery home. Jim was hopping about on his one good leg and shouting at the top of his voice for somebody to do something, for Lord's sake, to keep that big crab from escaping. I was barefoot and was very gingerly trying to kick the crab back into the boat without getting nipped, and between us we almost swamped the boat. Finally Jim got hold of an oar and attacked that crab as if he were killing a snake. We finally got our badly battered prize into a bag, and next day we enjoyed a huge crab salad.

We also caught these shallow-water species in traps similar to our fish traps, except that they were made of expanded metal lath, instead of welded wire mesh, and had differently shaped entrances. The entrances to our crab traps were broad and low, as were the crabs, while the entrances to the fish traps were high and narrow, like a fish. The Kanaka crab and the white crab are smaller, consequently more tedious to eat, than the huge Samoan crab, whose teeth-filled claws, as large as your hand, are capable of shearing off a finger at one pinch. But all provide excellent food, and any surplus finds a ready market in the Islands.

The Kona crab is considered by many to be the best-tasting crab in the Islands. To my taste, the Samoan crab runs it a close second. Unlike the others, the Kona lives a bit offshore in water 50 to 150 feet deep. We sometimes caught them in circular crab-nets such as we used for capturing the other species, but it was a long haul up from a 150-foot depth, and the crab sometimes managed to get off the net before we could get him to the surface. After considerable experimenting we devised a rig that worked well in catching this finest of crabs. It was a coarse net about 10 feet long and 3 feet wide with a length of bamboo fastened along the upper edge to serve both as a net spreader and as a float to keep the net upright. Along the lower edge we fastened a piece of reinforcing iron heavy enough to carry the whole rig quickly to the bottom. A bridle was rigged with a line running to each of the four corners of the net, and from the bridle a fairly heavy line ran to a little buoy on the surface. We fastened a few fish heads along only one side of the bamboo and faced that side to leeward when we sank the net. We could lay a half-dozen such nets before it was time to pull up the first one. As the buoy always lay on the leeward or bait side of the net, we could just start pulling up the line, and the whole net would fold up like a purse with the crabs inside. A large loose-footed net such as we used for lobster would inevitably have become tangled in the coral, had one attempted to use it for this purpose, but these short nets seldom became fouled on the bottom, and if one caught, it could be yanked loose at the price of a few broken strands that could easily be repaired later. In water so deep there was no diving down and freeing a snagged net.

When all these "fish stories" are put in juxtaposition in this way, they make it appear that I was becoming a full-time commercial fisherman instead of a beachcomber, and for a while it was a close thing. I escaped by gradually transferring the ownership and responsibility for the fish business to Jim and his son Hugo, while retaining the right to dip my finger back into the enterprise whenever I ran short of cash.

One of the greatest perils faced by the beachcomber is the chance that one of his penny-grubbing little gambits will turn into a profitable business that will involve him full-time. I have seen too many beachcombers' careers wrecked on this shoal not to be aware of its dangers. I had one friend, a young beachcomber of the very highest type, who was well on his way to becoming a model to the profession when he took up coconut defruiting as a means of acquiring a little cash. This is an odd job that must be peculiar to the Hawaiian Islands.

Everyone, everywhere, as I've mentioned, recognizes the coconut as one of the prettiest trees in the whole plant kingdom, so this feathery palm is highly valued in the Islands as an ornamental. However, in our affluent society, most people deplore the fact that this beautiful tree bears fruit which drops off when ripe, cluttering up the lawn. To avoid the mess and bother of falling coconuts they hire drifters and beachcombers to climb their trees and remove all the fruit and developing blooms. A plant breeder could make a good thing of developing a fruitless coconut for these tropical suburbanites.

My friend, by straining his credit to the limit, acquired a pair of lineman's spurs and an old pickup truck, and went to work defruiting coconut trees. To a man of his energy and enterprise it inevitably became a profitable business. It hurt his foraging sensibilities to see all those good coconuts merely hauled to the dump and thrown away, so he bought a brood sow and began feeding the by-products of his business to her. Within three years he was not only the coconut-defruiting czar of Honolulu, but he also was the owner of a large and profitable pig farm, was married, owned a new Oldsmobile convertible, and was building a new house in a fashionable suburb. It was an ironically conventional ending to what had promised to be an outstanding career of beachcombing.

4. Fishing for Fun

IN my association with Jim's fish-oriented family, and with Island fishermen of all races, I was almost daily hearing of strange and interesting techniques for taking fish and I couldn't wait to give each of them a trial.

On these expeditions I was sometimes joined by Falani, for she was not only our technical adviser, netmaker, and cook, but she was a pretty good fisherman in her own right. There are a number of the smaller shore and reef fishes in Hawaii that are seldom caught in commercial quantities but have exceedingly delicious flesh, and these were the fishes Falani celebrated. If our nets and traps failed to provide enough of the kind of fish Falani preferred, she would go out and catch them herself.

These tasty little inshore fishes, the *manini*, *maiko*, *mamo*, and *moi*, and others not so alliterative, are each caught by different methods, but Falani was master—or mistress—of all these different techniques. It is worthwhile to detail the methods used for the four species mentioned, for they beautifully illustrate at least a small segment of the vast wealth of fishing lore possessed by these Island natives.

MANINI

The manini is one of the most abundant fishes in the Islands and can be seen swimming about the shores and reefs in large schools in

5 to 10 feet of water. Individuals are usually 5 to 6 inches long, and an 8-incher would be a whopper. Their bodies are oval-shaped, their mouths are very small, and they have five dark stripes running vertically from their backs toward the under parts. So compressed and transparent are their bodies that a skin-diver can, when the light is right, actually see right through the fish and make out the stripes on the far side of his body. They are a dull-greenish color above and lighter below. The word "manini" is used in Hawaiian and pidgin to denote anything small or underdeveloped, somewhat as we use the term "runt."

These fish simply will not bite on a hook, regardless of the bait used. Sometimes we caught maninis in a surround net or hukilau, and sometimes Hugo or I would be able to drop the throw-net over a school of these tasty little fish while we were wading along the reef, but these methods seldom provided enough to satisfy Falani. She insisted we move two of our fish traps into good manini territory. These traps, unlike our others, were baited. The bait was a chunk of stale bread bought from the baker at reduced prices. Even this augmentation often failed to provide as many of these little fish as Falani wanted, and then she would go out along the reef and spear her own.

Like most Polynesians, Falani had learned to swim before she had learned to walk and could not remember a time when she was not perfectly at home in or under the water. She often went along when we were running the fish traps, and we would leave her on a bit of projecting reef where she would spend the morning spearfishing. She used a bamboo sling powered with strips of old inner tube and loaded with a special manini spear about 7 feet long, made of steel wire and having a folding toggle barb near the business end. This long spear enabled her to approach the fish closely enough so the point could be placed almost against his side and the fish was impaled at point-blank range.

After being gone for several hours, we would return and find Falani still diving or floating about the surface in shallow water, usually with a great string of maninis tied to a cord about her ample waist. She was always in a muumuu, the Mother Hubbard dress of Hawaiian women, when she was swimming. I once asked her why she didn't dispense with this cumbersome swimming dress, and she informed me that she often did just that after we were out of sight, but she always donned the wet dress again when we were expected to return.

Falani always wound up our manini-fishing trips by drying the catch in the sun for two days, then broiling them a golden brown and serving them to us with generous bowls of poi, some sliced onions, hot wild peppers, and a dish of Hawaiian (coarse) salt.

MAIKO

This, too, is a small fish, not quite so diminutive as the manini, but still, a 10-inch maiko would be considered a large one. They are broadly oval, copper-colored, and are easily recognized by a conspicuous black spot just aft of the long dorsal fin. They are found along rocky, shallow shores and are best in late autumn, when they are very fat and delicious.

Angling for maiko with ordinary bait is a waste of time, but Falani knew how to concoct a witch's brew that sent these little fish wild and enabled one to pull them in one after another. Whenever we brought home an octopus, Falani would remove the ink bags intact and dry them indoors. She would then place a half-dried ink bag in an earthenware dish and cook it in an oven until it looked like thick, black tar. Then she would mix in a teaspoonful of finely grated and dried coconut meat, a pinch of salt, and a few drops of *okolehau,* the Hawaiian whisky made of *ti* root. A tiny dab of this gooey mixture on the point of a small hook will catch any maiko in the neighborhood.

MAMO

This little fish, peculiar to the Hawaiian Islands, can be found swimming about in large schools near the bottom of deep places in sheltered bays. The average length is about 6 inches, and the color is brassy green with several blackish bars running vertically down from the back. The underside is white, becoming yellowish near the anal fin.

In catching mamos, Falani again used octopus ink, but this time mixed an altogether different recipe. She would open a can of salmon and stir into it 2 cups of stale bread crumbs and one octopus ink bag; then she would combine this mixture with an equal quantity of beach sand. This made a respectable amount of chum, or *palu,* as the Hawaiians call it. Then we would go out in the dory and looking through a glass-bottomed box we would search the deep places in the bay until we spotted a school of mamos feeding near the bottom. Falani would then throw some of the palu into the water, and as it sank toward the bottom some of it would separate from the sand and become somewhat diffused through the water. A little of the chum was always carried all the way down to the school of fish by the sand, and as they sensed the magic mixture, they became absolutely voracious. Up they would come, following the trail of palu left by the sinking sand, and when skillfully baited in this way the whole school could be lured up near the surface. Out went our poles, rigged with fine, transparent lines and small hooks baited with bits of *opae*, which is a Hawaiian fresh-water shrimp. For the next few minutes we were likely to be extremely busy pulling in fish, dislodging the hook, and as quickly as possible rebaiting it and getting it back in the water. Falani would judiciously scatter more palu every few minutes, to hold the school about the boat as long as possible. By the time the remnants of the school decided to leave us, we usually had the bottom of the boat covered with flapping mamos.

The mamo contains too little oil to make a good fish to sun-dry, but its firm flesh makes mighty good eating when cooked fresh. The best way to cook mamos is to roll the cleaned fish in cornmeal and fry a large platterful; then dive in.

MOI

Moi is the Hawaiian word for king, and gastronomically the moi is truly the king of fishes, considered by many to be the most delicious fish caught in Hawaiian waters. He is a little larger than the species mentioned above, ranging from 8 to 15 inches in length and weighing from 1½ to 3 pounds. Apparently they sometimes far exceed these limits, for there are records of 18-pounders being caught, but I have never seen such a moi.

In color they are a light yellow with a silvery sheen, becoming lighter toward the belly, with many narrow wavy horizontal dark lines running from the gill openings to the tail. They have very large eyes, and the projecting snout with the mouth on the underside gives them a sharklike appearance about the head. There are two degenerate fins near the bottom of the gill openings, just back of the mouth, in which the rays have become threadlike and the connecting membrane has disappeared altogether, and these hang down like little chin whiskers.

Because of his build, the moi easily becomes entangled in a net, and it was with the gill-net, hakilau, and throw-net that we obtained most of the moi we procured. Their favorite habitat is a sandy-bottomed hole along a rocky shore, and Hugo knew every moi hole along a considerable stretch of coast. He was so confident that moi would be lurking in some of his favorite fishing holes that he always sneaked up and cast his throw-net before looking to see if the moi were actually there, and he usually brought home moi after one of these forays, unless he consumed them on the way, for he dearly loved to eat them raw, and I have seen him clean one with a pocketknife and gobble down the tasty flesh while it was still quivering with life.

Falani, however, liked to take her moi with a hook and line, and her methods were even more ritualistic than for the species described above. She would angle for moi only during the autumn months, for she claimed they were much fatter, tastier, and more easily caught at that time. Even then, she would fish only when the moon was on the wane, and her favorite times were just before dark and just after moonrise.

Before going fishing she had to procure the bait, and this was quite a ritual, performed with an almost sacramental air. At low tide she would go along the shore catching minnow-sized fish called *pao'o* from the tidal pools with a dip net. This requires an alert eye and a quick hand, for the pao'o can move like lightning and can accurately jump into another tidal pool 10 feet away.

When sufficient pao'o had been procured, she started stalking the little black rock crab called *aama*. To catch these she used a 6-foot bamboo wand, cut so two long slivers protruded from one end. These slivers were wedged apart with a spreader and a fine, almost invisible, black thread stretched between their tips. Despite her great bulk, Falani could move lightly and quietly, and she would gently approach a crab perched on a rock and slowly move the Y-shaped end of the bamboo pole toward him until the fine thread touched his eyestalk. The instant the crab felt the thread he would pull his eyestalk back into its socket, carrying the thread with it, and he was held fast.

To prepare a bait Falani would split a pao'o from end to end and wrap half of the little fish around the shank of a hook, tying it fast with a piece of fine thread. Then, she cut off the two ends of the largest leg of an aama and sliced a thin sliver from the sharp, inner edge of the leg. This would permit the shell to be opened, and the leg meat could be removed from the joint in one piece. This tiny piece of aama meat was threaded onto the point of the hook.

Falani would seldom permit anyone to go moi-fishing with her, for she claimed that even a whispered conversation would scare these timid fish away, but by promising to maintain absolute silence I persuaded her to allow me to watch her in action.

It was well after sundown when I watched her approach her favorite moi hole in a crouching waddle, keeping out of sight of the fish in the sandy hole. With a long bamboo pole she tossed the line with the attached hook and magic bait up over the rocks and among the fish. Almost instantly the bait was taken, and after considerable struggle she pulled a 3-pounder clear of the water and swung him in against herself.

It was a weird sight, this fat old lady in the gathering darkness standing at the water's edge, an occasional wave running in over her bare feet and wetting the bottom of the muumuu in which she was dressed. The moi is a fierce fighter for his size, but she played each one skillfully, and as soon as she could get it clear of the water would swing it straight in toward herself, where it struck with an audible smack. She would quickly disengage the hook, toss the fish to me, then inspect the bait and renew it if necessary, and have the hook back in the water in an unbelievably short time.

I have heard *haoles* refer to the moi as "sleeping fish"—a most inappropriate name, as this big-eyed, active fish is anything but sleepy. I imagine this term arose because a foreign ear confused the word "moi," which means king, with the word "moe," which means sleep. I once heard a self-styled expert explain that this fish was called "moe" (which it is not) because it made a snoring sound that was audible from the shore. He said that Hawaiian throw-net fishermen often located schools of "moe" by this sound at night. This is pure poppycock. If the moi makes any sound at all, I have never heard it. I suspect this delicious little fish earned his name because the ancient Hawaiian kings knew a good thing when they tasted it and reserved the moi catch for their own use. It *is* a dish fit for a king.

It was in my outrigger canoe that I made the closest approach to conventional, tourist-style, big-game fishing, and on these expeditions my favorite companion was Hugo.

Although ignorant of all bookish subjects, Hugo was almost a genius in nonacademic fields. He was absolute master of the guitar and could make that instrument perform in amazing ways. His voice was good, and he had a repertoire of literally hundreds of songs in English, Hawaiian, and Samoan. He was a superb dancer and, at a luau, he could do a comic hula that would have the guests rolling in the grass with laughter. He worked in the Navy Yard as a mechanic, and the intricate insides of an internal-combustion engine, which are still a mystery to me, were familiar ground to him. A strong swimmer and a skilled diver, he had forgotten more about fishing and hunting than I will ever know. Any new skill, as long as it required only muscular coordination, mechanical ability, or manual adroitness, was learned with great speed and ease. He was even a good cook and could prepare the food for a luau with a finesse that is seldom equaled.

Hugo not only easily mastered all nonacademic subjects, but in those fields was also an excellent teacher. In our association I learned a great deal more from him than he did from me. I did teach Hugo to sail, and he became an excellent and daring sailor, but he taught me hundreds of things about the mountains, jungles, and sea, and their furry and finny inhabitants.

It was Hugo who taught me *awa*-fishing and this became for me not only a thrilling sport but a lucrative source of income. The awa is called "milkfish" in English, but that name is never used in the Islands, and this streamlined race horse of a fish is found in all tropical seas, although it is seldom taken by sport fishermen because it refuses to bite the baits they ordinarily use.

The awa attains a length of 5 feet and a weight of more than 50 pounds, but most of those I caught in Hawaii were in the 10- to 40-pound class. In outline the awa is narrowly elliptic with a pointed head, a small, toothless mouth, a graceful V-shaped tail, and a single, spineless dorsal fin. It has large scales, and in color it is greenish on the back, shading to silvery on the sides and white on the belly.

In fishing for awa, Hugo and I would sail the outrigger canoe about a mile offshore on the Honolulu side of Oahu and anchor it in about 40 feet of water. This is no sport for one subject to seasickness, for a small boat, anchored in the open trade winds, gets tossed about unmercifully. After stowing the sail and making things secure, we would break out a gunnysack of stale bread, purchased from the baker at giveaway prices, and start tearing this bread into small pieces and tossing them overboard. The steady trade wind caused these pieces to drift away from the boat in a straight line. Sometimes it was an hour or more before we ever put a hook in the water, and by that time the line of floating bread reached a mile or more to leeward.

Sooner or later a school of awa would cross our breadline and start swimming toward the boat, eating the crumbs as they came. They could be seen long before they reached the vicinity of the boat, leaping, playing, and competing with one another for the bits of bread. As soon as the fish were in sight we would take handfuls of the soft insides of fresh loaves of bread, bought hot from the oven that morning when we obtained our bag of stale bread, and we would wad, knead, and roll these soft crumbs into doughy balls. These were molded about three-prong hooks that were fastened to stiff wire leaders about 2 feet long with a cork float near each end of the leader. This peculiar rig was used so the leader would float flat on the water and hold the bait near the surface, for the awa is a surface feeder. These leaders with their baited hooks were attached to stout fishlines on good, heavy, saltwater rods and reels, and then the bait was floated downwind toward the fish. Although the awa seemed voracious when feeding on the free-floating pieces of bread, they became cautious in the vicinity of the canoe and nosed about the bait in an exasperating manner, often swimming from Hugo's bait to mine and back again, several times, while our excitement mounted.

Finally, gluttony would overcome caution, and a big one would gulp in the bait. The second he felt the hook, this slow-biting fish was transformed into 40 pounds of pure dynamite. Off he would go on a thrilling run that would leave the line smoking and the reel almost bare. Or he would dive down, then rush up and break water in a great rainbow arch of a leap, shaking his head like a terrier with a rat, trying to dislodge the hook. This might go on for thirty minutes, with a dozen runs and as many leaps, before the fish was brought to gaff.

The secret of playing an awa is to keep a fairly loose drag on him, and when he wants to run, let him go, for this fish has a soft mouth and only a little too much pull will tear the hook away. Don't be tempted to tighten the drag when the reel begins to look empty. Remember, that growing length of wet line is furnishing an increasing drag on the fish, anyway. Let him tire himself out dragging that long line through the water. On the other hand, the line must be kept gently taut at all times, especially during his mighty jumps, or he will shake himself free of the hook and escape. You have to be alert near the end of a long run so that when he turns and speeds back toward the boat, you can reel in line as fast as he moves. The reward comes when an exhausted fish finally comes to an exhausted fisherman and the gaff is slid down his side, the point turned under his belly just back of the head, and the fish is heaved aboard the boat with a single, sweeping motion.

If one continues to scatter some bread on the water, the school can be kept about the boat even after one of their number has been hooked and is being played. It was not unusual for Hugo and me to catch eight or ten of these big fish in a day, and buyers were always waiting at the docks when we came in and were eager to take them off our hands at fifty cents per pound. The awa is the favorite fish for making Chinese fish cakes, while a small one makes excellent raw fish.

Whenever we went awa-fishing, Hugo and I always saw many huge sea turtles; sometimes they surfaced right by the canoe. Hugo dearly loved turtle steak, and he determined to devise an easy way of capturing these monstrous reptiles. At first he used a small harpoon, and he actually caught a few with it, but too often the turtles we sighted were just out of throwing range. Finally he acquired a heavy bow fitted with a fish-reel and a harpoonlike fishing arrow attached to a stout nylon line. Hugo had never practiced archery, but as in all endeavors calling for athletic skill, he quickly mastered it and was soon an expert bowman. Whenever a turtle surfaced within range of this rig, Hugo would put an arrow with its trailing line straight through its hard shell and deep into its flesh. He would then hand over the bow with its attached reel for me to play the turtle while he plunged into the water to give the awkward beast a battle right in its own element. When Hugo got his hands on the turtle he would slide onto its huge carapace and put an arm under each front flipper. After some practice he learned not only how to keep the turtle from diving, but to guide it right back to the boat, where I would secure it by slipping a noose over its head. Then Hugo would come aboard, and together we would heave the heavy monster into the boat.

It is illegal in Hawaii to sell turtles taken with the bow, but our activities kept two families and one bachelor beachcomber well supplied with turtle meat, and occasionally we had some left over to present to neighbors and friends. Turtle is excellent meat, and these huge sea turtles would furnish large, boneless steaks that could be deliciously fried or broiled. Sometimes when we cleaned a female turtle we would find her filled with eggs, and these were an extra bonus. Turtle eggs are very good boiled, fried, or made into an omelette.

Another occasional visitor to our awa-fishing grounds was the *niuhi* or man-eater shark. We saw sharks nearly as long as the canoe, and some we caught weighed more than 500 pounds. We carried a shark line and always kept a high-powered rifle wrapped in a waterproof poncho and stowed in the hull of the canoe. When a shark appeared, all the awa would skedaddle for safer parts of the ocean, so then we would turn to shark-fishing. Our shark gear consisted of a heavy hook on a length of flexible steel cable, which in turn was fastened to a strong nylon line. For bait we used awa head, a chunk of meat, or even a dead cat. When no other bait was available, we caught shark by using a loaf of bread, wrapper and all, on the hook.

Sometimes a shark will take a bait as soon as it is offered, and sometimes it will ignore all baits completely. I have heard people say that the shark won't fight when hooked, but this is a mistake. True, the man-eater doesn't make long runs or leaps, but its steady, strong pull can wear you down. To shorten this dull and uninteresting fight, one of us would hand-play the shark while the other stood by with the rifle and pumped lead into him every time he showed himself. A shark can carry an amazing amount of lead without showing any effect from it—unless he is hit in his tiny brain or in his cartilaginous spine. When we finally killed a shark, we could not possibly lift him aboard the canoe without swamping it, so we would suspend him partly in the water, under the outriggers, and sail him home.

What do you do with a 500-pound shark? Well, you do several things. Fish dealers will buy the liver to sell to drug companies, who process it for its vitamin D content. The skin, when tacked to a board and dried flat, makes excellent, if somewhat smelly, sandpaper. The fins, salted and dried in the sun, can be used to make shark-fin soup, a great delicacy with the Chinese. I once believed that the Chinese ate shark fins for superstitious reasons, under the impression that the fins would impart the strength and courage of the shark, but this is not true. The Chinese make this gourmet soup simply because the shark's fin, composed largely of an exceedingly good gelatin, makes excellent soup. Try it sometime. You'll be surprised how good it is.

The shark's huge jaws, each with five rows of large, serrated, triangular teeth, make a fine trophy, if you go in for that sort of thing. I don't. The jaws should be skinned out and cleaned, then left for a day or so in shallow water near the beach, where little crabs and other minute ocean life will clean them of every shred of clinging meat.

Shark meat, though not usually eaten, even in the Islands, is really not at all bad. When scraped fine, or ground in a food chopper, and kneaded with a little salted water, it will assume a spongy consistency and can then be mixed with chopped green onion and formed into little Shark Balls, which are very good fried, or dropped into boiling soup to make a sort of South Sea Bouillabaisse. Once I was preparing to serve some of these fried fish balls, but was afraid my guest, a fellow beachcomber and, like me, a former Texas cowpuncher, might be prejudiced against eating shark. I tentatively asked him if he liked shark balls, and he surprised me by answering, "Why, shore. That's the best part of the fish."

Good as these shark balls were, we couldn't possibly eat 500 pounds of them, so the bulk of the meat from the sharks we captured went to feed Hugo's two huge dogs, which we used to help us hunt wild pig in the mountains; thus, after a fashion, we were able to trade shark meat for pork.

One day, when Hugo and I were out awa-fishing, we sighted a huge flock of seabirds of several kinds moving slowly along in the distance, screaming, diving, fighting, and apparently feeding on small fish from the surface of the sea. Hugo became quite excited and said these birds were following a large school of *aku*. This is the Hawaiian name for the ocean bonito, or skipjack, as he is called by sport fishermen. We immediately hoisted anchor, set our sails, and gave chase.

The aku moves through the open ocean in large schools feeding on any small thing that moves. Small fish in the neighborhood of a school of aku are really "between the devil and the deep" for they are either eaten by the aku below, or leap into the air only to be eaten by the camp-following seabirds. This is the most important commercial fish in Hawaiian waters, supporting the large sampan fleet that supplies a huge modern cannery in Honolulu.

The aku is a member of the tuna family and makes some of the best canned tuna on the market. Fresh, it is one of the most common fish found in Island markets. It is eaten fried, steamed, boiled, baked, dried, and raw, and enjoyed in all these ways. The fish caught by the commercial sampans usually weigh from 10 to 20 pounds apiece, an ideal size for canning, and the supply of aku in Hawaiian waters seems unlimited.

On this day we set our course to cut across the head of the school. Hugo removed our bread bait, with which we had been angling for awa, and rigged the lines with feather lures from the tackle box. When we came in front of the school, Hugo let out the lines while I sailed the canoe. As our course was a reach, with the wind dead abeam, I was using our large spinnaker sheeted back like a Genoa jib. As I slowed the craft to let the fish overtake us, one of the reels began buzzing as a fish carried out the line. Hugo leaped for the rod and started playing the fish in, and just then the other reel started to sing. I dropped the spinnaker, letting it lie half in the boat and half in the water, and clambered over the tangled gear to get at the other rod. We were both pretty busy for the next few minutes, and I was sure our lines would become entangled with one another as our fish ran back and forth. By some miracle the two fish stayed clear of one another, and we soon had both of them alongside the canoe. Selecting a short-handled gaff from among our gear, Hugo managed to hold his fish with one hand and gaff him with the other. He then gaffed my fish, and we looked around for the school of aku, but they were nowhere to be seen. There seemed to be an unusual number of birds in the sky, but they were pretty evenly distributed over the firmament, with no noticeable concentration anywhere.

We trolled our feather jigs as we tacked back and forth a few times, but the aku were gone and we had captured only two from that immense school. The ones we had caught would weigh 18 to 20 pounds apiece. They were bluish-black on the back, paler on the sides, with a silvery belly, and on the lower parts of each side they had four parallel dark stripes running lengthwise of the fish. Although not called aku in other places, this same fish is found in tropical seas throughout the world, and no matter where you select the site for your own tropical beachcombing adventure, you will probably find large schools of this excellent fish roaming offshore. During the summer months they often come quite close to the shore, at least in Hawaii.

This little taste of tuna trolling only whetted Hugo's appetite for aku, and he began prodding me to prepare for a real expedition against them. As this involved building a live-bait well in the canoe with screened holes so the seawater could run in and out and be continuously changed, and also involved sailing this frail canoe farther offshore than I thought safe, I was reluctant. However, it was a challenge that promised rare adventure, so I finally relented. In midsummer, when Hugo had accumulated a few days' vacation time from his job in the Navy Yard, and when schools of aku were reported close inshore, we set out to do some aku-fishing in earnest.

Our first task was to fill the bait well with *nehu*, or shiners, a silvery little fish about 3 inches long that congregates in tremendous schools in sheltered bays and harbors. We used fine-meshed nets on long handles and, standing on the platform between the main hull and the outrigger, we would bring this net down over a school of these little fish with enough force to carry it some distance under water. The net was then turned sidewise and swiftly retrieved with a sweeping motion upwards. Even the most successful dips yielded only a small handful of these little silvery slivers, so we spent the entire first day just filling our bait well.

The next two days, from daylight until after dark, we were out searching the sea for aku without once sighting a flock of betraying birds. This time was not a loss, however, for I had decided we would troll for other fish as we sought the elusive tuna. We had borrowed a couple of extra rods and reels for the occasion, and so we had four lures trailing in the water. Two of the rods were in the regular rod sockets located on either side of the after end of the cockpit in the main hull, but the other two were rigged with ingenious devices made by Hugo. These were no more than short pieces of board, pointed at either end like a child's toy boat. On the under sides of these boat-like floats were metal keels affixed at a slight angle to the centerline of the tiny hull, so when they were fastened to the fishing line some distance back of the canoe, they would carry the lure far out to the side of our line of travel. With the two keels angled in opposite ways we had a lure off each side of the boat as well as two behind it.

On the first day, although we didn't see the aku, we did catch a couple of his relatives. After we had trolled for several hours, a *kawa-kawa* (little tunny) took one of the side lures, and I brought him to gaff. He fought savagely from deep in the water, and when we finally boated him I was very surprised to see that he weighed only about 5 pounds. Only a short while later, another reel sang as something took the lure for a long run. This time Hugo played the fish, which fought with authoritative strength and skill, and when he was brought alongside we saw we had an *ahipalaha*, or albacore, weighing about 30 pounds. This wasn't a bad day's fishing, even if we did fail to get the game we sought. We had 35 pounds of fish, and both the species we had caught were excellent eating.

The second day was one of the most successful days of fishing I have ever experienced, although we failed again to so much as even sight an aku. We slipped our moorings when daylight was barely showing in the east, and for the first three hours we put all our ener-gies into sailing, for we had decided to look farther offshore than we had gone the day before. We crowded on sail, and since we were sail-ing a close reach, it was rough and wet going, with all hands alert to prevent a capsize. We welcomed the warm sun that day as it mounted into the sky, for with wet clothes in the chill trade wind we felt frozen.

It was about 9 A.M. when we shortened sail and Hugo went aft to rig the trolling lures. These were barely in position when we saw a school of bluish flying fish break the surface and come sailing toward the boat, and the next instant something big and fast had one of the lures and was running away with it at the speed of a race horse. Hugo seated the butt of the rod in his harness and started pumping the fish in. He put up a valiant fight, close to the surface, and long before we had him we could see that it was a big bull *mahimahi*, or dolphin, although I dislike using the latter name because it tends to confuse this streamlined fish with the mammal called dolphin.

As we watched him struggle in the perfectly clear water, we could see behind him a large school of the same species as he was, following the hooked fish curiously. As he was brought alongside, we didn't gaff him, but slipped a noose made in the end of the shark line over his big V-shaped tail and tightened it around the smallest part of his body and heaved him aboard with that.

Hugo was all excitement, and promising me, "You ain't seen nothin' yet," he quickly threaded the shark line through the fish's gills, looped the heavy hook around the standing end of the wire cable to make the fish secure, then tossed him back overboard. He paid out the line until the mahimahi was being docilely led about 50 feet behind the canoe. Immediately, the school, which had seemed to disperse when the hooked fish had been brought close to the boat, reassembled about their captured comrade. Hugo floated a lure back among them, and in a few minutes he had another on the line.

Eight big fish were hooked and landed before the remnants of the school decided they had business in some other part of the ocean and veered off. All this wasn't done nearly as quickly as it has been told, for each fish had to be played, gaffed, and boated, and all of them put up stubborn fights before coming in. We didn't weigh the fish before they were decapitated and cleaned, but I would judge that the ones we caught would average about 25 pounds apiece, not large for mahimahi, but still pretty big fish.

The mahimahi is a beautiful creature, paddle-shaped, broadest at the head and sloping back in perfect streamlining, with a large forked tail as his prime mover. He has a continuous dorsal fin, high in front and sloping down aft, running from almost on top of his head to the base of his tail. When first lifted from the water, he has dark spots against a background of silvery blue on his upper parts, while below he is yellow with black spots; then, as he dies, the color changes rapidly, running the gamut of iridescent yellows, greens, and blues. The males are easily distinguished from the females because the "kane kind," as the males are called in pidgin, have erect high foreheads giving them a real highbrow look, while the "wahine kind" have un-intelligent-appearing sloping foreheads. The flesh of the mahimahi is firm and white, and a steak cut from the forward part of its body and breaded and fried is excellent, far surpassing in flavor any sword-fish steak I ever tasted.

After our grand mahimahi haul we tacked about that part of the ocean trying to relocate the mahimahi or to sight a school of aku, but we failed in both endeavors. As the morning waned and the afternoon began, we decided it would be wiser to get our mahimahi back to port while it was in marketable condition rather than continue to hunt for the aku that were so elusive I was beginning to believe they were nonexistent.

On the third day, or the fourth, if you count the day we spent collecting bait, we sailed even farther offshore, and it was midday before we began to troll, but nothing so much as smelled of our feather lures. About 3 o'clock in the afternoon the trade wind died to no more than a pleasant breeze, and the sea became relatively calm. Under these conditions the canoe was easy to handle, so I turned the tiller over to Hugo, inflated an air mattress, spread it on the outrigger platform, and lay down to catch forty winks in the shade of the sail. I had drifted off and was in the middle of a pleasant dream when I was awakened by Hugo shaking my shoulder. I came up with a start and, following Hugo's pointed finger, I saw a huge flock of seabirds circling and diving far off in the distance.

I doubted that we would ever overtake the school of fish in this weak breeze, but we began piling on sail until we had everything flying but the cook's apron, and the canoe started slipping through the water at a pretty smart clip. The school seemed to be moving in a great semicircle, so we made a chord of our course, and in about an hour we were ahead of the screaming, hungry birds. As the school came about us we began throwing nehu from our bait well into the water. In a few minutes dozens of voracious fish were about the boat competing with one another for the little shiners we threw to them.

Then came the most amazing exhibition of fishing I have ever seen. Hugo removed the hatch cover from the afterdeck of the canoe so he could step down inside and have a secure place to stand. He had a stout bamboo pole about 10 feet long and a line about the same length terminating in a bright, shiny, barbless hook. As I steered with one hand and tossed out bait with the other, he dropped that bare, shiny hook among the fighting fish. Mistaking it for another nehu, one of the tuna grabbed it. Hugo brought him aboard with a mighty

heave, caught the fish under his left arm, disengaged the hook, and
tossed it back among the fish and at the same time threw the big
aku behind him into the cockpit that was to serve as our fishhold.
By the time the first fish was out of his hands, another was on the
hook. Hugo was working like a galley slave, with sweat pouring off
him, but his timing was perfect and there was no lost motion. Catching and disposing of each fish took only a few seconds, and the cockpit was rapidly filling with fish as the canoe sank lower and lower in
the water. Finally I called a halt, although the fish were still biting
freely, for I was afraid the weight of fish we were taking aboard was
going to sink the canoe under us.

We were a long way from home, the hour was late, the wind was
still falling, and the canoe was sailing sluggishly with its huge over-
load of fish. Fortunately the course home was a downwind run, but
this run soon slowed to a walk and finally to a crawl. After sundown
the wind died almost completely, and there was barely enough breeze
to billow our light spinnaker. We even broke out the paddles to lend
an ash breeze to our motive power, but we could do little with this
overloaded canoe. Before darkness descended completely, we picked
a star to steer by that would lead us into the harbor. It was long after
midnight when we reached the entrance to the yacht harbor. Fortunately the tide was running in and fairly sucked the canoe into the
safe haven inside the reef. We were so tired that we stretched out
on the outrigger platform and slept until sunrise.

I have told of these three successful days of fishing because they
were successful and therefore worth the telling, but I hope the reader
doesn't get the idea that one can go out any day in the Islands and
make such fabulous catches. Deep-sea fishing in Hawaii is like the
little girl with the little curl. "When it is good it is very, very good,
and when it is bad it is horrid." In all the time I remained in the
Islands, I never again caught as many mahimahi or as many aku in
one day as I did on the days I have described. Trolling and other
methods of deep-sea fishing can be grand fun when the fish are biting,
but there were times when Hugo and I would troll for a month of
Sundays without getting a nibble.

Not all big-game fishing in Hawaii is done from boats, for the
mighty *ulua*, or jack crevally, both the black and the white species,

is usually taken from the shore, and he certainly ranks as a big-game fish. The o'io, or bonefish, is also taken from the shore, and while much smaller than the huge ulua, this is one of the gamest fishes in the ocean, a favorite of sports fishermen in all warm seas.

Shore-casting is one of the most common sport-fishing methods used in the Islands, and any weekend one can see dozens of little fishing camps, each with its line of poles stuck in the sand, all around the Islands. I was reluctant to adopt this method, partly because it was so conventional and partly because, although I had passed a great many of these little fishing camps while driving about the Island on weekends, I had never seen anyone catch anything. I should have known better. An enjoyable weekend of shore fishing is one of the arts of gracious tropical living, and many Island people are past masters of this amenity.

It was at the importuning of Jim and Falani that I finally consented to go shore fishing, and after only one trip I was converted and soon became an ardent fan of this sport. Most Islanders, like most mainland Americans, work all week and enjoy shore casting and other such sports only on weekends. We three, however, were foot-loose and fancy-free, not allowing our lives to be regulated by calendars, factory whistles, or time clocks, so we usually went shore fishing on weekdays, when we could take our pick of all the good spots.

Our favorite place was on the leeward or dry side of the Island, where the weather was nearly always perfect. There was an uneven rocky shore along this section, and we pitched our tent on a clean stretch of sand in a little valley where there grew a few scraggly coconut palms that bore scant crops of nuts but were usually able to furnish our camp with the few drinking nuts we needed.

Never go shore fishing by merely casting out your bait and then sitting nervously by, chewing your fingernails, while waiting for a strike. This is deadly, for sometimes two days and nights will pass without a bait being bothered. Cast out your lines, then relax; enjoy a long, cool drink or a tasty snack of food, some pleasant conversation, or just plain, lazy lolling. This is a sport to be enjoyed neither alone nor in a large party. Take along a couple of congenial companions and enjoy the intimacy that a camp by the surf and a night under the stars always engender.

Jim, Falani, and I would arrive at our favorite shore-fishing spot in the early afternoon, and at first everything would be business. They would set up camp while I was casting out the lines. We finally acquired nine complete shore-fishing rigs among us. Each of these consisted of a long rod, homemade from special bamboo selected from thickets in the mountains and fitted with agate line guides, a huge saltwater reel that would hold 500 yards of strong fishline, and a strike alarm. This last piece of equipment was a little battery-powered siren on a sharpened stake that could be stuck into the sand behind the rod. There was a line from a switch on the siren that was secured around the rod with a slipknot that could be removed with a single pull on its running end. When a fish struck, he pulled the rod forward and tripped the switch, and the screaming siren brought one of us running.

To make a cast with one of these long shore-fishing rods, I would bait the hook with an octopus tentacle, back up a few steps from the water's edge, then, with a quick little run, bring the weighted bait over my head, using both my own speed and the centrifugal force generated by the long pole to give the bait greater impetus. Using this technique, one can cast the bait an unbelievable distance before it strikes the surface and sinks into one of the sandy little channels that cut through the coral near the shore. I would then secure the pole upright by sticking it into the sand or by piling lava rocks about the butt, if the sand was too shallow, and then connect the alarm switch.

On returning to camp I would find Jim taking his ease in the shade of a tent fly, sipping iced panini swipes or okolehau mixed with lime juice, while Falani might be off searching the tidal pools for pao'o and aama to prepare her magic moi bait, for there were some excellent moi holes in that neighborhood. Jim and I would fire up the hibachi with charcoal we had made ourselves from *kiawe* wood, and when the fire had burned to glowing coals, we would prepare a sumptuous supper of food that had been collected from the sea, the mountains, and the jungle, and had never been degraded or devitalized by being sold at a profit.

After our picnic supper, Falani would go off moi-fishing while Jim and I would go to the top of a nearby height to watch the sunset and the surf beating on the wild, deserted shoreline. Swimming was very dangerous along this coast, so we would perform our ablutions in bathtub-size tidal pools, lathering with homemade coconut soap. We didn't reel in the lines to inspect the baits, but before darkness fell we would send a sliding bait slipping down each line. The sliding bait is an ingenious Island invention that eliminates the necessity of reeling in the lines more than absolutely necessary and risking snagging or cutting it on the rough coral. It is no more than a baited hook on a short length of leader with a snap swivel attached to its upper end. This is snapped around the line and allowed to slide down until it is stopped, either by the bait touching bottom or by the snap striking the original swivel above the first bait. After dark, Falani would sing the plaintive songs of the Islands, or Jim would regale us with tales of his adventures while traveling in the South Seas.

It was rare for a night to pass without a striking fish setting off an alarm, but even when the baits lay unnibbled the whole night through, we never allowed this fact to get us down. We would arise at dawn, send down a set of new sliding baits, and prepare ourselves a good breakfast. Then if the tide was low, Falani and I would leave Jim in charge of the fishing poles while we went off hunting *opihis*. The opihi, or limpet, is an excellent little shellfish that clings to the seaward surface of rocks that are pounded almost continuously by the surf. It is a univalve with a shell shaped like a little squat Indian tepee, and is collected by sliding a knife blade under the shell and prying the creature loose from the rock. They have firm, sweet flesh and are delicious raw, stewed, boiled, or fried. I did the opihi collecting while Falani gathered *limu*, or edible seaweed, at the water's edge, and kept a weather eye peeled toward the ocean to warn me of the approach of any large waves that might knock me loose from the rocks and carry me out to sea, for this was an exceedingly dangerous stretch of coast.

We would work our way along the shore and around a point of high rocks to another small cove that sheltered a calm little lagoon behind the reef. We would wade about in this knee-deep little lake capturing *aloalo*, or squilla, a kind of mantis shrimp that lives in vertical holes in shallow water. To hunt these we each carried a small, fine-meshed dip net such as Falani used to catch pao'o for moi bait. In the other hand each of us would carry a slender switch with a piece of opihi attached to one end of it for bait. Aloalo holes were everywhere on the bottom of the shallow lagoon, so we would stick our bait down one hole, then slowly withdraw it to lure the squilla into the open. He is a gamy little creature 6 to 10 inches long. As the bait is being moved, he apparently thinks it is alive and attacks it by doubling himself up, then suddenly uncoiling and striking the bait with a force that can be felt all the way up the slender wand. By moving the bait gradually into the net, we could persuade the aloalo to catch himself. Squilla make delicious food, far more delicate and tasty than the comparatively coarse lobster. We would return to our fishing camp with one bag full of opihis, another full of aloalo, and the gathered-up front of Falani's muumuu bulging with limu to add to our raw fish or salads. When we added these treasures to the moi that Falani had caught the night before, and then tallied them with the fun we had had, the sights we had seen and the love we had shared, our attitude was, "The devil with the ulua and o'io. They can bite or not, just as they please." Even if these gamy fish never took the bait, they had given us an excuse for a night of congenial companionship in a pleasant camp on the beach, and this left us deeply in their debt.

If the fish still pleased not to bite, we would confer on whether to stay a second night or return home. If the decision was home, we would take in the lines, stow our gear, and drive back at a leisurely pace, taking little side excursions onto dirt roads and stopping at wayside trees to gather the wild fruits that happened to be in season, and although we may have failed to so much as see the kind of fish we had set out to catch, we always came home with no regrets.

However, all our fishing trips didn't end in this way. Some of them were more than mere excuses to fool around the shore and enjoy one another's company, for sometimes the huge ulua and the gamy o'io would give us exciting sport and a great weight of fish to carry home. I remember one of these trips when low tide was at dawn, so Falani and I returned from our aloalo fishing before 9 A.M. As we neared the camp I heard a strike alarm whining and broke into a run, leaving fat Falani to pant after me. When I reached the poles, I saw that Jim was already playing one fish while another alarm was screeching its message of a fish on the hook. I shut off the alarm and started playing a speedy fish that I instantly knew was an o'io. Then, just as Falani came puffing up, a third alarm started to wail. Falani grabbed the rod eagerly, stuck its butt between her fat legs and joined in the exciting three-way fight, laughing, screeching, and having herself a ball, but handling that fish skillfully as a veteran withal. Falani had really had very little practice at reel fishing but that woman just naturally had good fish sense.

The o'io plays rough, running straight out to sea, then suddenly, without warning, turning and heading straight for the shore so swiftly it is difficult to take in the line as he comes, and if he ever loosens it, you have lost a fish. After four or five such runs he is tired out, but he still has a trick or two up his sleeve. As he is being brought close to the shore, if a wave happens along and loosens the tension for a moment, he will go into a roll and free himself of the hook. The proper technique is to hold him tautly, but without too much pull, for he has a tender mouth, just beyond the breaking point of the waves and then, when a good wave comes along, bring him quickly to shore on the crest of it.

The o'io often bites well when there is a rising tide in the early morning, especially if the day happens to be cloudy. These were exactly the conditions that prevailed on the day I am telling about, and in the next thirty minutes we caught twelve o'io weighing from 6 to 10 pounds apiece.

Although the flesh of the o'io is delicious, it is considered a poor food fish in most parts of the world because its numerous soft bones become brittle and hard when the fish is cooked. The Hawaiians circumvent this difficulty by eating the fish raw, and the o'io is highly valued for this purpose. The raw flesh can also be scraped from the bones and made into some delicious fish cakes.

O'io fishing is good fun, but it is the huge ulua that furnishes the real thrills in the kind of shore fishing I have been describing. One night, after a windy squall had left the sea confused and choppy, an alarm siren started its wail. I went sprinting through the darkness at grave risk to life and limb, and Jim came after me with a large focusing flashlight. The reel was still singing when I reached it, and as I got a feel of the fish on the line, I knew I had hold of a big ulua, and I tightened the drag as much as I thought the line would stand. My fish soon came to a stop, and I started trying to pump him in.

Ulua-fishing is thrilling sport, but it's also godawful hard work. When my arms were aching from pumping and my crotch was beginning to get raw from the chafing butt of the rod, I had gained only a few yards, and then he headed out to sea again as if the drag was nothing to him, taking out many times the length of line I had gained. Finally I brought him to a second halt and started the slow grind in again. The ulua has a habit of turning broadside to the line of pull, making it nearly impossible to move him. Almost inch by inch he came toward shore. After about forty minutes of this he was within thirty feet of me and was about exhausted, and so was I. Falani had arrived by this time and was holding the light while Jim handled the gaff. Finally the tired fish slid in on his side on top of a wave and Jim slipped the business end of the gaff under him, heaved the point in between his ribs, and we had him.

Our big fish was a white ulua and he weighed 64 pounds, the largest one I ever caught, although later that same night we landed a second one that weighed only a few pounds less. The white ulua is one of the finest large food fishes in the Islands. It is found on the menus of the fanciest seafood restaurants and commands premium prices on the market.

During the war, when fishing boats were not allowed to operate, the prosperous but fish-starved Islanders would pay any price for a taste of seafood, and despite a vigilant O.P.A., there was a flourishing black market in shore-caught fish. I knew one beachcomber who, during those times, once caught six big ulua in a single night, yielding over 200 pounds of dressed fish that was easily disposed of at a dollar a pound. Two hundred dollars for a night of good sport is not bad pay. Still, success in shore fishing is too sporadic and uncertain for the beachcomber to depend on it as his sole source of income. Fish trapping, lobster netting, and awa-fishing, to mention only the piscatorial pursuits, are much more dependable, and that occasional grand haul of shore-caught fish should be considered a welcome bonus that can add to the amenities of the already pleasant life the beachcomber is leading.

Not all the fishing I did for fun was wildly exciting; some of it was just interesting and pleasant. To slide from the perfectly divine to the utterly ridiculous, let's move from ulua to crawfish. The crawfish *is* a ridiculous creature, and yet this miniature fresh-water lobster seems to intrude into my life wherever I go. I don't know when I first became interested in these little crustaceans; from as early as I can remember, I considered myself no mean threat to the crawdads in the streams and ditches of eastern Texas. By the time I was five years old I had caught hundreds of crawfish on chunks of bacon tied to twine strings. In my family we scalded the crawdads to kill them quickly, removed the tails, which contain the bulk of the meat, peeled the shells off these tails, rolled the meat in cornmeal, and fried it. I thought fried crawdad tails the finest of delicacies and I still do.

Later I caught crawfish in Oklahoma, Arkansas, Louisiana, and New Mexico. When I moved to the Pacific Northwest and found the lakes there teeming with crawfish, I felt right at home. In Seattle I was a professional crawfisherman for a while, furnishing the local fish companies up to 1500 of these tasty little crustaceans per week. This business was limited only by the size of the market, for during the summer I could have caught almost any quantity the market would take. It was there that I learned to use ring nets for crawfish. These ring nets were made by lacing a net inside a wire barrel hoop and attaching a bridle and lifting line of mason's cord. I have raised such nets that contained over fifty crawfish at one time, and ten to twenty market-sized crawfish were common catches each time the net was lifted. I could easily tend a dozen such nets, running them every twenty to thirty minutes. More than once I have caught 1000 crawfish in a single afternoon, and I could have greatly expanded even that kind of catch had there been sufficient market for my product.

When I started beachcombing in Hawaii and learned that crawfish were plentiful in the taro fields and irrigation reservoirs, I figured that I had at least one dependable source of food just waiting for me to exploit it. Shortly after I had settled into my thatched hut, I made up ten ring nets with a finer mesh than we used for catching crabs, and taking a companion I set out to show him how to catch crawfish in quantity. We arrived at an irrigation reservoir and started walking around it setting out our nets, each one baited with a fish head. The crawfish were there, for as we walked around the little lake we could see them by the dozen darting away from the shallows into deeper water.

I was so sure of my prowess that I promised my companion that when we ran the nets the first time, he would see more crawfish than he had ever seen in his whole life before. Imagine my chagrin when after leaving the nets down about thirty minutes, we pulled them in and found not a single crawfish in any of them.

For half a year I couldn't even read the word "crawfish" without blushing. I did, however, learn that crawfish are considered a great pest in Hawaii, as they destroy much taro in the fields by hollowing out the roots and eating them from the inside. There are strict laws against introducing crawfish into any Island area they have not already invaded. Strangely, the Islanders who eat raw fish, octopus, eels, and sea cucumbers and seem completely catholic in their taste for seafood are only now learning to eat this finest of crustaceans. Crawfish are vermin there, and who wants to eat vermin, even if it happens to be perfectly delicious? It would bring tears to the eyes of a French chef or a New Orleans Creole cook to see how this delicate crustacean, with which they can do such wonderful things, is spurned in Hawaii.

Finally I swallowed my shame and returned to the scene of my discomfiture, this time alone and unboastful. On analyzing my former failure I decided the trouble had been in the bait I had used. It seems that Hawaiian crawfish, unlike those I had fished for in the State of Washington, preferred a vegetarian diet. No wonder they had scorned my fish heads. This time I took along some taro root so I could bait these Kanaka crawdads with their favorite food, but I never used it. When I arrived at the reservoir, I found it drawn down with a wide ring of leaf-covered mud between the water and the surrounding trees, and in this open space were crawling literally thousands of crawfish. Using no equipment whatever, I simply walked out on the mud and picked up two bushelbasketfuls of crawfish.

After that, my only crawfish tackle was some covered baskets in which to bring them home. By gifts of choice ocean fish and jungle fruit, I persuaded the plantation workmen in charge of the irrigation reservoirs to notify me whenever the crawfish were walking about on shore. At these times I would gather crawfish by the Jeep load. You may wonder what a lone beachcomber could do with bushels of crawfish in an area where these tasty tidbits enjoy no market whatever, but I wasn't overdoing it nearly as badly as it sounds, for a bushel of crawfish will yield only about three pounds of cleaned crawfish meat. During the crawfish runs, I would package enough of this meat to make gourmet dishes the year round and store it in my landlord's freezer.

Cleaning crawfish is a tedious operation at best, but with the proper technique it can be done fast enough to make it worthwhile. Cover the live crawfish with boiling water, which quickly kills them and turns them from a dull green to a bright red. Then drain them and quickly cool them by running cold water over the shells. Remove the tail next, with two quick sidewise bends, and discard the forward part of the body. The shell on the tail is cracked between the thumb and first finger and peeled off. Then, holding the tail meat dorsal side up, one presses along each side of it with the thumbs until it splits, so one can remove the midgut or "vein." The meat is then washed under running water, and it is ready to prepare in many wonderful ways or to freeze for future use.

I have mentioned octopus and octopus ink a number of times in this section, but I haven't told you how we caught our octopuses. The octopus is much more than merely the makings for some of the best fish baits in the world, for in the Islands the octopus is also highly valued for food. Even mainland Americans, if they can get past the senseless prejudice against eating this queer creature, enjoy octopus flesh. I consider octopus especially valuable as a change from either fish or meat, for this odd dish has a delicious taste and texture that are its very own, with little resemblance to fish or fowl or good red beef. Turn to the chapter on seafood preparation and see how many ways this versatile food can be prepared.

The octopus is incorrectly called a "squid" in Hawaii, and any kind of octopus-fishing is called "squidding." Two kinds are commonly caught and eaten, the *he'e*, or day squid, and the *puloa*, or night squid. The he'e is usually a grayish-brown color, but he has such a chameleon-like ability to change his color to blend with his background that I can give no assurance what color he will be when you first see him. The puloa is a dull-reddish color with white stripes on his head and white spots on his tentacles.

We caught our octopuses in several ways. Hugo and I managed to spear quite a few while skin-diving about the reef, and sometimes when Falani was out manini-spearing she would bring back an octopus or two. At low tide on calm days I would wade along the reef searching the bottom through a glass-bottomed box and spearing he'e. I wore high-topped, bellows-tongued boots with a cloth bound around their tops. These didn't keep my feet dry, but they did protect my feet and legs from coral cuts, and they kept out the sand. Ordinary sneakers won't do, for the sand sifts through the eyelets and packs about your feet, making very uncomfortable walking. I was armed with a 5-foot spear with four barbed prongs, and I carried a bag attached to my belt in which to bring home the game.

It takes practice to see an octopus on the reef, even when looking through a glass-bottomed box into that perfectly clear water. Search for holes with cleaned-off areas about them, and don't neglect a hole with a heap of empty crab shells near it. Poke your spear into all such holes, and if the octopus is at home, he will come out with the spear through some part of its body. All those stories about the octopus squeezing someone to death, or holding the fisherman until the tide came in and drowned him, are pure hogwash. I have seen Hawaiians remove octopuses from their spears, place them on their own chests, backs, or shoulders, and allow them to seize, then go on fishing, paying no attention to the clinging horrors about their necks and arms. In Hawaii, octopus-fishing is considered a tame and pleasant pastime with practically no element of danger in it. The best time of the year for this kind of squidding is during the autumn months.

We also fished for octopuses in deeper water from the dory or the canoe. We used a homemade cowrie-shell lure, for the octopus has a weakness for cowrie meat and will seize on any of these shiny shells he sees. Falani was very particular about the size, color, and pattern of the cowrie shells she used and would carry along a number of these lures, changing them according to light conditions, time of day, or the condition of the water. Frankly, I never believed that this fussiness made much difference, for if octopuses were biting, they would take any shell that passed, and if they weren't, a gold-plated shell wouldn't tempt them, but I must admit that Falani invariably caught more octopuses than I did.

Whenever I was gathering opihis I would also keep an eye out for cowrie shells large enough to make octopus lures. Cowries are found in holes in rocks below high-tide level. We had to be careful about feeling in holes that were below water level, for eels might be hiding there, which meant that we could get a painful bite or even lose a finger. When a large shell was found, it was first thrown in a shady place for a day or two, so the ants would clean the meat out of it. Then a hole was drilled end to end of the shell and a stiff steel wire inserted through the shell. The after end of this wire was fashioned into a strong, sharp hook with the point uppermost, and the forward end of it was bent into an eyelet in which to fasten the fishline. A heavy piece of lead was fastened to the flat bottom of the shell so the lure would stay upright in use.

This lure was slowly dragged along the bottom in some 50 to 150 feet of water while we gently paddled the boat or just allowed it to drift. When the weight of an octopus was felt, a quick jerk imbedded the hook and the octopus was pulled in as quickly as possible. He had to be held well clear of the boat as he was brought over the side, for if he could get a tentacle onto the outside of the boat, he would seize a hold there and be very difficult to loosen.

Probably the most interesting way of all to catch octopus is by torch fishing on the reef at night. On any calm, moonless evening in autumn, with a low tide expected between the fall of darkness and midnight, I could expect Hugo to arrive at my thatched hut with a proposal that we spend the low-tide hours out on the reef torch fishing. Our equipment for this sport was the same as I used for daylight squidding, with the addition of the torch. This was a knapsack affair with a brightly burning asbestos wick above one's head, fueled with kerosene.

The reef at night is a strange, almost unbelievable place with brightly colored fish darting about and many improbable creatures, never seen in the daytime, crawling, swimming, or lying about the coral. We often speared many excellent small fish of several species on these excursions, but our chief game was the puloa, the octopus of the night, which is seldom taken by day; after dark, he lies exposed on the coral. When Hugo speared an octopus, he would bring him quickly to his mouth and bite him in the eyes, claiming this was the quickest and easiest way of killing them, but this was one Polynesian custom I could never bring myself to adopt.

Those still evenings out on the reef were precious moments to me, whether we caught much or little. Even now, when I think of the

Islands, the picture that oftenest comes to mind is of the weird watery world of the night, with all those exotic and colorful creatures exposed to my gaze in the flickering light of the fishing torch. Beachcombing at its best is for those who love lagoons, reefs, boats, surfy shores, and strange methods of catching strange fish.

5. Tropical Seafood Preparation

I ALMOST used the term "cookery" in my chapter heading and then realized that in many Island dishes the fish is not cooked. I have never been able to understand the prejudice of most mainland Americans against raw fish. Recently a charming young lady asked me, "Did you actually eat *raw* fish in the Islands?"

When I assured her that I not only ate it, but liked it immensely, and thought it the very best way to utilize certain kinds of fish, her comment was a sound of disgust. Only a few moments later, she was telling us about a trip she had just made to Maryland's Eastern Shore. She used glowing terms to describe the fine cuisine there and was especially enthusiastic abgout the unique fresh flavor of Chesapeake Bay oysters on the half shell. I asked her if she realized those oysters about which she was so ecstatic were not only raw, but actually alive. She assured me that she was fully aware of this, but since she had known it all her life, she seldom thought about it, and it in no way aroused her disgust or diminished her appreciation of these succulent bivalves.

Again, I was recently dining with a friend who knows and appreciates good food, and he was telling me about his vacation in Hawaii and how much he had enjoyed the many kinds of excellent cooking available there. He then said there was only one Island dish he could never bring himself even to try, and that—you guessed it—was raw fish. I asked him if he knew that the pickled herring on his plate, which he was consuming with such relish, had never been near a fire. He answered, "Of course I know that, but any fool knows that pickled herring is good food."

Any fool also knows that raw fish is good, if the fool has been eating it since childhood and has no built-in prejudices. Anyone who is not a fool should also be able to figure out that a concoction that is enjoyed by millions of people all over the world must have some intrinsic worth.

Although I now live in Pennsylvania, I still eat raw fish whenever I can obtain the proper sort for this purpose. Fresh salmon makes excellent *lomilomi* and fair *sashimi*; red snapper is also good as sashimi, excellent as *nahu-pu*, and very good in lime juice.

In the recipes given here, I will mention only the fish introduced in earlier chapters, but I hope the reader realizes that these are a very small part of the piscatory wealth of the Islands. There are several excellent books on marine fishes of the tropics that can help the novice beachcomber to identify his catch. One of the best for the waters of our fiftieth state is *Sport Fishing in Hawaii,* by Edward Y. Hosaka. This handy little volume has a synoptic key for identifying the fish and lists over a hundred edible fishes found about the Islands, with suggestions as to the best way to prepare each kind for eating. As a help to identification there are line drawings by the author of each fish mentioned.

SASHIMI

This is a Japanese dish that is now appreciated by many people of all races in the Islands, even including some haoles who refuse to allow prejudice to dull their sense of taste. Many kinds of fish can be used, but the very best sashimi is made of aku, kawakawa, or ahi-palaha, all of them varieties of tuna. The fish should be skinned and filleted, then cut into long strips about 2 inches wide by 1 inch thick. Take care to exclude the dark-colored meat, which has a strong taste. These strips are cut crosswise in slices about $\frac{3}{16}$ inch thick. Arrange slices of fish and thin slices of crisp palm heart on a bed of lettuce and chill thoroughly. Sashimi is served either with Mustard Sauce or Ginger Sauce, or even better, small dishes of both. To make Mustard Sauce, obtain some pungent mustard from a Chinese store or restaurant, or use Coleman's dry mustard, made with vinegar rather than water, according to the directions on the box. (Ordinary prepared mustard is very good on hot dogs, but it simply won't do for sashimi.) Thin the Chinese mustard with soy sauce to a watery consistency, and the sauce is made. Ginger Sauce is merely grated fresh gingerroot, and I don't mean freshly dried—I mean the green kind just as it comes from the ground—mixed with soy sauce. Serve these sauces in small, individual dishes, and dip each slice of sashimi into one or the other as it is eaten. Learn to do this with chopsticks— sashimi just doesn't taste right when eaten with a fork. The slices of palm heart can also be dipped into the sauce or just lightly salted and eaten. Serve this dish with bowls of fluffy, Oriental-style rice.

NAHU-PU

The best Nahu-pu I ever ate was made of young ulua, although this fish is never called "young ulua" in the Islands. The Hawaiian language is rich in terms one can use to talk about fish, and an ulua under about 10 pounds is always a *papio*. The papio was cleaned, skinned, and washed, and the meat was diced into bite-size cubes. These were salted generously and allowed to stand for an hour; then the excess salt was rinsed off. A few hot peppers were crushed and added to some ice water, which was poured over the fish. The little wild peppers used in this dish are really pungent, so one should eat nahu-pu with plenty of cold poi to keep the peppers from biting too sharply. Red snapper, or any other white-meated fish, could be prepared this way.

LOMILOMI

The Hawaiian word *lomilomi* means "knead" or "massage," and it very well describes this method of preparing raw fish. Aku, as well as some other species, makes good Lomilomi, but the very finest massaged fish I ever tasted was made of o'io. After the o'io is cleaned and skinned, salt the whole fish and leave it in the refrigerator for a day. Rinse under running water to remove the excess salt, then pull the flesh from the bones with the fingers, cutting the longer strips into chunks about an inch long. Add some salt water, either seawater or fresh water with one teaspoon of salt added to each cup of it, to the flesh and knead and mash the fish meat with the fingers. When it is pretty well worked apart, add some grated onion, some finely chopped limu, and a few crushed wild peppers. Mix well, chill, and serve with kukui-nut relish (see index) and large bowls of poi. Actually, fish prepared this way may closely resemble lox, in final form.

FISH IN LIME JUICE

This was Falani's favorite way of preparing moi, that eminently esculent king of fishes, and while not exactly raw, it is never near a fire. The fish is skinned, the flesh removed from the bones, cut in bite-size chunks and put into a jar, then covered with the juice of fresh limes. The lime juice actually cooks the fish, and since the operation is performed in a clear glass jar, you can watch the cooking process. You can see the flesh lose its clear translucency to become white and opaque like fire-cooked fish. After standing in the refrigerator for several hours, the fish is cooked through. It is then drained, covered with well-salted and freshly made coconut cream, and served while still well chilled. It is as delicate and delicious a dish as the most finicky person could demand.

HOW TO EAT AN OCTOPUS

An octopus has its "innards" in its head, and the body cavity of this bodiless monstrosity can be opened by cutting a few muscles down where its neck would be if it had one. Turn the whole head inside out, and remove all internal organs, including all the dark spots of "ink." Lay these ink bags in a shady place to dry, so they can be used to make some of the magic fish baits described in the preceding chapter. Now, dump a goodly amount of coarse salt into a dishpan and scrub the octopus in it. A slimy froth or foam will form as the boneless horror is vigorously rubbed with the dry salt, so it will have to be rinsed under running water from time to time. Keep up this scrubbing until the octopus stops lathering, the tentacles start to curl, and the skin begins to slip and tear off. If you want to keep some octopus for later use, remove all the skin, cut the tentacles in convenient lengths, and then package and freeze.

A good method of preparing Boiled Octopus is to drop the whole, cleaned beast into a pot of salted, boiling water and cook until it is tender. Personally, I always tested it to see when it was tender and never really timed my cooking. It took from one to two hours to reach the tender point, as a rule, but this would probably vary from cook to cook, since "tender" is a relative term. Actually, octopus cooks superbly in a pressure cooker, becoming wonderfully tender very rapidly.

While your octopus is steaming away, cook a pot of taro tops until medium-tender, then drain. I had Hawaiian friends who raised taro, and they would give me all the taro tops I cared to pick. Cut the octopus into convenient lengths, combine with the taro tops, salt to taste, cover the whole with a cup of freshly made coconut cream, simmer for a few minutes, then serve. Don't tell your Hawaiian neighbors that you are cooking this dish, or they will all come to dinner.

Another way to serve Boiled Octopus is to boil the octopus in salted water as described above, then cut the tentacles into pieces about a half-inch long, and serve with *mizo* thinned with soy sauce. Mizo is a fermented soybean paste and can be bought in most stores in the Islands. Again, use chopsticks when eating octopus prepared in this way; it is boorish to eat such Oriental food with a fork.

The octopus can be eaten raw, too. For Raw Octopus, slice into small bite-size pieces, and for two cups of sliced tentacles add a half-cup of finely chopped limu, a tablespoonful of grated onion, and one finely crushed wild pepper. Stir well so the condiments are evenly distributed through the meat, and allow to sit in the refrigerator for a few hours until the flavors blend. Raw octopus is a bit rubbery in texture, but a taste for it is easily acquired if you hold your prejudices lightly.

To make Fried Octopus, first cover the bottom of a heavy skillet with peanut oil, and when it is hot, slice a clove of garlic into it and fry until the garlic turns brown. Remove every shred of the garlic and discard it. (If even a tiny piece of garlic burns in the pan, it will give the finished dish a bitter, disagreeable taste.) Slice the octopus in thin pieces, frying each one in the hot oil for only a minute or so. When the thin pieces begin to curl up, they are done. Serve with a relish of freshly grated green ginger thinned with soy sauce.

ON EATING OPIHIS

This little limpet is difficult and tedious to gather from surf-beaten lava rocks, but it is one of the most delicious shellfish eaten by man.

You will need at least two dozen per person for any kind of meal, so gather as many as you can find. Wash them thoroughly to remove any clinging grit. This is a univalve, so it doesn't need to be opened like a clam or an oyster. Run a sharp knife with a thin point around the shell, under the opihi, to cut it loose from its moorings. Turn it the other way up in its shell, and season with a tiny sprinkle of paprika. Put a layer of crushed ice on a plate, and imbed the points of the shells in it so they will stay upright and in place. Give them a pleasing arrangement, garnish the plate prettily with sprigs of parsley and thin lemon wedges, and serve immediately before the ice begins to melt and get messy.

I know this sounds like a mighty fancy dish for a beachcomber, but what's wrong with a beachcomber living it up in high style, now and then, if it costs no more than a little extra effort? Actually, I probably ate more raw opihis by just scooping them out of the shell with my fingers and eating them as they were gathered than in any other way, and surely that is primitive enough to satisfy the savage streak in anyone you'd care to have around.

Broiled Opihis are, as far as I know, my own invention. It is another rather fancy dish, but this little limpet is delicious enough to deserve extra attention. In the local variety store I was able to buy some round pan racks, each perforated with 24 holes about a half-inch in diameter. The opihis were washed, cut loose from their fastenings, and turned over in the shells. They were placed on the racks with the points of the shells through the holes, so they would sit upright, then each opihi was seasoned with just one drop of Tabasco sauce. These racks were placed in the broiler for only a few minutes, until the shellfish just started to brown. A full rack was needed for each person served, for each opihi furnishes but one delicious bite. The racks were placed on dinner plates and garnished with green sprigs of parsley and bright-red tomatoes, cut in bite sizes, for the rack furnishes a poor surface on which to cut food. There are a few drops of a delicious nectar in the bottom of each shell, and after the opihi is eaten this should be drunk from the rim of the shell.

Opihis can also be fried like clams or made into a stew like oysters, but I'll leave you to adapt some common cookbook recipe if you want to eat opihis in these ways; as for me, I like them raw or broiled too well to spare any for such plebeian pottage.

CRAYFISH, KING OF CRUSTACEANS

Crayfish, crawfish, crawdads, fresh-water lobsters or crabs, whatever you call them, they are fine food wherever found when properly prepared. I consider them the finest of crustaceans, but even their goodness is not so intrinsic as to be independent of the cook's skill. Once, in the South, a Creole cook served a group of us a huge dish of crawfish that had been boiled whole in water flavored with white wine, bay leaves, and mace. They were arranged on a bed of shredded lettuce like the spokes of a wheel, their heads pointing inwards toward the central red tomato stuffed with tartar sauce that formed the hub, and they were lavishly decorated with sprigs of parsley and tiny cherry tomatoes. It was a beautiful sight, fairly making one's mouth water, and a painting of this dish would serve very well as a symbol of luxury.

But alas, its looks belied its taste. It was messy to eat, dripping from pockets of water entrapped in the shell. I don't like watery shellfish even if the water *has* been flavored with wine and herbs. Being overcooked and then served whole, I found that the contents of the midgut, which was still intact, was a more powerful flavoring agent than the wine and spices, without being nearly so good. After appearing so appetizing, the darned things tasted muddy.

I managed to eat my portion, but I honestly believe that gobs of good, organic, Mississippi mud would have been as good had they been as well spiced and as tastefully served. Some of the other guests were ecstatic about this dish, but I fear their judgment was clouded by the outrageous price we had paid. There really is something more to fine cooking than high prices and lavish decoration.

Later, when raw crawfish were available in the Islands, I decided to see if I could salvage the good features of Crawfish in the Shell and make it live up to its looks. The crawfish were covered with boiling water and left in it about two minutes to kill them and slightly coagulate the meat. Then each crawfish was turned on its back and a deep cut was made from the snout to the end of the tail; the shell was then forced open, and the spongy gills, the little bag just back of the head, and the straight gut that runs to the end of his tail, were removed. The meat in each half was sprinkled lightly with salt and a pinch of chopped fresh tarragon, and the crawfish were placed on a broiler, cut side up, 2 inches below the flame for 6 or 7 minutes until the meat had just started to turn a tawny yellow. They were then removed from the fire and brushed with melted butter, and the two halves of each crawfish were fitted back together.

I kept most of the arrangement of the beautiful but poor-tasting dish of the Creole cook. A red tomato was scooped out and filled with tartar sauce. Arranged around the central stuffed tomato were crisp leaves of romaine lettuce, trimmed so they would just overhang the round platter I was using. Then a reassembled broiled red crawfish was placed on each lettuce leaf with its nose touching the red tomato in the center. Interstices were decorated with halves of cherry tomatoes with the cut side up and on each half I put a few grains of salt, one drop of olive oil, and a sprinkling of chopped fresh basil.

Of course this was an entirely different dish from the one I had formerly been served, but it looked just as good and tasted heavenly. I prepared this dish only one time, and that was as an antidote to prevent that muddy-tasting mess I had formerly eaten from ruining my taste for crawfish altogether. Cleaning crawfish to serve in the shell was terribly tedious work, but the result was pretty and delicious enough to be almost worth it.

I commonly eliminate all this fuss and bother by cleaning and deveining my crawfish catch as outlined on page 103. These tiny pieces of delicate meat, small as a finger joint, can be prepared in a number of tasty and attractive ways.

Crawfish Coconut Cocktail is decorative and delicious, and it uses only ingredients gathered and processed by the beachcomber himself. Cut some paper-thin slices of coconut-palm heart, using an ordinary potato peeler and cutting across the grain, or use heart leaves of romaine lettuce. Line as many cocktail glasses as you will need with these slices. Drop cleaned crawfish tails into salted, boiling water, cook for just two minutes, then remove and chill. Cut the chilled crawfish into dainty bite sizes, fill the centers of the cocktail glasses with these tender and tasty little tidbits, and cover with guava catsup (see index).

Crisply fried Crawfish Tails Tempura make a tempting main dish. Beat 2 eggs slightly, add ¼ cup of water, then stir in 1 cup of biscuit mix, ½ teaspoon salt, 1 teaspoon monosodium glutamate, and a little freshly ground black pepper. Dip the crawdad tails in this batter one at a time, and drop them into smoking hot fat until they turn a nice golden brown. Drain on paper towels for a minute, but serve them while they are still hot. They puff up wonderfully in frying, so this will make your precious crawfish tails go a long way.

Crawfish Newburg is an exquisite luncheon or dinner dish. Heat 1 cup of cleaned crawfish tails in 1 tablespoon of butter or coconut butter for just two minutes, then add 1 cup of sherry wine. In a small mixing bowl beat 1 egg yolk, then stir in 5 tablespoons of light, sweet cream. Gradually add the egg-cream mixture to the crawfish, stirring constantly. When slightly thickened, season with salt and freshly ground black pepper, and serve on toast triangles.

I have said that the crawfish is the finest of crustaceans, but the *aloalo*, or squilla, runs him a close second—if, indeed, he is not entirely the crawdad's equal. The aloalo is cleaned, preserved, and prepared exactly like the crawfish; it can be substituted in any of the above recipes and the result will still be a bona-fide gourmet's dish. It will have a different taste and texture, for crawfish and aloalo are different foods, but both are delicious. This is some of the fanciest eating the beachcomber will do, and I, for one, get a kick out of "putting on the dog" at no cost to myself except a little extra effort and ingenuity that is part of my recreation.

SUN-GLAZED FISH

I have mentioned dried fish several times, and that is what the dish is usually called in English, but this Island method of preparing fish has no relation to the rock-hard, aged product one sees (and smells) around foreign markets in mainland U.S.A. The Hawaiian suffix -*kala*, which is being translated "dried," really means "sunned," and the purpose of this method is to improve the flavor and texture, not to preserve the fish for indefinite storage.

Fish suitable for this kind of preparation include manini, moi, eel, aku, and best of all, maiko. Small fish are merely split in half and cleaned, but large fish, like the aku, are cut into long, thin strips. Soak the fish overnight in a brine made by adding two tablespoons of Hawaiian or other coarse (or kosher) salt to each quart of water.

Next morning wipe the fish dry, place it on a rack in a screened cage, and keep it in full sunlight. Don't allow any of the fish to touch the outside screen, or the flies will spoil it for you. The hot sun partially cooks the fish, firms it, and subtly enhances and changes the flavor. Some like their fish sunned more, and some less, but I think that just two days in full sunlight gives most fish exactly the right kind of glaze and the best flavor.

Hawaiians like to eat sunned fish with no further preparation, serving it with poi. I like it broiled over charcoal, on a hibachi, and served hot with a big gob of thick coconut cream on each piece. When one is surfeited with fresh fish, as a beachcomber is sometimes apt to be, this Sun-Glazed fish serves as a delicious change of diet.

CHINESE FISH CAKES

The very best Fish Cakes are made of o'io (the Hawaiian name for bonefish) or awa, with little choice between them, and a fair product can be made of chilled chunks of man-eater shark, ground in a food chopper. To make fish cakes of o'io or awa, clean and skin the fish, and leave it in the refrigerator overnight. Then, starting at the head and working toward the tail, scrape the flesh from the bones with a tablespoon.

Put the boneless scraped flesh in a large mixing bowl and stir and work it while gradually adding water that has been salted at the rate of 1 teaspoon of Hawaiian salt to 1 cup of water. As you work this mushy fish, it will assume a spongy texture and can be kneaded almost like dough. Mix in some chopped green onions, then wet the hands and form the fish into small balls. These are delicious fried, or you can use them to make an extra fancy fish soup. Boil the head and the scraped bones of the o'io or awa for 30 minutes in just enough water to cover them. Melt 2 tablespoons of coconut butter in a skillet and sauté 1 sliced onion and 2 sliced tomatoes until the onion just starts to turn yellow. Now strain off 1 quart of liquid from the fish heads and bones and add this liquid to the onion-tomato mixture. Pour in 1 cup of dry white wine, and season with salt, freshly ground black pepper, and a pinch of saffron. As soon as the soup boils, drop in a dozen or more of the fish cakes. Simmer without boiling for 10 minutes, then pour into a deep dish lined with slices of buttered toast, and presto, you have a Beachcomber Bouillabaisse with a tropical taste that would delight an epicure. Striped bass or any other well-flavored fish could be prepared this way.

BROILED FISH STEAKS

Both the ulua and the mahimahi furnish excellent steaks for broiling, but since neither of these fish is particularly fat, some oil needs to be added during the cooking process. Slice the steaks straight across the fish, making them at least 1 inch thick. Fish steaks are better cooked in the broiler of your range than over a hibachi or grill. Salt each slice and cover it generously with thick coconut cream, and place 3 inches below the broiler flame. Turn after 10 minutes, cover the other side with coconut cream, and broil for 5 minutes more. Arranged on a plate with a mound of rice sprinkled with saffron, and prettily garnished with parsley and cherry tomatoes, this is a dish you should be proud to serve to anyone.

LAULAU

The Hawaiian word *laulau* means "two leaves," and the two kinds of leaves involved in this indigenous dish are taro tops and *ti* leaves. The taro tops enter into the dish, and the ti leaves furnish the container in which to cook it and the plate from which to eat it. Boil the taro tops in salted water for 5 minutes, then drain. Line a bowl with ti leaves and put a large serving-spoonful of the taro tops on the leaves to hold them in place. Next, add a half-cup of diced fish, then 2 slices of bacon cut small, or some thin slices of fat pork (wild or domestic). Season with salt and pepper, and cover all with about four tablespoonfuls of rich coconut cream. Gather up the ends of the leaves and tie them with a ribbon of ti leaf to make a little green bag of the whole laulau. Traditionally, these are cooked in the *imu* or underground oven, but you can do a good job using the oven of your range. Make one laulau for each person to be served, place them all in a pan without added water, and bake them for 45 minutes in a 350° oven. Serve them still tied, so each person can open his own and enjoy the marvelous aroma that arises when the laulau is untied. Most Island fish can be used to make laulau. Use a little less coconut cream and fat pork with oily fish, and a little more with the dry kinds.

The number of ways in which fish can be prepared are unlimited, and there are Island fish that will taste good in nearly any fish recipe you can find. Fish is fine food, with many essential and easily digested proteins. Eating plenty of fish also assures one of getting an ample supply of many minerals that are essential to health and are hard to come by elsewhere. For health's sake, for fun's sake, and for goodness' sake, the beachcomber should catch and eat lots of fresh ocean fish.

6. Bananas for the Taking

THE BANANA is as essential to the South Sea life as the coconut. No tropical island can be called a paradise unless bananas grow there. According to ancient tradition, the banana grew in the original Paradise, and this, not the apple, was the very fruit with which Eve tempted Adam and started us on our merry way. Bless her!

Our European ancestors seem to have known that the banana was the fruit through which man fell from pristine innocence. When English-speaking soldiers first encountered this fruit, in the East, during the Crusades, they quickly called it "apple of paradise." It was only in more recent times that the term "banana" was borrowed from a Congolese language. Trying to describe this fruit by calling it some kind of apple was a mistake, for the home folks thought these travelers were talking about just another variety of *Malus malus* (or ordinary apples), and ever since, Eve has been portrayed offering Adam a big, red apple.

There are no truly wild bananas except for a few almost inedible seed-bearing species found in tropical Asia. Long ago the true banana gave up the ability to bear seed and came into a kind of symbiotic relationship with man, offering him immense quantities of nutritious food in exchange for his aid in the banana propagation and dissemination. The arrangement worked exceedingly well. Man has carried banana shoots into every part of the tropics to which he has penetrated, and the plant has proliferated into a vast number of varieties, with many flavors, textures, and uses.

Strangely enough, the "tree of knowledge" from which the banana springs is not a tree at all, but a gigantic herb. What appears to be the trunk is really a cylinder of tightly compressed living leaf-sheaths, and it is crisp and juicy throughout, with no woody part. These "trunks" may grow 20 feet tall and 8 inches in diameter in some varieties, but the largest of them can be felled with a single well-directed slash of a machete. Many newcomers to the tropics are horrified to see people harvesting bananas by cutting down the "trees," but a banana tree dies after maturing only one bunch of fruit. It is good practice to cut the old stem down to make more room for the growth of the little suckers or offshoots that spring from the base of the old plant. There are always too many of these young shoots, which are called *kiekis* by the Hawaiians, the same word they use for human children. Left to themselves, bananas tend to crowd too thickly for their own good, so, for best production, the *kiekis* must be drastically thinned. The excess shoots are either used for new planting or discarded.

Among the hundreds of varieties found growing in the tropics one can find tall plants and dwarf plants, big ones and little ones; the fruit varies in size, color, shape, quantity, and quality. There are short, round bananas, and long, skinny ones, red, yellow, and green fruit, as well as all shades between, hard bananas and soft ones, sweet kinds and starchy kinds. Some are crisp, and some are mushy. Each of these numerous kinds presents a new and different experience to the palate. Never say, "I don't like bananas," until you have sampled the great variety of kinds to be found in the lands where they grow.

Bananas are now known and used all over the world, but it seems very strange to me that among the hundreds of varieties in existence, the people of northern climes are acquainted with only one, the Gros Michel, or Bluefield, as it is called in Hawaii. I must admit that this common supermarket variety is a good banana, one of the very finest for eating out of hand, although I prefer other kinds for cooking. While in the Islands, I learned to prefer certain varieties for certain uses. Some are good raw, while others must be cooked before they are edible. Some are better fried, and some are better baked, while

still others are best for salads, ice cream, or puddings. Also, I found
that any one variety, when used exclusively, was likely to pall, and
then another kind came as a refreshing change.

When the first Polynesians landed in Hawaii, they no doubt had
live banana shoots in the holds of their great double canoes. In almost
every well-watered valley in the Islands you find survivals of these

first plantings. The Hawaiians used the fruit from the wild groves
both as food for great feasts and as reserve stores in case of famine.

When I went in search of wild bananas, I usually had in my knapsack a kieki or two from some good variety of cultivated banana and
set them out in any favorable location I happened to find. Future
foragers in the hidden valleys of Hawaii who find wild bananas of a
variety usually found only in cultivated fields may be sampling offspring from shoots I once planted. Don't be too quick to give me
credit, however. Apparently others anticipated me in this activity, for
I have found recently introduced varieties such as the Bluefield, the

Cavendish, the ice cream, and the ridiculously named apple banana growing far from the modern haunts of men.

While I was beachcombing, I ran out of bananas only when I was too interested in other activities, or too lazy, to go out and find them. Wild bananas are more plentiful in January and February than in other months, but if you search the mountain valleys long enough, at any time of the year, you are sure, eventually, to find bananas at just the right stage for cutting and carrying home for the final ripening. However, a seasoned beachcomber would never hunt for bananas in such a haphazard fashion. Whenever I was out in the jungles, I kept my eyes peeled for wild bananas. When I found bunches of immature fruit, I made a memorandum of their location and attempted to estimate just when they would be ripe for gathering. After some practice I became quite skillful at guessing when any given bunch would reach maturity. On returning home, I always marked these locations and estimated dates on my calendar; then, when the date rolled around, I would return for the harvest.

Once, I had located two beautiful bunches of Bluefields growing a mile or so from the nearest road. When, according to my calculations, they were ready for the plucking, I drove to the mouth of the valley and started working my way inland to bring out the booty. I had made my way a mile or more up the valley, mainly by leaping from rock to rock in the stream bed, and was beginning to wonder if any bunch of bananas was worth carrying out over such terrain. About this time I met a huge Hawaiian coming down the valley; across his shoulder was a carrying-pole, and on each end of it hung *my* bananas. I could only accept the loss with good grace and go in search of better-hidden fruit.

I suppose the reader is wondering who owns the land of which I made such free use both in planting and harvesting. Frankly, I never inquired. I was always careful never to do anything that would detract from the value of the property on which I was foraging, and no one ever objected to my free use of the wild produce that otherwise would go to waste. If your sense of the rights of private property so cramps your conscience that it wouldn't permit you this freedom, you would make a very hungry beachcomber.

Because of the availability of the Gros Michel of the supermarkets, Northerners are already familiar with the banana as a fresh fruit, over cereals, in salads and fruit cocktails, in pies and cakes, and with or in ice cream. Since the reader already knows how to use bananas in these ways, or can find recipes in any general cookbook, we will concentrate on how to use bananas as a vegetable and in combination with other tropical fruits.

Few Northerners ever think of the banana as a vegetable, but millions of people in the tropics use this "fruit of paradise" as their staple starchy food, and with them it replaces the potatoes and bread of our own diets. I suspect that one reason why those outside the area where bananas grow never learned this use of them is that the variety available to us is not the best for this purpose. Not that the Gros Michel cannot be cooked; baked, boiled, or fried when barely firm-ripe, it is a perfectly acceptable vegetable, and I have often eaten it in these ways, but it is definitely not the best kind for these uses. My own favorite cooking banana is the *Maiamaoli*, a Hawaiian variety and fortunately the most common wild banana of the Islands. The beautiful, orange-colored flesh is delicious when well-cooked, and this banana is a good source of vitamin A, contains some B_1, and is a fair source of vitamin C. It is also a good source of phosphorus, a fair source of iron, and contains some calcium, so these wild bananas are not only good, they are good for you.

Bananas can be baked or boiled right in their own skins. For Boiled Bananas, just drop ripe cooking bananas in boiling water and simmer for 25 minutes, and they are ready to serve. They can be peeled and seasoned with butter, salt, and pepper at the table.

Plain Baked Bananas are simply laid, unpeeled, in a baking pan with no water and baked in a 350° oven for 45 minutes. By then the bananas will be very soft and the skins beginning to burst in places. They can be peeled and seasoned at the table, just like boiled bananas.

If you want to make a little fancier dish of baked or boiled bananas, remove the skins after they are cooked, slice them lengthwise, and cover them with freshly made hot coconut cream sweetened with a little sugar or jaggery.

A good dish that can be served hot or cold is Baked Bananas with Orange Sections. For this method, peel 4 bananas and slice them lengthwise. Next, peel 2 oranges, divide them into sections, and remove the membrane from each section. Place the sliced bananas in the bottom of a baking dish, arrange the orange sections on top, sprinkle with ¼ cup of sugar, then pour 2 tablespoons of orange juice and 2 tablespoons of lemon juice over all. Bake at 350° for 45 minutes.

Sautéd Bananas are an excellent accompaniment for wild pork, and they also make an easily prepared and delicious vegetable with any meal, even breakfast. Melt 2 tablespoons of clarified coconut butter in a frying pan, then peel and cut 4 bananas in half lengthwise. Brown the halves in the fat, then add the juice of half an orange, the juice of 1 lime, and 2 tablespoons of sugar or jaggery. Simmer until bananas are very soft, then serve piping hot.

Besides the obvious uses of bananas in desserts, and the ways I have outlined, this fruit combines well with most tropical fruits, meats, and other foods. While living in my thatched hut, I seldom cooked bananas twice the same way. I would place ripe cooking bananas around the loin of a wild boar, as I roasted it in an *imu* or underground oven. I used bananas, cooked or raw, with whatever other fruit I had on hand. I even added banana to such unlikely dishes as meat casseroles, crab salads, and poultry stuffing. Most of these odd concoctions were edible, and some of them were actually delicious. The banana lends itself well to such experimentation. In banana cookery, just let yourself go, and the result will usually please you. The banana can be the beachcomber's standby. On a high tropical island there is no need for anyone to go hungry as long as wild bananas are ripening back in the mountain valleys.

Besides serving as a staple food for half the people of the world, the banana plant has many uses in folk medicine. In *Medicinal Plants of India and Pakistan* [1] I counted fifty different medicinal uses of this "tree of knowledge," utilizing every part of the fruit and plant. From time immemorial, primitive man in the tropics has poulticed his wounds with a pulp made of the pounded peelings of ripe bananas. Medically sophisticated Western man long ignored this use of the banana, even though the banana skin has been spoken of as "nature's bacteria-proof wrapper." Now, science has vindicated this ancient usage by discovering that the skins of ripe bananas contain powerful antibiotic substances that are effective against both disease-causing fungi and pathogenic bacteria. Thus, once again, as so often happens, primitive man, ignorant of the germ theory of disease and guided

[1] *Medicinal Plants of India & Pakistan*, by J. F. Dastur, F.N.I. D. B. Taraporevala Sons & Co. Ltd., 210 Hornby Road, Bombay, India.

by unaided observation and intuition, has anticipated the findings of modern science by thousands of years.[2]

In many tropical countries, the huge green leaves of the banana are used decoratively, as tablecloths, place mats, dinner plates, and napkins. I have eaten many a meal from sections of banana leaf and have even served my guests on this same kind of green chinaware. What a joy it is simply to throw the tablecloth, napkins, and dishes into the trash at the end of the meal and forget the dishwashing and laundry that usually have to be done after the guests depart. Truly, bananas are wonderful.

2 "Antibiotics That Come From Plants" by P. S. Schaffer, William E. Scott & Thomas D. Fontaine. *Yearbook of Agriculture*, 1950-1951, page 732.

7. Guavas by the Ton
(Psidium guajava)

AMONG tropical fruits the guava is one of God's greatest gifts to greedy man. Originating in tropical America, it has been introduced all over the tropics, and in Polynesia it has gone native with a vengeance, becoming a pest in pasturelands and forming veritable jungles in localities suited for few other plants. Its tenacity of life and its iron-hard wood make it very difficult to eradicate, once it has gotten a start. Its roots find their way down through the porous rocks of Hawaii and anchor this plant so firmly that often the guava bush is the one trustworthy handhold one can use in climbing the crumbly, volcanic hills of these islands.

It varies from a mere shrub a few feet high to a maximum of 30 feet in height. The leaves are ovate or oblong and covered with a soft down that gives them a grayish appearance. The fruit is lemon-yellow, or occasionally almost white, round or slightly pear-shaped, from 1½ to 3 inches in diameter, and it is the most abundant and easily obtainable wild fruit in the Islands. Due to seedling variation, and all these wild trees form from seedlings, the color of the flesh may be white, yellow, pink, or red. The predominant taste varies from sweet to sour, but all guavas, white or red, sweet or sour, have a characteristic guava flavor that is unmistakable.

Each micro-locality matures its guavas at a different time of the year and, while this fruit is more plentiful from April to October, the mobile, Jeep-borne beachcomber will be able to find guavas in their prime the year round. Most people like guavas at the first taste, and the beachcomber will do well to cultivate a taste for it, for, nutritionally speaking, this is one of the finest fruits in the world. It is nature's vitamin pill. The guava is a splendid source of ascorbic acid (vitamin C), a fair source of vitamin A, and even furnishes significant amounts of thiamin (vitamin B_1), which is rarely found in fruits. It is also an excellent source of iron and a fair source of calcium and phosphorus. A single guava, eaten fresh from the tree, or a small glass of canned guava juice, will give you your full daily quota of vitamin C, and a goodly portion of some of the other needed vitamins and minerals.

Glowing, energetic health is absolutely essential to enjoyable beachcombing, and the guava can help provide and protect this kind of health in a most painless and pleasant way. During the height of the guava season, which varies from locality to locality, one can gather guavas by the bushel, by the barrel, or by the ton. There is little competition for this wild fruit, for in the Islands the guava is a pest, and who wants to eat a pest, no matter how delicious and wholesome it happens to be?

I have known several beachcombers who made a fair portion of their cash income by gathering wild guavas and selling them to commercial canneries that preserve guava juice and make guava jelly, mostly for export. Besides selling them, what could a beachcomber do with bushels of guava? The ripe fruit is very perishable, and even when kept in the refrigerator will remain in edible condition only a few days. The answer is, eat what you can ánd can what you can't, and be sure to can your surplus as soon after picking as possible, if you want to retain the maximum amount of those healthful vitamins and minerals.

Canning guavas is easily done, and the rankest amateur can be certain of success if he observes a few simple precautions. Slice the guavas into a kettle until it is two-thirds full. Slicing the fruit enables one to detect and discard all worm-eaten parts, for the larva of the Malayan fruit fly sometimes infests the guava. Barely cover the slices with water and bring to a boil, then reduce the heat and simmer for 15 minutes, and you will find the fruit perfectly soft. Put the fruit, juice and all, through a colander, ricer, or food mill to remove the seeds and skins. Reheat the juicy pulp to the boiling point, then pour immediately into hot, sterile, quart fruit jars, filling them to the very brim, and seal with two-piece dome lids. The reason I recommend filling the jars so full is that we must exclude every bit of oxygen-bearing air, for even a small amount of oxygen can cause considerable loss of vitamin C.

Wrap each jar in several thicknesses of newspaper and store in a dark closet, for light also causes deterioration of the vitamin C content. Even when guavas have been properly preserved and stored, there is a gradual loss of ascorbic acid if they are left too long uneaten, but this age-loss is of little significance unless the canned fruit is kept for a year or more.

If guavas, canned as directed, are left undisturbed for a time, the pulp settles to the bottom, leaving the clear juice on top. This is good, for it means that you have succeeded in canning two products with different uses in one jar. Guava juice and pulp are some of the most versatile foods ever to come out of a fruit jar, and the ways in which they can be prepared are endless, as you can surmise from the sample recipes I give below. An ingenious cook can discover many new ways to serve this palatable fruit. I found that by constantly varying the dishes and drinks, I could consume an average of one quart of this combined juice and pulp every two days, and I'm sure such copious consumption of this wholesome fruit was one reason I remained healthy and vigorous in a climate that is traditionally supposed to render the white man languid and apathetic.

One tends to tire of even the finest of flavors, and the excellent flavor of guava products is no exception. I tried adding a thumb-sized root of fresh ginger and the outside, yellow part of the peel of one orange to each kettle of guavas as I cooked them for canning, and I found that this ginger-orange-flavored guava could be eaten for a long time without palling. After that, I always included these flavors in part of my canning.

When the pulp has settled to the bottom of the jars, then Guava Juice, that peer of all breakfast juices, far exceeding orange or tomato juice in vitamin C content, is already made. Cautiously unwrap a jar of canned guavas, holding it upright all the time so as not to disturb the settled pulp. Open the jar and carefully decant the clear juice into another container. Save the pulp, for you will soon see that it, also, can be prepared in many delicious ways. I like to drink guava juice diluted with a little water and sweetened with a spoonful of honey.

If you are expecting company, why not make a Hawaiian Fruit Punch? Slice a thumb of fresh gingerroot and boil with 3 cups of water and 2 cups of sugar for about 10 minutes, then strain out the slices of ginger to leave a thin, strongly ginger-flavored sweet syrup. Allow this to cool, then add 2 cups of guava juice, the juice of 1 large pineapple, the juice of a dozen Hawaiian oranges, and the juice of half a dozen limes. If available, add ¼ cup of finely chopped mint leaves. You can also add a pint of *okolehau* or a quart of *panini swipes* without spoiling the flavor too badly. This fruit-juice mixture is purposely made strong so that it can be poured over ice cubes without the melting ice diluting it too much.

On some cool, rainy night try serving your guests cups of Hot Spiced Guava Juice. Take a finger-joint's length of fresh gingerroot, chopped fine, half a stick of cinnamon, crushed, and about a dozen whole cloves; tie them in a small bag, and boil in 2 cups of water in a covered pan for about 10 minutes. Remove the spice bag, then add 2 cups of guava juice, the juice of 1 Hawaiian lemon, and enough raw sugar or honey to sweeten to taste. Heat just to the simmering point, then serve in demitasse cups or small punch glasses.

The best-known product of guava juice is Guava Jelly, for in this form the guava has found its way all over the world. It can usually be found in most grocery stores, so give it a trial some day, although I must say that I prefer the homemade product, especially if a bit of ginger and orange peel have been added as the fruit was cooking. The secret of good jelly is small batches and rapid evaporation, and this prevents commercial companies from ever achieving the very finest in jellies.

Carefully pour 2 cups of clear juice from a quart of canned guavas. If a little of the pulp gets in, too, it won't harm the flavor, though it might make the jelly slightly cloudy in appearance. Bring the 2 cups of juice to a boil, then add 2¼ cups of sugar, all at once. Guavas need no added pectin, so the jelly is usually made by the "long-boil" method which, under ideal conditions, can be just as "short-boil" as any other method. Boil the juice until the jelly test tells you it's ready to jell, then pour into glasses and cover with paraffin, or even better, pour into straight-sided half-pint jars and seal with two-piece dome lids.

Do you know how to make the jelly test? It's easier done than explained, but I'll try. After adding the sugar, bring the jelly to a good rolling boil and keep it boiling for at least 1 minute. Dip up a bit of the liquid with a cooking spoon and wave it about to cool it slightly, then pour it back into the pot from the side of the spoon. If it runs off like water, you are nowhere near the finishing point. When the last of the jelly drips off the spoon in two places, you are getting there but haven't quite arrived, but when the last few drops coalesce and drop off in a sheet, snatch the jelly from the fire. Overcooked jelly is dark and gummy.

To make Guava Syrup, add 2 cups of water and 3 cups of sugar to 2 cups of guava juice and boil until it is the right consistency, usually about 30 minutes. This syrup is excellent served hot over pancakes or waffles, and makes good sauce for puddings or topping for ice cream. To store this syrup for future use, pour it boiling hot into sterile jars and seal with sterilized dome lids. You can use this syrup to make a nourishing Beachcomber's Drink by simply adding 2 tablespoons of it to a glass of coconut milk and stirring well. Be sure you use real coconut milk, squeezed from grated coconut meat, for this is a nauseating mixture if you use the water from the cavity of the nut.

Coconut-Guava Sherbet can be made in the ice trays of your refrigerator. Dissolve ¾ cup of sugar in 1 cup of guava juice and boil for about 3 minutes; then cool. Add another cup of guava juice and the juice of 2 limes. Place this in an ice tray and freeze it into mushy ice. Just before it reaches that stage, beat 2 egg whites until they form soft peaks, then add ¼ cup of sugar, and beat to stiff peaks. Now, pour the frozen guava mixture into a chilled mixing bowl and beat until it is fluffy. Add one cup of rich coconut milk and fold in the egg whites. Return this airy mixture to the ice tray and freeze stiff, and you will have a smooth, delicious sherbet.

Now that we have learned a few ways of using the juice from the top of the jar, let's see what we can do with that pulp, which has settled to the bottom.

The simplest and most widely known product of guava pulp is Guava Butter. You will need 2 cups of guava pulp, 1½ cups of sugar, the juice of 1 lime, ¼ teaspoon ground cinnamon, ¼ teaspoon ground allspice, and if the guavas have been cooked without ginger, add 1 teaspoon grated fresh ginger. Just combine all ingredients and boil until it is thick, stirring often to prevent scorching. Pour boiling hot into straight-sided half-pint jars, and seal with two-piece dome lids. This butter is excellent on pancakes or toast, with hot biscuits or rolls, and when combined half-and-half with peanut butter, it makes a tasty and filling sandwich spread.

Guava Candy is a rare treat and is certainly more healthful than most commercial confections. Combine 2 cups of guava pulp with 3½ cups of sugar and cook over low heat until it is very thick, stirring constantly to prevent burning. Meanwhile, soak 1 teaspoon unflavored gelatin in 2 tablespoons cold water for 5 minutes, then melt over hot water. When the guava-sugar mixture becomes so thick that it seems to leave the sides of the pan, stir the gelatin into it and remove from the fire. Allow the candy to cool until barely lukewarm, stir in ½ cup of chopped Indian almonds, and pour into a buttered pan to harden. When cold, it will have the consistency of smooth gumdrops and can be cut into squares; then wrap each piece in wax paper. For variety, and to make the product more "beachcomby," substitute Hawaiian raw sugar, or better yet, coconut jaggery, for the sugar called for in the recipe. Each of these substitutions will produce a different flavor and a slightly different texture, but all are delicious. This is a real show-off recipe.

The flavors of guava and papaya combine exceedingly well in a tasty product called Guava-Papaya Jam. Make 2 cups of papaya pulp by pressing the edible parts of a soft, ripe papaya through a colander or food mill and mix it with 2 cups of canned guava pulp. Boil the fruit until most of the water has evaporated, then add 4 cups of sugar and the juice and grated peel of 1 lemon. Cook until thick, then pour into glasses or jars, and seal. Surely I don't have to tell anyone how to use jam so delicious. Just eat it.

While living alone in my thatched hut I rarely bought bread, as I quickly learned to prefer poi or rice as a starchy food. When I bought a loaf to make sandwiches to carry on a hike, hunt, or fishing trip, I had trouble using it all before it became stale. I couldn't bear to see anything purchased with money go to waste, as I was jealous of every joyful moment of my time and wanted to spend as little as possible of it in earning money to buy things. I found that by crumbling leftover bread into a bake pan and drying it slowly in a low oven and then sealing it, still hot, into jars, I could have bread crumbs for cooking that would keep perfectly fresh for months.

I most often used these bread crumbs to make Guava Betty, a simple dessert of which I am so inordinately fond that I would sometimes make a whole meal of it. Start making it by cooking together 2 cups of guava pulp and ¼ cup of jaggery until the mixture is very thick. Then melt ¼ cup of coconut butter and blend it with a heaping cup of bread crumbs. Mix ½ teaspoon of cinnamon and ½ teaspoon of nutmeg with ¼ cup of ordinary white sugar. Now, start building your betty. Cover the bottom of a baking dish with a layer of buttered crumbs, then add a layer of the guava-jaggery mixture, and sprinkle with some of the sugar-spice mix. Continue adding layers in this order until the ingredients are used up, topping it with a layer of the crumbs. Now, mix the juice of 1 Hawaiian lemon with 2 tablespoons of water and pour this over the betty; cover the dish and bake for 20 minutes in a 350° oven, then remove the cover and bake for 10 minutes more to brown the crumbs on top. Serve slightly warm with whipped coconut cream. —All right, so you could use butter or margarine, regular sugar, and whipping cream from the store, instead of the coconut products that are so much labor to prepare, but it wouldn't feed your soul or your body nearly so well. Why become a beachcomber if not to have time for such nonprofit activities that are so profitable in the satisfactions they yield?

Obviously I am not a fanatic on this subject of natural foods, or I would have found a more primitive substitute for the bakery bread, refined sugar, and purchased spices. Even my wild guavas were preserved in machine-made jars, and the betty was baked in an electric oven. If my beachcombing days proved anything, it was that the primitive and the modern, the wild and the domestic, the savage and the civilized, could be blended together harmoniously in my food, my home, my life, and my very soul.

One man's blend is another man's blunder. Some may long to subsist entirely on raw food from wild sources, while others are satisfied to enliven their food with occasional bits of foraged fare. If you find the labor of gathering and preparing wild products becoming burdensome, then ease up on this activity, or you might begin to hate the life you expected to love. On the other hand, if you feel that your life is becoming too artificial, then enjoy more of the good things that you can receive as a gift from nature with your own hands, for some of us have a very broad streak of the primitive in us that needs considerable nourishment.

A good blend of the exotic and the commonplace is Guava Tapioca. Add ½ cup of sugar to 2 cups of guava pulp and cook until it is only slightly thickened, that is, until it is no longer watery. Meanwhile, in the top of a double boiler, combine ¼ cup of minute tapioca, 1½ cups of water, ¼ cup of sugar, and a pinch of salt. Bring to the boiling point over direct heat, then place over boiling water until the tapioca is transparent. Combine the products of both pots and add the juice of 1 lemon and a bit of the grated rind. Cool until lukewarm; then pour into dessert dishes or sherbet glasses and chill. To add a further Island touch, serve with whipped coconut cream.

Guava-Coconut Ice Cream is a delicacy for those who like to use all natural ingredients. You will need 2 cups of guava pulp, 2 cups of rich coconut milk, 2 tablespoons of Hawaiian lemon juice, and 2 cups of palm sugar or jaggery. Just mix all ingredients together and stir until the palm sugar is dissolved, then freeze in an ice-cream freezer, using 8 pounds of ice to 1 pound of rock salt. Of course, cane sugar and whipping cream could be substituted for those derived from the coconut palm and the result would be good, but it would also be an entirely different product.

If you have no ice-cream freezer, then make a Coconut-Guava Mousse, which can be frozen in your refrigerator. Use 1 cup of guava pulp, 1 tablespoon of lemon juice, ¼ cup of palm sugar, and 2 cups of whipped coconut cream. When the coconut cream is whipped fairly stiff, mix the other ingredients together and fold them into the whipped coconut cream. Pour into ice trays and freeze.

Not all guava products come under the classification of sweets or desserts. Guava Catsup is a spicy condiment that can do much to improve the esculent qualities of a hunk of wild beef from some old bull slain in the mountains of Lanai, or a roast of wild goat meat. I also enjoy avocado diced and covered with guava catsup in lieu of salad dressing.

Cook 1 finely sliced, medium-sized onion and 1 chopped or crushed clove of garlic in ¼ cup of water until they are soft. Then add 2 cups of guava pulp, 1 small red pepper, ¼ cup of vinegar, ½ teaspoon allspice, ¼ teaspoon cinnamon, ⅛ teaspoon ground cloves, 1 cup of sugar, and a pinch of salt. Cook all together over low heat for about 40 minutes; then pour into hot, sterilized bottles and cap, or into hot sterilized fruit jars and seal.

Guava pulp, like applesauce, can be used in innumerable recipes for pies, cakes, fillings, dumplings, conserves, and marmalades, but this section is already beginning to resemble a conventional cookbook. However, I can't leave guava pulp until I tell you about a delicious Guava Chiffon Pie filling that can be made from it. Soak 1 tablespoon unflavored gelatin in 3 tablespoons cold water for 5 minutes. In the top of a doubler boiler combine 1 cup guava pulp, ⅔ cup sugar, and the yolks of 2 eggs. Cook and stir over boiling water until it thickens, then add the soaked gelatin and stir well. Allow to cool, then stir in 2 tablespoons lemon juice, and put in the refrigerator to set.

When the mixture has congealed enough to mound slightly when spooned, beat 2 egg whites until they form soft peaks, add ¼ teaspoon of salt and ¼ cup of sugar, and beat until the eggs are glossy and form stiff peaks. Now, beat the congealed guava mixture until it is foamy; then fold in the egg whites. Pour into a graham-cracker crust or baked pastry shell and chill in the refrigerator until it is firm.

To make a delicious Guava Icebox Cake, place thin slices of lady-fingers, plain cake, or dessert shells in individual dishes and cover generously with the same chiffon pie filling. When served, either as a pie or as an icebox cake, it can be garnished with whipped coconut cream or guava jelly—one, both, or neither—for it's a pretty rich dessert just as it is.

One would think, from the way I have been going on about them, that I ate guavas only after they were canned, but the guava, as a fresh fruit, should not be overlooked. As I was driving or hiking about the Islands, no matter what my errand, I always had time to stop and eat a few guavas whenever I saw a tree loaded with prime fruit.

There is a belief (I'd call it a superstition) among the old-timers in the Islands that fresh guavas cause constipation, but they certainly never had that effect on me. Some of my Portuguese friends on Maui told me that as children they had subsisted largely on diets of dried beans, dried codfish, Portuguese sausage, polished rice, and home-baked bread made of imported white flour, with little or no fresh fruits and vegetables. Despite this obviously vitamin-short diet, these children were under strict orders from their parents to eat no wild fruit or vegetables, as these were considered unwholesome. All my friends confessed that these orders were seldom obeyed and that they stuffed themselves with guavas and handfuls of wild parsley at every opportunity. Such disobedience probably saved many lives.

Besides just eating them straight from the tree, you can use guavas in many fine fresh-fruit dishes, and they blend exceedingly well with bananas, papayas, pineapples, and coconuts. When they are available, I always include guavas in fruit salads, and while I was in the Islands I often dined on fruit salad alone.

One of my favorite dishes, which I call Ambrosia, was made of guavas, bananas, papayas, coconuts, and sometimes Surinam cherries, five fruits that are usually available to the sharp-eyed tropical forager all year long. Peel 6 large, ripe guavas and cut them in halves. Scoop out the inner pulp and put it through a sieve to remove the seeds. Mix this pulp with ½ cup of sugar. Now cover the bottom of a serving dish with thin slices of the guava shells, add a couple of slices of banana, cut lengthwise, then a layer of thinly sliced, peeled papaya, then another layer of guavas, and continue in this manner until you run out of materials or the dish begins to look too formidable in size. Pour the sweetened pulp over all, cover the dish and chill thoroughly in the refrigerator. Serve with about ½ cup of whipped coconut cream topped with 2 or 3 raw Surinam cherries cut in small pieces to add color and piquancy. When I used homemade palm sugar or wild honey for sweetening, I was able to make this delicious and wholesome salad meal with no cash outlay whatever, and I daresay that on the evenings I ate this concoction few people in the Islands dined better than I.

Guava Shortcake must bow to few other desserts. Peel and halve the guavas as directed for ambrosia, then cut the shells in small squares or chunks. Put the pulp through a sieve, measure it, and add an equal quantity of sugar. Mix the pulp, guava chunks, and sugar all together, and allow them to sit in the refrigerator for several hours. Prepare a rich biscuit dough from a commercial mix, or by your own recipe, and bake a rather large biscuit for each person to be served. Hot from the oven, break the biscuits open, butter them lightly, then add a generous helping of the sweetened fruit, cover with whipped cream or whipped coconut cream, and serve immediately.

In the diet-conscious America of today, I know that many will be thinking that all these rich desserts I am describing will not help in taking off weight. That is true, but the only ones who need worry about this are those who purchase the ingredients from the market instead of going out and gathering them from the wild. When one climbs a palm for the coconuts, scales cliffs or crashes through jungles for the guavas, and descends into wild canyons for the bananas, those excess calories are burned up. Overweight is seldom a problem in a food-gathering culture, for those who work at it, not because the people are underfed, but because the rugged exercise of gathering wild food will keep anyone slim and trim, despite those extra calories. Indeed, you will find that you sorely need the extra energy they can provide. Even today I seldom indulge in a rich dessert unless I feel that I have earned the right to do so by gathering at least part of the materials for it with my own hands.

THE CATTLEY OR STRAWBERRY GUAVA
Psidium cattleianum

This sprightly little fruit almost never appears in the Island markets, and it is seldom cultivated except in a few high-altitude gardens where it is grown as an ornamental. If you want to enjoy this beautifully colored little guava with a flavor that combines just the right amounts of sweet and sour, you will have to get out in the hills and pick them from wild trees. Fortunately, if one is thoroughly acquainted with the areas where it grows, ripe strawberry guavas can usually be found from May until November.

Originating in Brazil, the worth of this refreshing little fruit was early recognized, and it has been introduced into nearly every part of the world where it will grow. It arrived in Hawaii very early in the 19th century and promptly went native in that congenial climate. It does best at altitudes of from 500 to 2500 feet above sea level and is often found growing on rocky, volcanic hillsides where one wonders how it survives. With its glossy, dark-green leaves and purplish-red fruit it is an exceedingly handsome small tree, often no more than a slender shrub. Although in the same genus, it is quite different from the common guava. The fruit is round, about 1 inch in diameter, deep-red outside and bright-red inside. The center of the fruit is filled with a juicy pulp in which numerous small, hard seeds are imbedded. The flavor is excellent, but to my taste it has little resemblance to the flavor of a strawberry, despite its common name.

When I was living in my thatched hut, my favorite foraging grounds for strawberry guavas were on Tantalus, a "tamed" mountain that stands within the confines of Honolulu. There are good roads all the way to the summit, and the mountain is criss-crossed by well-kept trails maintained by the park department for the benefit of those who like safe, easy footing when they go for a hike. Despite this easy access, one has only to get a few yards from the well-traveled trails to discover that this park-like mountain is a veritable garden of wild fruit. Besides strawberry guavas, I have carried home common guavas, bananas of several varieties, papayas, avocados, and even macadamia nuts, from the forests that clothe the slopes of Tantalus.

One summer day, after I had married and given up my thatched cottage under the kamani tree, I decided to drive up Tantalus and see how the strawberry guavas that had fed me in days of yore were coming along. I found the fruit abundant, ripe and luscious, and at one point I made my way down the jungly hillside from a higher to a lower trail, picking strawberry guavas all the way. Arriving at the bottom with a shopping bag full of prime fruit, I discovered that somewhere in that dense brush I had lost my wristwatch. That evening The Wahine gleefully told our guests how I had acquired about a dollar's worth of fruit at the cost of only three hours' labor and a forty-dollar watch. The guests, however, after tasting the strawberry guava shortcake I served them, thought this not so bad a bargain and begged me to show them where such delicious fruit could be had for the picking. Next day I drove our guests up Tantalus, and as we were walking along a trail toward the guava groves, I recognized a spot where I had come down the hill between trails the day before. Going a few yards off the trail, I came under a guava bush on which I had swung down the last little cliff. There, parting the waist-high brush, I looked down and saw my watch, still running and with the correct time showing on its dial. I had the last laugh, after all.

The best way to use strawberry guavas is to eat them fresh, and because of their piquant flavor, beautiful red color, and refreshing quality, there are few fruits better for this purpose. The strawberry guava contains less ascorbic acid than its larger relative, but it is still a good source of this vitamin, and it is one of the best sources of calcium in the whole vegetable kingdom; thus the strawberry guava, like its larger cousin, can contribute to the health of the beachcomber, making it unnecessary for him to resort to commercial diet supplements.

Strawberry guavas are the best shortcake material I was able to find in the Islands. It doesn't taste like strawberry shortcake, and it doesn't have to, for the flavor of this little fruit is so good in its own right that it doesn't need to taste like anything else. Halve the strawberry guavas, spoon out the pulp, and put it through a sieve to remove the seeds. Add as much sugar as you have sieved pulp, and mix it with the guava shells, then chill in a refrigerator. To finish the shortcake, proceed exactly as directed for common guava shortcake on page 125, and you will have a dessert second to none.

If you pick more strawberry guavas than you can consume as fresh fruit, then by all means make some canned juice. Halve the guavas, barely cover with water, and simmer for about 15 minutes. Pour the cooked fruit into a jelly bag, then hang it over a container and allow the juice to drip out. Don't squeeze the jelly bag, or the juice will be cloudy; the clear red color of properly made strawberry guava juice is one of its attractions. Reheat the juice just to the boiling point, then seal in hot, sterilized jars with sterilized, two-piece lids. Wrap each jar in several thicknesses of newspaper, and store in a dark cupboard to preserve the color and the vitamin C content.

Strawberry guava juice is a pleasant hot-weather drink just poured over ice cubes and sweetened to taste. Made as directed, it is strong enough so that the melting ice will not dilute it enough to make it weak or watery. Combine this juice with that from other tropical fruits when you are concocting a punch for a party. It will always add a delicious sub-acid flavor and a pleasing color.

Strangely, jelly made of pure strawberry guava juice is not of the best quality. However, if one combines 1½ cups of common guava juice with ½ cup of strawberry guava juice and then proceeds as directed for guava jelly, on page 119, the result will be a very tasty product with an attractive pink color. Try it sometime. It's a pleasant change from ordinary guava jelly.

Occasionally one comes on a yellow variety of the cattley guava

(*P. cattleianum* var. *lucidum*) growing in the same localities as the red kind. The trees bearing these yellow strawberry guavas average slightly larger than those producing the red ones, but, aside from color, the two kinds of fruit are much alike and can be used in the same ways.

Surely I have said enough to convince any potential beachcomber that he should plan to add strawberry guavas to the amenities of life on a tropical island.

8. The True and False Nuts

THE KAMANI NUT TREE
OR INDIAN ALMOND

(*Termanalia catappa*)

MY botanist friends tell me that the tree under which my be-loved little thatched hut stood should be called a "false" *kamani*, and that the "true" kamani is the *Calophyllum inophyllum*, which belongs to a completely different family. Indian almond would be a good name for this common nut-bearing tree except that very few people in Hawaii would know what you were referring to, since the tree is not an almond, nor is it related to the almonds, and it is found in many places besides India. However, for the purposes of this book, I suppose we'll have to compromise on a point or two and call it an Indian almond to prevent confusion with the so-called "true" kamani.

The tree that sheltered my cottage was at least 70 feet high and had a total spread of more than 80 feet. My hut stood about 20 feet from the large trunk, and yet, from midday until evening, my cottage was cooled by the shade of its huge leaves, often a foot long and half as wide.

The Indian almond is that strange anomaly, a deciduous, or at least partly deciduous, tree that grows in the tropics. Along in October or November, most of the leaves on this highly decorative tree turn a bright red and fall off, giving a seasonal touch to this largely seasonless land. In a place where one season is so like another, I have never been able to figure out how these trees decide when the time has arrived to put on their autumnal show. Individual trees do seem to get confused at times, for here and there a tree will jump the gun and color up in August or September, while others procrastinate until late winter. Just to be on the safe side, most of these trees also keep coloring and dropping a few leaves, now and then, all year. There is never a time when the Indian almond is entirely bare, but the foliage does get a bit thin at times.

Along with the red leaves that fell from this tree annually, decorating my thatched roof with spots of color, each year bushels of Indian almonds also rained down, and added an effortless delicacy to my diet. As a matter of fact, when I started to renovate my little house, the yard, the roof, and even the floor under holes in the roof were inches deep in "almonds," which I raked up and stored in old cartons. (This "nut" is really a hard, corky fruit, ellipsoid-pointed in shape and slightly compressed, being about 2½ inches long, 1¼ inches wide, and about 1 inch thick, with three distinct seams running the length of the nut.)

I have a soft place in my heart for Indian almonds, not only because I enjoy eating their delicious seeds, but also because they furnished the basis for my first beachcomber business. This confirmed my hope that if I approached nature with a cooperative rather than a conquering attitude, nature would in turn treat me kindly.

One day, while I was still remodeling my house, I took a break, and carrying a carton of Indian almonds to an old stump nearby, I tried my hand at opening them. There is a definite technique to shelling these nuts that must be learned. Three longitudinal seams divide the almond approximately into thirds. If you strike a heavy knife into one of these seams, then give the nut a twist with the other hand, one third of the corky fruit will pop out, revealing the comparatively small edible seed. However, only *one* of the three sections will pop out in this way, so you have to learn which seam to strike and which way to twist the nut.

At first, shelling Indian almonds seems a discouraging business. A bushelbasket of them will yield only about a quart of the tasty little seeds. However, there is no shortage of material on which to work, for the Indian almond grows on all the Islands, and has even introduced its fruit onto tropical shores from India to Hawaii. Like the coconut, it has learned to make extensive ocean voyages. I have even picked up Indian almonds on the coast of Oregon that were still in edible (and presumably sproutable) condition. Of course such a tropical tree won't grow in Oregon, but when the seeds wash ashore in a hot country, they sprout and grow right on the beaches. They have developed a foliage that will stay shiny and green even when subjected to almost continuous ocean spray.

The edible seed of this sizable fruit is only about an inch long and a little over a quarter-inch in diameter, somewhat resembling in size and shape the pine nuts sold in some American markets. The flavor is delicious, closely resembling that of the pecan. Despite the tediousness of shelling them, I often spent a half-hour at the old stump that stood in the shade of a young coconut palm, combining a meditation with a delicious snack. You can't meditate too deeply while shelling Indian almonds, for a heavy knife being swung at a nut held by the other hand needs only to miss a little bit to chop off a finger instead of a shell.

When I discover a good thing I like to share it, so one day I presented a small jar of shelled nuts to a Chinese friend who owned a little store where I sometimes bought supplies. The store was filled with Eastern goodies and Oriental smells, and the owner was something of a gourmet and an excellent cook, as well as a merchant. When he discovered my interest in unusual foods, he often invited me to exotic dinners that he, not his wife, prepared. In return, when I discovered something good in wild foods, I either invited them to share a meal with me or gave them a sample.

When my friend tasted the Indian almonds I gave him, he was delighted with their flavor, and his commercial mind immediately began to devise ways to market this formerly unexploited native product. We obtained a quantity of small cellophane bags, and I put a scant ounce of nuts in each one. These were mounted with transparent tape on a display board that had a neatly lettered sign extolling the virtues of the Indian almond and offering this generous (sic) sample for only 10¢.

They enjoyed a brisk sale at this price, even though the purchasers could probably have picked up many pounds right in their own neighborhoods for nothing. The sophisticated Honolulans, both native and immigrant, have come to prefer the imported, processed, and partly devitalized foodstuff sold in the supermarkets, and allow tons of perfectly delicious native foods to go to waste all about them. It was only when the Indian almonds were shelled out and neatly packed in modern cellophane bags that they became acceptable merchandise. I took the profits in groceries instead of cash. Many of the odd but delicious meals I ate while living in my thatched hut were made from ingredients purchased in this fashion with Indian-almond income instead of money.

Indian almonds not only are good to sell and to eat fresh, but also combine well with other foods. Prolonged heating robs this nut of some of its delicious but somewhat delicate flavor, making it unsuitable for baking, but it can be added to cold desserts and salads, or stirred into icings, fillings, candies, or even soups and stews at the last minute, contributing subtle flavor and nutritive values.

I used to make a Tropical Filling that was delicious between layers of plain cake, between cookies, or on cupcakes, using three products that I gathered from Hawaiian roadsides and forests. When dates were plentiful, I would cook 1½ cups of pitted dates with ½ cup of Hawaiian orange juice for about 5 minutes, stirring constantly. By that time the mixture becomes very thick. Then I stirred in 1 teaspoon of grated orange peel, and after allowing the mixture to become almost cool, stirred in ½ cup of chopped Indian almonds. Anyone who doesn't like this concoction should have an operation on his taste buds.

I also made a Beachcomber's Candy of which I was inordinately proud, for all the ingredients were foraged fresh from the grounds right around my little hut. I boiled three quarts of sweet coconut-palm toddy (see index) until it was reduced by at least three-fourths, then let it cool a bit, and mixed it with 1 cup of thick coconut cream. I returned this to the fire, and cooked and stirred until it reached 235° on the candy thermometer. I then let it cool a bit, and beat it for a few minutes until the candy lost its bright gloss. At that point I stirred in 2 tablespoons of boiling water and 2 cups of shelled Indian almonds. This was dropped by the spoonful on wax paper, and when it had cooled and hardened, it was as delicious a confection as you ever tasted. It was a little like Southern pralines, but the palm sugar and the coconut cream add flavors and texture that make this candy a smooth, creamy dream.

The trunk of the Indian almond furnishes a beautiful wood with a wildly figured grain and is so tough that it can be turned into very thin bowls that never split, despite their delicacy. This was one of my favorite woods for making the ornamental dishes that I sometimes turned out on my lathe, which furnished still another part of the cash income needed to keep me in the beachcombing business.

THE "TRUE" KAMANI
Calophyllum inophyllum

I will not have much to say about this nut-bearing tree, for I made very little use of its seeds during my beachcombing days. This fruit also has a hard, corky endocarp that enables it to float across oceans, but it is globose in shape, instead of being long and pointed like the Indian almond, and it is about 1½ inches in diameter.

The small seed, though more easily extracted than that of the Indian almond, is, to my taste, not as delicious. I would describe it as edible, rather than as palatable. It has a slightly resinous taste and is very oily. I much prefer the Indian almond, and that is one reason I refuse to call that delicious little nut a "false" kamani. I want to avoid, at all costs, giving the impression that I *ever* prefer the false to the true.

The oil extracted from the "true" kamani nut is pleasantly fragrant, and the Tahitians sometimes added it to the coconut oil with which they anointed their hair and bodies. I think this tree must have established itself in both Tahiti and Hawaii before the coming of the Polynesians, for it is mentioned in some of their oldest songs and chants. Because of its ocean-crossing ability, it is found on seashores in tropical East Africa, in southern Asia, throughout Indonesia, and on out through the clouds of islands that dot the tropical Pacific to Hawaii.

The kamani belongs to the mangosteen family and botanically is unrelated to the Indian almond, although the two trees resemble one another superficially in habits, appearance, and uses. The kamani is the smaller tree of the two and tends to branch near the ground, thus seldom furnishing timber of any size, but the wood of the larger limbs is as beautiful as that of the Indian almond, although somewhat lighter in color.

The leaves are large and very resistant to salt spray, so it remains a beautiful tree where the foliage of most other species tends to spot and turn brown on the seashore. It is not as common a tree as the Indian almond, but since its ornamental qualities are coming to be recognized, it is beginning to be widely planted along spray-swept sections of the shore, so perhaps future beachcombers will be able to find a more abundant supply of these nuts than I was able to locate. Unlike the Indian almond, which bears small, greenish-white apetalous flowers with a slightly fetid odor, the kamani has white-petaled flowers, borne in clusters, that are deliciously fragrant.

Although I seldom ate the nuts of this kamani, I remember it fondly, for it once contributed handsomely to my support. One day, while walking along an unfrequented beach, I discovered a kamani stump that had been washed out by the sea and tossed on the sand by the waves until it had a fine driftwood surface texture. It was one of the most interesting pieces of driftwood I have ever seen, for the tree that produced it had no trunk whatever, but only a common center from which sprang a dozen limbs and several dozen roots. The root section was especially interesting, whorling in and out in fanciful forms, curves, and openings, with the roots growing out and back into one another in a dozen places in strange, curling, nature-created grafts.

I gave the stump a preliminary trimming with my machete and managed to load it on my Jeep and take it home. There I spent the greater part of two days sawing the roots and the branches on parallel planes about two feet apart. I purchased a 4-foot-by-6-foot piece of ¾-inch plate glass, and turning the root section of the stump down for legs, I balanced the glass on the spreading branches as a table top. Then, with a crayon, I outlined a pleasing free-form shape on the glass top to harmonize with the supporting branches under it. A glass-working shop cut the plate-glass top to the form I had outlined and polished the edges. This was an expensive business, and the top alone for this unique coffee table cost me $92. However, it was a fascinating piece of furniture; almost anyone with imagination, looking down through the clear glass top, could lose himself in contemplation of the strange contortions, curves, and configurations of the driftwood base.

I hated to part with this beautiful piece, which had largely been created by nature, but it turned out to be too cumbersome for my tiny cabin. When I showed it to a fashionable interior decorator and timidly asked $492 for it, he took it so quickly that I wished I had made the price much higher. However, the $400 profit I realized for about three days' work was enough to support me for many months in the kind of busy, strenuous idleness in which I then found my joy.

THE MACADAMIA NUT
Macadamia ternifolia

The macadamia is considered by many people the most delicious nut in the world. To make your own judgment on the comparative palatability of this dainty, which originally came from Australia, just step into the nearest fancy grocery shop that sells imported food and buy yourself a small jar of these shelled nuts. You will pay an outrageous price, but there are any number of people who think this particular taste thrill is worth it.

This is not a common "wild" nut in Hawaii, as it was only introduced into the Islands in the 1890s. By far the greater number of macadamia trees in the Islands are of the selected, thin-shelled varieties, propagated by grafting or layering, and raised commercially in orchards. These will not be available to the beachcomber unless he has both nimble fingers and an elastic conscience. However, besides bearing delicious nuts, this is also a very ornamental shade tree and there are plantings along the roadsides and trails where the nuts belong to the passerby with interest and ambition enough to gather them.

These wayside plantings of beautiful trees one sees while driving about any of the Hawaiian Islands didn't just spring up of themselves. Most of them were planted by members of a wonderful organization called the Outdoor Circle. It is this group who, by pressure of organized public opinion, have kept Hawaii's beautiful roadsides clear of unsightly billboards and hot-dog stands. They annually hold a flower show and plant sale, and the proceeds are used to landscape Hawaiian roadsides and to plant more ornamental trees, thus making Hawaii ever more beautiful, where "every prospect pleases," and at the same time demonstrating in a very convincing way that not every "man is vile."

Fortunately for the beachcomber, many of the more ornamental tropical trees, like the coconut, date, breadfruit, mountain apple, banana, papaya, Surinam cherry, and macadamia, also bear edible products of which he can make good use.

When mature, the macadamia tree is about 30 feet tall and forms a shapely, rounded top without pruning. The shiny, green, oblong-lanceolate leaves, about 5 inches long and 2 inches broad, with wavy edges, grow very densely, casting a deep shade. This tree usually branches high enough so that you can easily get in under the limbs, making the macadamia an ideal tree under which to spread a roadside picnic. The nut, a little over an inch in diameter and almost perfectly spherical, is borne in a thin husk that splits open at maturity and makes harvesting the nuts an easy pleasure.

While I was living on Maui I very fortunately discovered two heavy-bearing macadamia trees on an old abandoned farmstead in the Kula district that kept me well supplied with their fruit. The trees often bear two crops per year, maturing one crop in April or May and another in October or November. From these two trees I gathered several hundred pounds of nuts each year.

The only drawback to the macadamia nut is that it has an unbelievably hard shell. The products of the commercial orchards are shelled by machinery, but to do it by hand you need a heavy hammer and a good solid base, like an anvil, on which to lay the nut. Even then, one must strike it squarely and with just the right amount of force, or the unbroken nut may go flying off in any direction with the speed of a bullet.

I know no recipes for using macadamia nuts in cooking, and I loved them too well eaten alone to experiment by mixing them with other foods. Either raw or roasted, I found them well worth the trouble of cracking that iron-hard shell. Anyone who hasn't the patience and energy needed to shell macadamia nuts, or is too busy to find time to do it, shouldn't even try to be a beachcomber.

THE KUKUI OR CANDLENUT
Aleurites moluccana

The *kukui* is one tropical nut that is easily found and collected. Growing throughout the Old World tropics and on high islands across the Indian and Pacific Oceans and even in the West Indies, the tree that bears this oily nut is a common sight on volcanic South Sea islands. Even when one is still far offshore, the kukui groves can be plainly distinguished, dotting the mountain valleys. The light bluish-green leaves of this tree are covered with silver-gray hairs, giving a gray-blue-green cast that makes a kukui grove very conspicuous among the bright greens of most tropical foliage.

When you first climb to one of these groves, you will find that the kukui is a very unusual tree. Although the trunk is often smooth, straight, and unbranched up to a height of 30 feet or more, the branches tend to twist and curve in fantastic patterns. When I lived on the island of Maui, there was a kukui tree just near enough my bedroom window so that I could see the entire treetop while lying in bed. In the tropics I like to wake up at daybreak, for the very early morning is the most joyful part of the tropical day. Many a happy morning for me began with a quarter-hour's contemplation of the patterns made by the curled and twisted branches of that kukui tree against the dawn sky.

The fruit of this interesting tree is dark-green, spherical, and about 1½ inches in diameter. It hangs on the outer twigs and is borne abundantly. The outer hard covering is about ¼ inch thick, and this soon decays away after the fruit falls to the ground, leaving the seed proper, which is the nut. This nut has a wrinkled, hard, woody shell but it is not nearly as difficult to crack as the macadamia. The round nut-meat that easily separates into two halves is about ¾ inch in diameter.

The ground under a grove of kukui trees is usually covered with nuts the year round, and the foraging beachcomber could easily gather several bushels per day if he could use them. Unfortunately, this easily available and really delicious nut contains a laxative drug, which limits its popularity. Roasting the nuts seems to dissipate some of this laxative effect, but even roasted kukui products should be eaten sparingly until you have determined your own kukui tolerance. The kukui is regularly eaten and relished by the Hawaiians, but is considered a condiment or flavoring, not a staple to be consumed in large amounts.

A Kukui-Nut Relish or condiment that invariably appears at Hawaiian *luaus* is called *inimona*. To make it, take a dozen kukui nuts that have been roasted in the shell, hull them out, and combine them with 1 teaspoon of Hawaiian sea salt, and one small red pepper (*Cap-*

sicum frutescens). These red peppers can be found growing wild in many parts of the Islands. Put all ingredients through a food chopper, or pound them together in a mortar until you have a smooth paste. Used with discretion, this really adds something to meat, vegetables, or seafood. Sometimes the Hawaiians will add the dried ink bag of an octopus to this relish before pounding, but I have never learned to appreciate this addition, although I have no objection to eating octopus if it is prepared in ways that I like.

Although the kukui nut can make only a minor contribution to the beachcomber's diet, the utility of this odd tree extends far beyond its limited esculent properties. The kukui was a very valuable tree to the ancient Hawaiians, and it can still be useful to the modern beachcomber if he will take the trouble to learn its secrets.

Jim and I used to take up our fish and lobster nets three or four times per season, dry them thoroughly, mend all breaks and tears, and then tan them in an infusion of kukui bark. To make the tanning solution we would first scrape the outside bark from an old tree, then peel off about 10 pounds of the inner bark. This was pounded on an anvil, then steeped in a tub of water for several hours, with an occasional stirring. The bark was removed from the solution, and the nets were dipped in the infusion, dried, then dipped again. This dyed the nets a dull-red color that seemed to render them invisible to fish and lobsters, and, also, it had a wonderful preservative effect on the net twine that kept it from deteriorating in saltwater. A fish net regularly mended and tanned in kukui bark seems to last practically forever.

The kukui also aided our fishing in another way. We carried roasted kukui nuts in the boat and often, when we were fishing with rods or handlines, we would chew a few of these crunchy kernels and then blow the chewed particles out over the water. The copious oil in these fatty nuts would spread over the water, quieting its ripples and making the fish easier to see, while the oil slick and the settling particles of chewed nut seemed to attract the fish about the boat. Even when using the throw-net from the shore, I often spat chewed kukui nuts into the water to attract fish into convenient holes and make them more visible.

Probably the most important use of the kukui nut to the ancient

Hawaiians was as a source of artificial illumination, and from this use came the common English name, "candlenut." The kukui nut contains so much oil that the roasted or dried kernel can easily be set afire and burns with a clear, bright flame for several minutes before the combustible material is exhausted. These roasted kernels were formerly strung on the slender midribs of coconut leaves, and then at night the topmost nut of one of these strings was lighted, and the *kalikukui*, as the Hawaiians called this improvised candle, was stuck in a hole in a porous lava rock to hold it upright. When the top nut burned low, whoever was sitting nearest the light would invert the string of nuts until the second one kindled, then the old charred nut was knocked off with a stick and there would be a steady light for another three minutes.

To make a light that didn't require such constant attention they pounded the nuts in a mortar, then expressed the oil. This oil was placed in a shallow stone dish, and one or more wicks of bark cloth were laid from the oil to the edge of the dish and lighted. I remember my grandmother telling how her family used very similar "grease lights" in the Tennessee hills during the Civil War when neither oil nor candles were obtainable.

For outdoor lighting the Hawaiians used to make large torches by binding together a number of the *kalikukui* strings of nuts with dried banana leaves. These were the torches used to illuminate dances and rites in the old heathen temples. They burn with a bright, hot flame and are too hot, sooty, and redolent of roasting nuts to be used indoors.

The sophisticated natives of present-day Hawaii no longer use these ancient candles or lamps or torches. Like everyone else, they use electric lights where available, and in the few country districts beyond the power lines they use kerosene lamps or gasoline lanterns. However, they still remember that this oily nut furnished light for their grass huts in days gone by, for in the modern Hawaiian language an electric-light bulb is still called a "kukui."

The kukui produces what is known as a "drying" oil, like linseed, and it makes a fine vehicle for paints and varnishes. To make an excellent black paint, the Hawaiians collected soot on smooth, water-worn stones by suspending them over burning kukui nuts, then mixing this almost pure carbon with kukui oil. This paint was used for making designs on bark cloth and even for painting canoes.

After the Hawaiians came in contact with other peoples, manufacturing and exporting kukui oil became one of their first industries. There are records showing that as much as 10,000 barrels per year of this oil was shipped to Alaska and sold to the Russians who then occupied that part of the American mainland. This was in the early days of the monarchy; later, as labor became more expensive, this industry could no longer show a profit, and so today the kukui nuts lie rotting under the trees by the hundreds of tons.

Kukui-nut oil will impart a fine, hand-rubbed finish to the beautiful hardwoods found in the tropics. When I was making decorative dishes on my lathe from the local hardwoods, I always finished them with kukui oil. For this purpose you don't even need to extract the oil from the nuts. I simply placed a few crushed kernels of roasted kukui in a cloth, gathered up the corners and held the bag thus formed against the bowl or plate as it turned at slow speeds on the lathe. The friction heated the crushed nutmeats and made the oil flow through the cloth in just the right amounts to produce a smooth, rich finish with none of the cheap glassiness of commercial lacquer.

The kukui can, if approached in the right spirit, do even more for the beachcomber than merely furnish him with condiments, tanning materials, and wood finishes. I had one beachcombing friend in the Islands who used the kukui for most of his cash income by manufacturing jewelry of the nuts. He made a barrel-like contraption, rigged to turn slowly and driven by an electric motor. He would put several hundred kukui nuts into the barrel and tumble them with abrasives until they were worn smooth and shiny. Then the nuts were buried in a marsh for a month or so, where the shells would turn a jet black. After redrying they were given a final polishing and finished with kukui oil. There were usually a few shallow grooves, radiating from either end of the shell, that had failed to wear away completely. He inlaid these with gold leaf and then strung the nuts into necklaces, or leis, as they are called in Hawaii. The jet and gold of the beads were striking, and the leis commanded excellent prices in the jewelry stores and souvenir shops of the Islands.

The Hawaiians used to derive a number of herbal medicines from the kukui. The sap of the tree was used in a medicine for fungoid skin diseases, and the juice that exudes from the stem of the freshly plucked green fruit was used to treat "thrush," an infants' disease. The flowers of the kukui, and also the charcoal of the burned nuts, were thought to be efficacious against ills that we now know are caused by pathogenic fungi. This fungicidal property of the kukui should be investigated by modern science. We may be overlooking a medical treasure.

When the trunk of the kukui is hacked or bruised, a dark resinous gum exudes and dries. This gum was dissolved in water by the ancient Hawaiians and used as an adhesive or as a transparent varnish to protect the designs they painted on bark cloth, and to make the cloth more waterproof and durable.

The kukui nut also contributed, in no small way, to making honest men of the ancient Hawaiians. In a land where houses are flimsy and locks unknown, a thief cannot be tolerated. In the rare cases of thievery that formerly occurred, the victim could, for the price of a pig, persuade the priest, or *kahuna*, to perform the following ceremony: A new fire was kindled by friction and a dried kukui kernel was thrown into the flames; as it burned, a curse was pronounced on the thief; this was widely publicized and usually frightened the thief into confessing his crime, making restitution, and submitting to the punishment of a heavy fine. However, if the criminal was recalcitrant, a second, similar, ceremony was performed in which two nuts were burned and an irrevocable death curse was pronounced against the thief. No further action was taken, for everyone, including the thief, believed that his death was now inevitable. So effective was this belief that, according to Hawaiian historians, the thief invariably pined away and died. That faith can kill, as well as cure, is a fact well attested by those who have studied primitive societies where this kind of black magic is practiced.

This last bit of information, while interesting, will probably prove to be of limited usefulness. When a modern beachcomber from a civilized background starts resorting to primitive black magic, he has long since passed the process of "going native"; he is already far gone. However, even the most modern beachcomber, if he would live the life at its best, cannot afford to ignore the kukui. Whenever anyone grows tired of the secondhand sort of existence that depends on purchased products, and wants to resume the intimate relationship with nature that man once enjoyed, the kukui-nut tree stands ready to furnish him with food, flavor, tannin, oil, paint, varnish, medicine, and magic. A sojourner on a tropical island who refuses to make the acquaintance of this interesting and highly useful tree is probably wasting his time trying to be a beachcomber.

9. Hunting in the Islands

ONE of the unintentionally best-kept secrets about Hawaii is that it is a veritable hunter's paradise. At the time I was gleaning my living from land and sea, I foraged plenty of fresh meat from the mountains, where there was an abundance of big game and a year-round open season. I have seen a pack of wild dogs chase down and kill a wild goat on a ridge above Manoa Valley, within a mile of the campus of the University of Hawaii. Hugo and I have left home at daylight in the Jeep and returned by 9 A.M. with a fat wild pig apiece. I once shot an axis deer from the front porch of my Hawaiian host on the island of Molokai. A friend and I once very illegally landed his light plane on the island of Kahoolawe, and took off again in less than an hour with two fat wild lambs in the space behind the seats. On Maui I once saw Hugo kill two wild goats in five minutes with a bow and arrow. On several occasions I stuffed my landlord's freezer with wild beef from the island of Lanai.

Hawaii, like many island groups far from any continent, has no native land mammals. Probably the first such creature to set foot on these shores was the species *Homo sapiens*. However, this mammal came in huge seagoing canoes and carried with him pigs, dogs, and, as stowaways, rats. The pigs and dogs were both domestic meat animals, but they also soon ran wild and populated the mountains with feral swine herds and wild dog packs. The rat, as he always does, throve and prospered and replenished the earth with his kind. Hunting rats with a bow and arrow was *the* gentlemanly sport of the aristocracy of old Hawaii, and strangely enough, this was the only use to which the ancient Hawaiians ever put the bow and arrow. They fought their wars and did their heavy hunting with spears, clubs, and slings.

These few species were the only land mammals known to the Hawaiians until Captain George Vancouver arrived in the late 18th century and presented them with horses, cattle, sheep, and goats. These soon formed wild herds, some of which persist to this day. All the main Islands have wild goats and pigs. There are wild cattle on Lanai and Hawaii; wild sheep persist on Kahoolawe and Hawaii; axis deer are wild on Oahu, Molokai, and Lanai; and there are even naturalized wallaby on Oahu, but they are so wild that one seldom glimpses them. The axis deer is a native of Japan and was introduced into Hawaii during the monarchy as a present from the Japanese Emperor to the King of Hawaii Nei.

It was Hugo who taught me the secrets of hunting wild pig. These animals are still hunted with a spear or knife, not as a stunt, nor even in an attempt to preserve the old ways, but because these are still the best weapons for the job. The spears we used (for I simply haven't the nerve to come to close enough quarters with a wild boar to use a knife) had shafts about 5 feet long and laurel-leaf blades about a foot long, kept razor-sharp on both edges. We used these as sticking spears—never threw them. The reason firearms are not used in this sport is that wild pigs are hunted with dogs, and when one comes up to the pig, there is usually such a tangle of fighting dogs and pigs that one would be as likely to receive the bullet as the other.

Hugo kept two pig-dogs, and they were so huge and hungry that we were often hard-pressed to keep them fed on game offal and shark meat. He had originally obtained them from the local dog pound, and they were as mixed in breed as are most of the Hawaiian people, showing traces of mastiff, boxer, great Dane, and wolfhound in their makeup. Two strong dogs working together soon learn to seize a wild pig on either side, by his ears, and hold him until the hunter comes up and dispatches the animal. This sounds nice and easy when you say it quickly, but sometimes an old boar or a mother sow will decide to mix into the fight rather than run away, and then there is noisy, merry hell to pay.

Hugo was a skilled pig-hunter and knew the mountains well. He seemed to have a nose for game, and I remember only once that we came home empty-handed from a pig hunt, and that was because we found too much game rather than too little. Our dogs started what sounded like a big herd of pigs, but when we came up, an aggressive old boar with tremendous tusks was slashing our dogs unmercifully. He already had one of them entirely out of the action and had wounded the other so badly that his fighting was ineffective. When he saw us, the boar plunged off into the brush, leaving two helpless dogs behind. Did I say we came home empty-handed? We had to carry those two heavy dogs over our shoulders for more than a mile back to the Jeep, down the most rugged and boulder-strewn stream bed I ever walked over. When we finally reached the Jeep, one dog was unconscious, and the other was rapidly getting weaker, while Hugo and I were literally covered with their blood. We sped back to Honolulu, and though it was Sunday morning, we finally routed a veterinarian out of bed and he sewed, sterilized, and bandaged. Both dogs eventually recovered, but it was some weeks before they were able to go pig-hunting again. That round definitely went to the pigs.

Wild goats are an integral part of the South Sea dream. Ever since my Robinson Crusoe days, islands and goats have been inseparable in my mind. Coconut palms and sun-swept beaches might occupy the foreground, but in the background there is always the ubiquitous goat. The fact that wild goats are plentiful in Hawaii gives these Islands the final touch of suitability as a site for beachcombing.

Several times Hugo and I managed to stalk and kill wild goats on Oahu, but we were not as uniformly successful at this as we were at pigsticking, and we made many more goat hunts than we obtained goats. It was only after moving to Maui that this sport became a major source of fresh meat to my family and me. I have never been able to understand the prejudice of many Americans against goat meat, probably because I have eaten it all the days of my life. I consider it fully as good as lamb, and much better than veal. No meat is really good unless it has been properly butchered, cooled, aged, and skillfully cooked, but when these details have been properly seen to, the goat is a fine meat animal. Loin chops from a young goat are really delicious tidbits; a leg of goat, properly seasoned and roasted, is a Sunday dinner entree that is hard to beat; and a whole roasted kid has that sumptuous air that is essential for festive occasions.

Besides enjoying these fine fresh-meat dishes, I discovered another trick for using goat meat. In the Kula district of Maui I made the acquaintance of an old Portuguese man who had a secret recipe for making the best *linguesa* sausage from goat meat that I ever tasted. This Portuguese sausage is highly flavored with chilis and garlic, and the meat is coarsely chopped, rather than ground fine, as it is in most sausages. Strangely, once this meat is safely inside the familiar-appearing sausage casing, all prejudice against it disappears, and my most finicky guests would compliment this spicy sausage without probing too closely into the source of the meat from which it was made.

The old man who made this delicious *linguesa* had formerly been a great sportsman and a mighty goat-hunter before the Lord, but his old legs were no longer equal to the hills in which the wild goats hid, and he had become dependent on others to furnish the raw material for the spicy sausage he so skillfully compounded. I loved the strenuous sport of goat-hunting and was only too glad to give him half the meat for making my share into a sausage that was at least twice as good as any I could make myself.

Goat-hunting in Hawaii is wonderful sport, but devilishly hard work. I would park my Jeep at the very top of Haleakala, at about 10,000 feet altitude, and walk downhill several miles into the wild goat country. A 5-mile hike over sharp, crumbly, unbelievably rough *aa* lava at that altitude is an endurance test even when one is going downhill, and once a goat is killed, the walk back up with a heavy goat draped about one's shoulders can be sheer torture to anyone not in the very best physical condition. It is definitely not a sport for the very young or the very old, nor for the soft, the weak, or the lazy. But when it is done often enough to keep the right muscles toughened and the sinews flexible, it is extremely worthwhile in scenic treats alone.

The wild goats live in a tortuous, barren land where the scenery is awesomely strange and fantastically beautiful, resembling what I imagine a lunar landscape looks like. There are great frothy fields of *aa* lava, where every step is a hazard, and smooth rivers of *lapahoehoe* lava looking like chocolate fudge that has been poured out to harden. All of this subterranean slag was belched forth from the hot guts of the earth in recent geological time, and one is walking where the world is still very new. From this height the great island of Maui, unrolled from one's feet, occupies but a small part of the total field of vision, for there are vast expanses of an ocean of unbelievable blue, and in the distance the islands of Kahoolawe, Lanai, and Molokai stand sharply etched against the horizon. Around each shore the blue ocean shades to turquoise, then green, with a final ring of white around each island where the white surf attempts to tear down what the volcanoes have built.

How so many wild goats survive in this barren land I'll never know, but there they are, sleek and fat, bounding along the faces of cliffs so sheer and crumbly that it would be suicide for a human being to attempt to follow them. These agile animals are often saucy and bold, but they can also be elusive and so full of guile that they are among the most challenging of game animals.

One Christmas, after The Wahine and I had moved to Maui, I received a phone call from Hugo asking in his inimitable pidgin whether he and his family could come over from Oahu and spend the holidays with us. I wasn't surprised that no prior arrangements had been made, for Hugo would forgo any pleasure to escape the torture of writing a letter. Four years had passed since his marriage, so he now had three children and another on the way. The Wahine and I welcomed the prospect, for what is Christmas without children?

We met Hugo, his wahine, and their little kiekas at the airport, and after exchanging leis and kisses all around, Hugo told me what was on his mind. He had brought along his archery equipment and wanted to invade the goat country of Haleakala with bow and arrows. He had become very skillful at killing turtles with the bow, and now he wanted to try his bow hand on larger game. I heartily endorsed his plans, especially when he raised no objection to my being armed with my regular game rifle, for I am a poor hand with the bow.

I was tired of carrying dead goats up that mighty mountain, so this hunt was to be planned differently. We would have the wahines drive us to the top of the mountain and then meet us farther down where a spur road ran partway up the slope, making all our walk downhill.

One of the sights to see on Maui is the sunrise over Haleakala Crater, so we decided to combine this experience with the hunt. To avoid having to wake the small children at 4 A.M., we put them to sleep the night before in my station wagon. Hugo's children had never become accustomed to a set routine or schedule, so they adapted to new situations easily and went to sleep in these unusual beds with a minimum of fuss and bother.

Long before daylight next morning we piled in with the sleeping children and set out up the road that winds, turns, and twists its way to the summit. There is a good road all the way to the top, and we arrived at the crater's rim in the first gray of dawn. There is a plaque at the lookout that informs all who care that this crater is large enough to contain the entire island of Manhattan, but thank goodness it doesn't. This immense crater is miles across and more than a half-mile deep, and its floor is a moonscape of cinder cones and lava flows. Appearing dull-black in the early dawn light, the crater walls and uneven floor were transformed into a confusion of colors decorated with an ever-changing pattern of shadows as the sun rose over the eastern rim. Sunrise over Haleakala was exactly as advertised and very satisfying. We *oohed* and *aahed*, gazed in silence, and on the whole were properly impressed; then we ate a hearty picnic breakfast, and Hugo and I set off on our long downhill hike.

At first the trail was easy and we walked briskly, for at this altitude the weather is keenly cold in December, and a white frost covered everything, the first frost Hugo had ever seen. Walking down the western side of the mountain, we were immediately plunged back into its shadow and we looked forward to another sunrise. Two more hours passed before the sun melted the frost and drove the chill from our bones. About the time that it became comfortably warm, we discovered our first treasure, a great patch of *ohelo* bushes loaded with ripe berries. This was much tamer game than we were seeking, but we welcomed them nevertheless. We rested there an hour, filling our stomachs and knapsacks with the bright fruit. The *ohelo* is a relative of the blueberry that has adapted to life on these volcanic slag heaps, and for the ancient Hawaiians its fruit was sacred to Pele, the goddess of volcanoes. Its fruit is red, not blue, when ripe, and furnishes the raw material for pies the equal of the huckleberry pies baked by Pennsylvania Dutch cooks.

An hour after leaving the ohelo berries we were making our way through a narrow gorge when we sighted our first herd of goats. They were climbing up a trail halfway up the practically sheer cliff on our left. We hid behind some rocks and waited for them. As they passed almost directly above us they were still a bit out of bow range, so Hugo told me to pick one off with the rifle. I selected a young billy near the middle of the line, and when my bullet struck him, he came rolling down the hill practically to our feet. At the sound of the shot the herd scattered in all directions, performing impossible feats of cliff climbing. In a few seconds not a goat was in sight, but in their flight, friends and families had been separated, and these now made the gorge ring with their plaintive bleating as they signaled one another from their various hiding places. Hugo could imitate a goat cry perfectly, and he was outbleating the goats in an attempt to lure some of them from hiding. His goat call soon worked, for two half-grown kids came bounding almost straight down the cliff toward us. After each leap they would stop and bleat again, so Hugo carried on a regular conversation with these young goats until finally one of them was only 30 feet away. Hugo couldn't miss at that range, so he suddenly raised up and put an arrow straight through the goat. The nimble kid made one more leap and then fell dead, shot through the heart. The other kid ran a short way up the cliff and resumed his bleating. Hugo kept up his calling, and finally the other kid's curiosity or loneliness overcame his caution and he came within range of that deadly bow. Hugo raised up with his bow already bent and put an arrow into him. He wasn't hit in a vital spot and started scrambling back up the cliff. In the next second Hugo sent two more arrows after the first, and as the third one struck the goat, he lost his footing and came tumbling back down the cliff, snapping off the protruding arrows as he rolled.

Three goats to carry and still many miles from our rendezvous with the wahines! We decapitated and disemboweled our game to remove excess weight, and I wrapped my goat, which was the largest of the three, in a waterproof poncho and threw him across my shoulders. Hugo preferred the Island way of carrying loads and cut a stout carrying pole, tying a kid to either end of it and balancing it on his shoulder. Carrying a heavy load downhill, hour after hour, can be exceedingly tiring, and we rested often, but far in the distance we

could see the waiting station wagon parked by a high grove of euca-
lyptus trees. Finally, about 3 P.M., we two tired hunters walked quietly
up to the station wagon and surprised the two wahines taking a sun-
bath, while the three children slept in the shade. That year a whole
roast kid furnished the *pièce de résistance* for our Christmas feast, and
ohelo pie was the dessert.

Hugo wasn't my invariable companion on island hunts, for although this boy was naturally a devil-may-care soul, family responsibilities forced him to worship at the shrine of the great god Time
Clock five days a week. Fortunately, I had another friend, Leroy the
Flying Beachcomber, who was an enthusiastic huntsman, and in his
little two-seater plane the hunting grounds of all the Islands were
only a few hours away.

Leroy had served in the Air Force during the war and had flown
many fighting missions in the Pacific. Afterwards, he decided to remain in the Islands, and married a Chinese girl. He purchased a small
secondhand plane and a house in Damon Tract, near the airport.
He fed his family chiefly on game, fish, and wild fruit, and it was this
common foraging interest that brought us together. We flew many a
wild-food mission in his little plane and brought home great loads of
loot denied to earthbound foragers.

Some might think it pretty poor sport to bag feral farmyard animals
like the pig, goat, and cow, but don't be fooled; they are as wild and
elusive and sometimes even as dangerous as any game animals I ever
hunted. Indeed, it was that *legitimate* game animal, the deer, that
gave me the tamest hunting that I enjoyed in the Islands. Leroy and
I had been invited to visit a Hawaiian family on Molokai and go
deer-hunting with them. We arrived over Molokai Airport at dusk
and had to circle the field while a Hawaiian cowboy chased a herd
of white-faced cattle (not wild ones) from the runway. We finally
landed, were met by our host, and then were driven over a series of
small roads to his homestead. That evening we indulged in much talk
and laughter, so I was still very sleepy when a brown-skinned boy
came bursting into our room at daylight stammering something about
deer in front of the house.

We jumped from bed, grabbed our guns, and ran out. About 150
yards in front of the house, five deer were working their way cautiously
down a dry stream bed. Both bucks and does of axis deer have antlers,

but there was one large leader that I was sure was a buck. He had a huge rack that looked larger than the comparatively small deer beneath it. I rested my rifle on one of the porch posts, adjusted the sight leisurely, then killed him with one shot. It was as easy as that. At the sound of the shot, the rest of the herd bolted back up the dry stream. Leroy, more interested in tender venison than in trophies, took a lead on a good, big frying-size fawn and brought it down with another shot. Our deer-hunt was over before breakfast—indeed, before we were even out of our pajamas. I realize that this was sheer luck and another time one might hunt for a week without bagging a deer, but if one could judge from this one experience, one would conclude that island deer-hunting is about as exciting as knocking over mechanical ducks in a shooting gallery.

Herds of wild cattle still persist on several of the Hawaiian Islands, and while I was there they threatened to overpopulate their range on the island of Lanai. Nearly all of this island is owned by a pineapple company, and they announced in one of the Honolulu papers that a permit to hunt wild cattle on their lands would be given to any responsible person who applied.

We made arrangements by telephone for the rental of a Jeep, then rose early next morning and were over the wild cattle country by sunup. When on a hunt, I have often had the feeling that all those stories I had heard about the abundance of game in that region were so many myths. Looking over the game from the air prior to the hunt is the perfect antidote for that feeling; we could have taken a census of the wild cattle of Lanai from that little plane, and we flew about looking for the most accessible herd. Finally we selected a small herd that was drifting downhill toward a clump of trees a mile or more away. We figured these trees would make a landmark we could find and that the herd would most likely seek their shade during the heat of the day. We flew very low on our way back to the airport, searching out a Jeepable route by which we could return on land.

At first we stalked the clump of trees, but we needn't have bothered, for the herd had not yet reached them. It was difficult country in which to see game, being rough and rocky with black-wattle brush everywhere, growing just high enough to hide the cattle. I searched the slope above us with binoculars for half an hour, and then by sheer good fortune I saw a cow with a young calf cross a small opening, betraying the location of the herd we were seeking. We moved to one side so we would have a ridge between us and the cattle and started working our way silently upward, for these bovines are really wild, much more skittish than the deer of Molokai, and we knew that if only one of them caught sight of us, the whole herd would simply disappear. Fortunately, the brush that concealed the game also made good cover for the hunters.

It took a whole hour of cautious stalking before we again sighted our quarry. Leroy was ahead of me, and I saw him poke his head around a rock and then quickly withdraw it. Cupping his hands over the mechanism of his rifle to muffle the noise, he cautiously cocked the piece. I froze in my tracks with my hand on the safety of my rifle, ready to back him up in any move he made. We both simply stopped breathing, and in the utter quiet I could actually hear the cattle trampling, belching, and scraping against the brush on the other side of the rocks.

Leroy first tried to get to the top of the rock for a shot, but it was too high and steep, and apparently he was afraid that this attempt might make some noise that would startle the herd, for he gave it up. Finally he just crawled out into the open and suddenly stood up. He fired quickly, and this was my signal to move. I leaped out beside Leroy and found myself looking down a natural path between the high rocks. Charging straight up this path was a wild young bull Leroy had wounded. I snapped a shot at him and saw him swerve as the heavy bullet went home, but he kept coming. I think he was instinctively heading toward the higher hills, rather than actually charging us, for suddenly he seemed to see us for the first time and plowed to a halt. Just as he stopped, Leroy fired and hit him squarely in the forehead. So solidly was he standing on spread legs that the heavy bullet didn't knock him down. For a full second he stood there—so close that I actually saw his eyes glaze over—and then he crumpled in his tracks, dead before he reached the ground.

The most secret missions that Leroy and I ever flew were our wild-sheep hunts on Kahoolawe. This desert island off the coast of Maui was used as a bomb and shell target during World War II, and there is still plenty of unexploded ammunition scattered over its surface, so civilians are forbidden to land there. But the bait that lured us on was the wild sheep to be found there.

Before the last war, the lower parts of Kahoolawe were used as a cattle range, and the wild sheep were confined to the rugged hills, but since the island has been unused by cattlemen, the sheep have spread out and now range most of the island. We planned our first hunt in late summer, after *kona* weather had brought this usually barren island an unusual amount of rain. This was the season when *kiawe* beans would be ripe and the sheep would be nice and fat from feeding on them.

These Hawaiian wild sheep have little resemblance to the round, woolly animals we are accustomed to call sheep. They are slender and rangy, can run like a race horse, and in this warm climate very wisely grow coarse hair instead of wool. So much have these wild animals changed from their barnyard progenitors that a mainlander seeing one for the first time usually asks what kind of animal it is. However, when they are well-fed on sweet *kiawe* beans, their flesh is tasty and tender.

On our first sheep hunt we flew to Maui, where we had been invited to stay with some friends, and that first afternoon we merely flew over Kahoolawe and "cased the joint." The airstrip seemed perfectly usable, and we saw plenty of sheep, some of them very near the place we intended to land. Late the next afternoon we flew out, located the nearest herd of sheep, and after scanning the skies to be sure we were not observed, set down the little junk-heap and taxied it under the nearest *kiawe* tree so that it couldn't be seen from the air. Fifteen minutes' walk brought us into the neighborhood of the sheep, and we found a good hiding place close enough to the herd so that we could select at leisure the animals we wanted. After agreeing on the sheep we would fire at, Leroy counted off under his breath, as though he were directing a firing squad, and we fired simultaneously. Those were the only two shots fired on this hunt, as each of us connected with the chosen target.

One good thing about having such familiar animals as swine, sheep, and cattle as wild game animals is that I don't have to go into much detail on methods of cooking the meat, for every good cook knows how to prepare pork, lamb, and beef, and all conventional cookbooks contain innumerable recipes for using these meats. However, the primitive Polynesians developed a way of cooking pig that is a great improvement over any method we have. This is roasting in the underground oven, or *imu*, from which the pig emerges deliciously browned and with all the aroma and juiciness not only preserved but evolved by this method of cooking into their savory best. This is the famous *kalua* pig, served at every Hawaiian *luau*.

One Saturday morning, Hugo and I rose long before daylight and drove to a valley where wild pig could be found if you arrived early enough. It was still so dark when we arrived at the mouth of the valley that we had to depend on the tethered dogs to lead us up the brushy trail. We had hunted here before, and our dogs were confident, almost dragging us up the trail by their leashes. Just as the sudden tropical dawn made the trees and rocks about us visible, the dog that was leading Hugo made a low sound that meant "pig nearby."

We slipped the leashes, and the dogs dashed eagerly but silently ahead. A moment later we heard a great commotion as the dogs came up with the wild pigs. We ran as quickly as the narrow, overgrown trail would allow, and soon came up to the scene of action, which was in the bed of the shallow stream that threaded the valley. Usually the dogs would grab one pig, one by either ear, and when they worked together in this way, they could hold a pretty large wild boar, but this time they had each grabbed separate pigs, and neither would let go to help the other. The two pigs they had tackled were obviously of the same litter, only about half-grown, but they still had considerable power, so each pig was splashing madly round and round the dog that was holding onto his ear, in and out of the water, making the whole valley ring with their piercing squeals. It was no easy task to close with these mad, splashing pinwheels and distinguish pig from dog clearly enough to thrust home a spear. How we managed to spear those pigs without injuring the dogs, I'll never know, but we did it.

Afterwards, in the post-hunt quiet, we looked about us. This was one of the valleys formerly inhabited by Hawaiians but long since deserted. Iron-hard guava trees grew in the old taro terraces, telling us by their size that it had been at least fifty years since this land had been cultivated. However, many domestic plants still persisted on the valley floor. Great breadfruit trees hung full of fruit, and several varieties of bananas huddled in overcrowded clumps along the stream. The heavy-fruited papaya plants were probably self-sown from those abandoned by the Hawaiians as they moved out or died off, for these large papayas were of a variety that is seldom planted now. We even found a straggly row of coffee bushes loaded with unripe fruit.

As we washed our hands in the cold stream, Hugo noticed the thousands of darting *opaes*, the tiny fresh-water shrimp of Hawaii, which crowded the clear water. These little shrimp are the invariable accompaniment of a Hawaiian feast, and as Hugo watched them, I could see on his expressive face that an idea was being born.

Suddenly the idea ripened, and our words started tumbling together. "We stay give *luau*, us two guy; plenty pig, plenty *opae*, plenty banana, plenty breadfruit, plenty papaya—good kind da kind—"

Hugo knew that I would never be able to resist the idea of our giving a feast of all native foods foraged with our own hands from the sea and mountains, and I was soon as eager as he was. This wasn't to be a commercial luau for tourists, with hapa-haole food and paid hula dancers in cellophane skirts, but the real thing, with totally spontaneous entertainment and food fit for warriors and huntsmen.

We started preparing for this feast then and there. Hugo carried out both the pigs we had taken, while I filled my game bag with breadfruit and carried out two bunches of bananas besides. We filled our pockets with the tiny hot peppers found growing along the edge of the valley, and mentally we marked many other wild foods that we would gather later in the week, for we had agreed to give this grand luau the following Saturday.

On arriving home we scalded and scraped the pigs, then talked a butcher friend of ours into letting us hang them in his walk-in refrigerator for a week. Next, we had to secure permission from my landlord to hold this feast on his grounds. I approached this task with some trepidation, for he was a quiet, conservative gentleman, and a luau is often hard to contain, either spatially or acoustically. Here, I played into a bit of luck, for my landlord and his wife had already planned to spend the following weekend at Volcano House on the Big Island, and they gave their blessing to the impending riot that would be held in their absence.

Most of my nearest neighbors were Hawaiians, and to forestall any complaints from that area I invited them all to the luau. Jim and

Falani entered into the arrangements with gusto, Jim inviting his "sunshiner" cronies and his wife promising the presence of the most talented of her Samoan relatives from across the Island. Hugo's Hawaiian in-laws would be coming in droves, and I had invited my beachcomber friends with their wives of many races. I began to wonder whether the acre on which I lived would be large enough to hold the crowd.

All week we worked like slaves at the preparation. Falani fished for moi and helped me gather opihis, Jim helped with the fish traps and lobster nets, while Hugo rushed out every afternoon to gather wild fruit. We had great bunches of bananas, heaps of coconuts, piles of ti leaves and banana leaves, and a great stack of wood for the imu fire. It is customary for a guest to bring a gift of liquor or money to a luau, but we had warned those we invited that we wanted no money and would not tolerate imported liquors or brewery beer, for nature was furnishing all we needed at this feast. We suggested that generous guests bring flowers, so we could appropriately decorate the feast and garland all the guests.

On Saturday morning Hugo arrived at dawn and we started digging the pit for the imu. We built a tremendous fire in the bottom of it and another fire at the side in which we heaped the water-worn lava stones that would be the source of heat in this primitive fireless cooker. Many guests came early, for everyone likes to see the pigs go into the oven. Everybody turned to and helped with the work, making fish laulaus, smothered in coconut cream, esoteric dishes involving crabs, lobsters, and octopus, leafy packages of papaiee and kalolo, and many another strange ti-leaf-wrapped goody to be cooked in the imu with the pig.

About midmorning the pigs were brought, and the main preliminary event was under way. Expert Hawaiian hands made slits under the forelegs and hams and stuffed hot stones into the pockets thus made. The stones in the bottom of the imu were swept clean of ashes with a cluster of ti leaves, and more hot stones were placed inside the cleaned pigs. Then the bottom of the imu was lined with banana leaves, and the two pigs, resting on old lauhala mats, were lowered into place and surrounded with cooking bananas, breadfruit, and the leaf-packaged goodies the women had been making. Next came another layer of banana leaves, then more hot stones, and finally a covering of earth.

Work went on, for there was still many items of the feast to prepare, but with the covering of the pigs, the main task was done, and most of the crowd turned to other activities. They had responded to our request for flowers with mountains of fragrant bloom, and most of the older wahines brought out needles and started making leis. Some of the younger wahines turned to slitting the ti leaves to make pau skirts, for there would be many an impromptu hula dance later on. I made tremendous bowls of tropical punch, generously spliced with arrack or panini swipes. There was a keg of straight okolehau with a spigot at which the tipplers could help themselves.

By early afternoon all the guests had arrived, and they were a colorful crowd. There were Chinese, Japanese, Koreans, Puerto Ricans, Portuguese, Filipinos, Hawaiians, Samoans, American Negroes, and whites. The *tutus* and *mamasans* were apt to be racially pure, their sons and daughters of mixed blood; the little kiekas running about were complicated mixtures of many strains, healthy little hybrids of great vigor and beauty.

Everyone was ravenously hungry by the time we uncovered the imu and allowed its tantalizing smells to escape. With the aid of the lauhala mats on which they were resting, the pigs were lifted whole from the hot pit and lay steaming and crisply brown. The pigs were quickly carved, and soon everyone was seated around lauhala mats with banana-leaf plates and mountains of food before them. First there was the kalua pig, more succulent than any other roast pork ever tasted. Coconut-shell bowls of breadfruit poi were by every plate. There were great dishes of raw fish—nahu-pu, lomilomi, and sashimi. Laulaus of delectable moi, taro tops, and rich coconut cream were just asking to be untied so they could spread their fragrance around. Strange concoctions of lobster, eel, crab, and octopus were passed around and complimented. There were opihis with chopped limu, and crimson aloalos cooked in wine and spices. For condiments there were hot wild peppers, sliced onions, mango chutney, kukui-nut relish, and coconut shells filled with bright-red boiled opaes. Luau pineapples looking untouched but with the insides already neatly sliced were scattered over the lauhala mat that served as a ground cloth. There was a tremendous salad of palm heart, and a heap of baked bananas for those who still had a vacant cranny to fill, and okolehau, arrack, panini swipes, and palm wine flowed freely, while drinking coconuts furnished the perfect beverage for the more temperate. For dessert there was haupia, kalolo, papaiee, sweet melting mixtures of coconut, breadfruit, and taro.

The Hawaiians are a gay and happy people, full of talk and fond of laughter, but they are deadly serious about food, so for a time the only sounds were the munching of palm heart, the sucking of poi from fingers, and an occasional exclamation of appreciation. Finally

came repletion, and the guests sat about propped against trees or lying stretched on the grass, smoking or dozing, while the mysteries of digestion assimilated the huge quantities of food they had eaten. Only gradually did the party revive.

No mainland hostess would dare give a party of this size without carefully planning the entertainment, but a luau can be completely unprogrammed. Take a large group of Islanders, stuff them with their favorite foods, then season liberally with okolehau, and entertainment just naturally happens. Groups of young girls first barred themselves in my beachcomber's shack and then reappeared decked with flowers and wearing brief paus made of bright-green ti leaves. Other guests broke out ukuleles and guitars, and soon we were treated to hula after hula, each accompanied by its own song. Four Samoans performed a very dangerous-looking sword dance, before darkness came unnoticed, and a full moon rose—and still the fun went on.

The hazards of hunting, like the hazards of beachcombing in general, are more inside the hunter than outside of him. Some of my beachcombing friends refused to hunt wild pigs because they were afraid of being ripped by the tusks of a boar and bleeding to death in the jungle. Others wouldn't hunt goats because they feared breaking a leg on the vast fields of *aa* lava and possibly lying out there a day or two before being rescued. Some were afraid of being trampled by wild cattle, and others were afraid of being hit by a stray bullet fired by another hunter. Such fears never deterred me.

I am not particularly brave, and I certainly am not foolhardy; I took every reasonable precaution to minimize such dangers, and the dangers that remained inherent in hunting merely added spice to the sport. A few of my friends refused to hunt because they were too lazy to face the work of crashing through jungles or climbing over the high lava fields in search of game, while others were so jealous of time in their lives that they refused to devote the time necessary to make hunting zestful and productive. I couldn't worry much about the lazy or time-hoarding objectors to hunting. They simply weren't cut out to be beachcombers, anyway.

In my experience, the chief hazard to hunting that the beachcomber faces is a kind of chicken-heartedness that I prefer to call compassion, since I'm afflicted with it, and I, at least, insist that my defects be described in beautiful terms. To continue hunting, one must love the sport, the joy in one's own prowess as a hunter, and the gourmet dishes that can be prepared from wild game, more than one loves the animals while they are wild, free, and unharmed.

After moving to Maui I remained, for a while, a great goat-hunter. Then my neighbor, another great goat-hunter, captured a tiny kid by the outrageous method of shooting its wild mother. For a time they gave this new pet a great deal of attention, and the pretty little creature almost instantly became tame, trusting, and lovable. Then the novelty of the new pet started to wear off, and they began to neglect the little goat. His pen was against my yard fence, so I gradually became his chief caretaker. I would gather armloads of browse and throw them into his pen, see that he had water, and play with him by the hour. I have never seen an animal who loved the company of human beings as much as did this little wild kid. He was an inveterate show-off. He taught himself a whole repertoire of tricks and would exhibit them all for my benefit every time I came close to the pen, pausing after each stunt and looking up for applause. He soon learned to know me and to love me, and as soon as I came in sight he would start cavorting and bleating with every sign of joy. One cannot help returning at least a small measure of such unstinted devotion.

Then one day I went goat-hunting again. Far up on the slopes of Haleakala I sighted a herd of goats and stalked them so carefully that I was able to approach within a hundred yards. Slowly poking my rifle over a rock, I found my sights coming to rest on a half-grown kid that could have been the twin of my goat at home. I simply couldn't pull the trigger and blast the life out of that pretty wild animal. I moved my sights to an old billy goat, but then the thought occurred to me that this might be the father of my pet kid, so I lowered the rifle and lay there observing the colorful wild goat herd until they drifted over a ridge. My car was several miles away and several thousand feet above me, on the road to the crater, and as I struggled back up that difficult trail I consoled myself that it was much easier than it would have been had I been burdened with a heavy, bloody, poncho-wrapped goat draped across my shoulders.

Oh, well, at least I could still hunt pigs. A few days later I was working my way up a jungly valley that once was home to a community of Hawaiians, but had long since been deserted. I was looking for wild bananas, but was perfectly willing to accept any other gifts that nature had to offer. As I traverse such wild spots, I always pause occasionally for a minute or two of absolute quiet, to see if nature has anything to say to me. During one such silence I heard snuffling and grunting up ahead. I was unarmed, but decided to stalk the creatures and see if I could catch a glimpse of them. I left the stream and sneaked along the edge of the narrow valley, pausing now and then until I heard the animal sounds ahead. A shrill squeal had already informed me that the animals I was approaching were wild pigs.

I saw movement under a breadfruit tree, crept forward through the brush, and found a hiding place where I had the pigs in full view. It was a big wild sow with five little pigs. The sow and four of the pigs were noisily gobbling ripe breadfruit that had fallen from the tree, but the fifth pig apparently didn't relish this food, as he was under his mother trying to seize one of the hanging teats. He was the noisemaker, shrilly squealing a protest whenever his mother moved enough to jerk him loose from that fountain of plenty. The pigs never suspected my presence, and presently, when all the fallen breadfruit were eaten, the sow gave in to the importunate one and flopped on her side. All the pigs rushed in to the feast, each seizing a teat and sucking on it as if his life depended on it, which it did. I was so close I could actually hear their noisy sucking sounds as they scrambled, rooted, pushed, and chewed with apparently no regard for the mother's feelings, though really she seemed to be enjoying the process as much as the pigs were.

An old boar has the fiercest and most repulsive appearance of any wild creature I know, and a wild sow is certainly no thing of beauty, but a tiny pig, with pink ears and curly tail, is one of the cutest and most appealing of all the wild young. As I sat watching this charming scene, I suddenly realized that my pig-hunting days were over. When the pigs moved on, I came out of hiding, cut a stalk of wild bananas, gathered a knapsack full of breadfruit, and walked back down the trail wondering whether a vegetarian could actually get enough protein to keep up his health and energy.

If there is any moral to these stories, it is that the beachcomber who intends to get any of his food from hunting should avoid becoming too intimate with the creatures he intends to kill. Otherwise he might find himself in the predicament of Alice, who found herself unable to eat the leg of mutton after she had been formally introduced to it by the Red Queen, for who can eat an acquaintance? I can still go fishing, but recently I built a lily pond in our yard, and my wife tells me she intends to release some native fish in it as pets. Does anyone want to buy some fine rods and reels?

10. Some Fruits You Don't Want to Miss

THE VERSATILE PAPAYA

(Carica papaya)

THOSE who have traveled to the British West Indies or other English-speaking tropical countries will know this fruit as the papaw, but in the United States the name papaw is applied to the *Asimina triloba*, of an entirely different family. Why are we so unimaginative when it comes to names for unfamiliar fruits? Is it because we fear strange foods and can only eat them if they are linked to something familiar by giving them a variation of the same name?

The papaya could hardly be called a truly wild plant of Hawaii, although I have picked some excellent fruit from naturalized trees found growing in wild gulches on Oahu, Hawaii, Maui, and Molokai. It is a fast-growing and short-lived tree that manages to persist by resowing its own seeds from falling ripe fruit. They are sometimes spread to new localities by animals, birds, or far-sighted beachcombers.

The papaya is a native of tropical America, and it had been a cultivated plant for centuries before Columbus came along and made it known to the rest of the world. Almost everyone who tasted it recognized its worth, and the papaya started a triumphal round-the-world tour that soon made it a truly pan-tropic fruit.

The tree on which this luscious, melon-like tropical fruit grows is not a tree at all in the botanical sense, but a giant hollow-stemmed herbaceous plant that sometimes, in some varieties, reaches a height of 30 feet. Left to its own devices, the papaya is usually a simple un-branched plant, the pseudo-trunk covered with old leaf-scars, and the top a spirally arranged cluster of large, lacy leaves borne on long, hollow stems. Like many another tropical fruit, the papaya is a very ornamental plant as well as a fast and efficient producer of great quan-tities of nutritious and tasty fruit. If the top of the plant is cut out or accidentally destroyed, the main stem immediately puts out a num-ber of branches. If several of these are allowed to grow, the plant assumes a weirdly beautiful shape, like something out of the Car-boniferous Age.

The papaya often ripens its first fruit in less than a year after the seed is planted, and after that it is a continuous producer, the same tree bearing ripe fruit, green ones, tiny baby ones, and finally blossoms and buds in the axils of the newest leaves at the top. Having been a cultivated plant from prehistoric times, it has proliferated into dozens of horticultural varieties, some bearing ripe fruit no larger than your fist, while others have watermelon-sized fruit that some-times weighs more than 15 pounds apiece, and the color of the ripe fruit varies from a light yellowish green on some kinds to a deep orange on others. On many varieties the staminate and pistillate blos-soms are borne on separate trees, and in local pidgin these are called "kane kind" and "wahine kind," or "men trees" and "women trees." One would naturally assume that the male trees would bear no fruit, and as a general thing this is a correct assumption, but this perverse tree refuses to obey rules and sometimes skinny little fruits appear between the staminate blossoms! To top it all off, some of the most commonly raised of the modern varieties have perfect blossoms, with the complete male and female principles in a single bloom.

While living in my thatched hut I did not depend on wild plants for my supply of papayas, although I took the wild fruit whenever I came across it in my exploring. On the grounds that I tended as rent on my beachcomber's shack I planted papayas at strategic places where my landlord could enjoy their ornamental beauty and I could use most of the fruit. I have actually reached out of my kitchen window and plucked a luscious, ripe papaya for my breakfast.

Many dislike the papaya on first acquaintance, finding it too perfumy, but with very little persistence a taste for it is easily acquired. When eaten alone, the fresh ripe fruit tastes a bit flat, because of a lack of acidity, so as a breakfast fruit it should always be served with wedges of lemon or lime to liven it up. I prefer lime juice over my papaya, for it not only furnishes the needed acidity, but also contributes a hint of delicious bitter to titillate the tongue, and there are few fruits more delicious than a firm but sweet papaya bathed lightly in lime juice. Novices usually like their papayas dead ripe and soft, but as one learns really to appreciate this fruit the barely ripe, still-firm fruit is preferred. Of course, as with all other fruit, there are papayas and papayas, and the quality differs not only with variety, but also with the locality in which it was grown. Papayas grown in wet sections at fairly high altitudes are apt to be watery and tasteless, while fruit from drier, sandy sections is very flavorsome and sometimes almost too sweet.

The papaya is much more than a fancy breakfast fruit to be served on the half-shell, and the prospective beachcomber should by all means plan to add this versatile fruit to his cuisine. It is a salad fruit extraordinary, combining smoothly and tastefully with both fruits and vegetables. The ripe fruit can be made into jams and marmalades or combined with other fruits in some most delicious beverages. The green fruit can be boiled or baked and served as a vegetable, and it furnishes a wonderfully efficient and flavorsome meat tenderizer. The blossoms can be made into an interesting confection, the young leaves can be boiled like spinach, and even the tip of the trunk can be sliced and cooked as a vegetable.

One of my favorite salads was made by peeling and dicing one firm-ripe papaya, then adding one finely chopped onion, one cup of shredded palm heart, and a little salt. This was thoroughly chilled in the refrigerator, then garnished with a whorl of mayonnaise mixed with a little guava catsup.

A wonderful drink called *Ono-ono* by the Hawaiians combines a number of tropical fruits. After discovering by experiment that the relative quantities of the various fruits were not critical, I made this drink without using a very strict recipe. Usually I would peel and dice

1 large papaya, scoop the juicy flesh from 3 or 4 passionfruits, and add the juice of 1 orange and 2 limes, plus the juice of 1 large pineapple. Then I would pour in the juice from 1 quart jar of guavas, and sweeten it all with a cup of sugar, palm sugar, or honey. All this was whipped at high speed for 2 minutes in a knife-type blender and served over cracked ice. If any of your guests fail to appreciate it, strike a heavy black line through their names in your address book.

For a mellow, mouth-watering Milk Shake, mash the pulp of 1 very ripe and sweet papaya with 1 ripe banana, the juice of 2 limes and ¾ cup of sugar. Add 1 pint of rich milk, a dash of nutmeg, a generous scoop of ice cream, and blend at high speed for 2 minutes.

A cooked papaya sauce with lime juice added makes a marvelous Papaya Shortcake. Dice a firm papaya, add ¼ cup water, ½ cup sugar, and boil about 15 minutes until the papaya is soft. Remove from heat and stir in the juice of 2 limes. Make a rich biscuit dough using your own recipe or a commercial mix; roll the dough pretty thin, butter the surface, then fold it over before cutting out large rounds to be baked as shortcakes. When these biscuits are golden brown, break them open, butter, and generously heap the papaya sauce between and on top of the biscuit; then cover with whipped coconut cream, and beware that you don't overeat.

My favorite jam combines papaya, pineapple, and coconut. Dice 1 large firm-ripe papaya and 1 peeled and cored pineapple and add 6 cups of sugar. Grate the meat of 1 coconut, pour 1 cup of boiling water over it, then squeeze out all the milk you can get. Add this milk to the papaya-pineapple mixture, and boil it down. This makes quite a kettleful at the beginning, but the longer it boils, the less there is of it, and by the time it has reached the proper thickness, you will be wondering what became of the fruit. However, all this cooking serves to concentrate and blend the three delicious flavors, and this Papaya-Pineapple-Coconut Jam is heavenly on toast, pancakes, or hot biscuits.

For a Tropical Ice Cream, press the pulp of 1 very ripe papaya through a sieve, add the juice of 1 orange, the juice of 1 lemon, 1 cup of sugar, and 2 cups of rich coconut cream. Freeze in a mechanical freezer, using 8 parts ice to 1 part rock salt.

For luscious Papaya Pickles, slice 4 cups of half-ripe papaya, making the pieces about 2 inches long by 1 inch wide. Cover these with water and boil for 5 minutes, then drain. Make a syrup of 2 cups sugar, 1 cup vinegar, six cloves, 8 whole black peppercorns, and 2 bay leaves. As soon as this is boiling, add the drained papaya and cook for 12 minutes, then pour into hot, sterilized jars and seal.

Papaya Catsup is excellent on meat, fish, avocados, and a number of other foods. Take 5 tablespoons of mixed whole pickling spices, 1 chopped onion, and 1 chopped clove of garlic, and tie them in a small square of cheesecloth; then simmer them in 6 cups of sieved papaya pulp for about 20 minutes. Add 2 tablespoons of sugar, 1 teaspoon salt, ⅔ cup vinegar, and ⅛ teaspoon tartaric acid. Cook slowly until thick, about 30 minutes. Remove the spice bag, pour the hot catsup into sterilized jars, and seal.

A few pieces of green papaya added to a stew can make a hunk of meat from a tough old wild bull tender as baby beef. This meat-tenderizing ability of the papaya is due to the presence of papain, a protein-splitting enzyme, in the unripe fruit. Some Islanders buy cheap cuts of meat and then wrap them in papaya leaves and store them in the refrigerator for a day or so before cooking them. The best way I found to tenderize some of the tough meat I acquired by hunting the feral game of Hawaii was to liquefy a green papaya in the blender, pour this over a steak or roast, and then fork it in, that is, prick the meat all over with a fork. Long soaking is unnecessary, as most of the tenderizing is done after the meat heats up in the cooking process.

Now let's explore the papaya as a cooked vegetable, beginning with Boiled Papayas. If full-grown but still green papayas are peeled, diced, and boiled in salted water until they are tender, then drained and seasoned with black pepper and butter, they make a very palatable vegetable with a delicate squash flavor.

When papayas are just beginning to ripen, but are still quite hard, is the right time to use them for Stuffed Baked Papayas. Use half a papaya for each person being served. Cut each fruit in half lengthwise, remove the seeds and fill the cavity with a stuffing made of ½ pound of ground beef to 1 cup of cooked rice, seasoned with salt, pepper, a touch of chili powder, and a sprinkle of oregano. Fill each half just level full and cover each one with a little square of aluminum foil. Place in a baking pan, add enough water to cover the bottom of the pan, and bake for 40 minutes in a 350° oven. In practice

I often varied this stuffing by using bread crumbs instead of rice, or by using Portuguese sausage to replace the ground beef and seasonings. For plain Baked Papaya to serve as a vegetable, omit the stuffings and sprinkle the papaya halves with lemon juice, salt, and melted butter; bake as above, without the foil covering.

The young, tender leaves from the very top of the papaya tree make very good boiling greens. Remove the stems, press the leaves into a pot, and cover with boiling water. Place over high heat, and as soon as the water boils again, drain it off and cover the vegetable with fresh boiling water. Papaya Greens are rather bitter unless they are given this treatment. Allow them to cook in the second water 10 minutes, then drain again and season with butter, salt, and a little freshly ground black pepper. Try using coconut butter or coconut cream, instead of butter, for a delightful change.

Whenever it is necessary to remove papaya trees, or when you are cutting them back to make them branch, always salvage the tender, growing tip of the trunk. This crisp Papaya Tip, when peeled and sliced, then boiled for 20 minutes and seasoned with coconut butter and salt, is an excellent vegetable, and its enzymes will help you to digest the protein eaten at the same meal.

And finally, there are the flowers. Papaya flowers are large, fleshy, and ivory-colored and have a faint but delicious fragrance. Gather them on a dry day, being careful not to bruise them. Make a syrup, using 2 cups sugar, ½ cup water, and ½ cup lemon juice. When it is boiling, drop in the flowers and cook them until they are translucent; these Candied Papaya Flowers are better if one candies some firm-ripe papaya at the same time. To make Papaya Squares, pare the fruit and cut it into 1-inch squares. Drop a few of these squares into the syrup with the cooking blossoms, and they will improve the flavor as well as making some additional and very good confections. Remove from the boiling syrup when the flowers and the papaya squares acquire a clear look, and dry them on wax paper for a day, then roll in granulated sugar. Dry for one day more; then store in a tight container until you are ready to eat them or offer them to a very special guest.

Besides its protein-digesting enzymes, the papaya is a very good source of vitamin A and an excellent source of vitamin C, so this luscious fruit is not only a taste thrill, but makes a genuine contribution to your health. All in all, I would say that the papaya is far from being the least of the luxuries which the beachcomber can enjoy at no cost, while winterbound Northerners either do without it altogether or buy green-picked, imported papayas at outrageous prices. I have never tried canning papaya except in jams, for there is no need to preserve the fruit of this truly tropical plant that offers you fresh, tree-ripened fruit every day of the year.

BREADFRUIT ISN'T BREAD
Artocarpus communis

The breadfruit has an appetizing but very misleading name. A favorite scene in the South Sea dream is of trees loaded down with round loaves of bread, making baking or buying unnecessary. Why the early explorers fostered this illusion I can't imagine, unless it was to encourage the slaves in English colonies to eat this food that could be so cheaply grown. I have before me an early account of this fruit, which says that the inside of a breadfruit baked in an underground oven "closely resembles the crumb of a tuppenny loaf." All I can say is that either the author was totally devoid of eyes, nose, and taste buds, or else a "tuppenny loaf" is vastly different from any bread I ever saw or tasted. Breadfruit is wonderful, and after a taste for it is acquired, it is even delicious, when properly prepared, but it in no way resembles bread.

The *fruit* part of the name also promises more than it delivers, for the breadfruit in no way replaces fruit as we generally use the term. In use, the breadfruit is a high-carbohydrate vegetable, and in the diet of the Polynesians it replaces or supplements the use of taro and sweet potatoes. The carbohydrates in green breadfruit are in the form of starch, but as the fruit ripens, this is all transformed into sugar. It is always cooked before eating, as raw breadfruit is fit for nothing except pig feed.

Speaking of pigs—another tree that has been introduced into Hawaii bears large cylindrical fruit with rounded ends, hanging on long stems, so from a little distance this fruit looks exactly like large bologna sausages hanging on strings. Of course this tree is called a "sausage tree," although the fruit is really not edible. An old legend in the Islands relates that when Captain Cook first sighted Hawaii, he looked through a telescope and saw a sausage tree growing between two breadfruits, and that is why he named this group the Sandwich Islands. In reality, Cook named these islands for his patron, the Earl of Sandwich. This English nobleman dearly loved his food, and apparently he was the first to put cold cuts and tidbits between two slices of bread for between-meal snacks, so the modern sandwich was named for him.

Actually, breadfruit *was* the staff of life for many Polynesian peoples, although it played a supplemental role in ancient Hawaii, where the natives depended more on taro, sweet potatoes, and bananas than they did on breadfruit.

This really excellent food is borne on large, beautiful trees with lacy, lobed leaves. The fruit is spherical and usually from 6 to 8 inches in diameter, with its skin figured in tiny polygons giving the surface a mosaic-like appearance. These little polygons are really separate fruits, for the breadfruit is a compound, or collective, fruit made up of literally thousands of tiny fruits grown together.

There is no reason why a beachcomber should not enjoy all the breadfruit he can use during the season when it is available, for the tree grows bountifully on all the islands and there is little competition for the fruit. Although individual trees ripen their whole crop over a comparatively short period, the wide-awake beachcomber who gets around can find trees with ripe fruit from about the beginning of July until well after Christmas, and sometimes a tree gets confused and ripens a crop at some other time of year. It is simplest to pull breadfruit from the tree with a pruning hook on a long pole, as described in the chapter on coconuts, rather than climb the tree, for the breadfruit has very brittle branches that break easily.

A taste for breadfruit must be developed before one can really enjoy eating it, but acquiring this taste is no formidable task. The recipes given below present the breadfruit in the forms most acceptable to Northern palates, and most find these dishes acceptable from the first taste, while some, after a time, actually acquire a passion for this food.

Probably the native breadfruit dish most appreciated by the uninitiated is a sort of sweet pudding called *Papaiee*. For this you will want a dead-ripe breadfruit, so bring one in the house and lay it on the window sill for a few days until the outside is brown and crusty and the inside is semiliquid. Grate the meat of 1 large coconut, pour 1 cup of boiling water over it, and after kneading it with the hands to loosen the oily juice, squeeze out as much milk as possible through two thicknesses of cheesecloth. Scrape the soft flesh from the almost overripe breadfruit and mix it with the coconut milk, then add ½ cup sugar and ½ teaspoon salt, and mix again. Pour into a buttered casserole and bake in a 350° oven for 1 hour. What does it taste like? Well, it's a little like sweet potatoes baked with cream, but really one shouldn't compare it to any other food, but just enjoy it for its own sweet sake.

For Fried Breadfruit use a ripe but not overripe fruit. Cover it with water and boil for 1 hour, then drain, and as soon as it is cool enough to handle, remove the stem, core, and skin. Slice what is left into pieces about ½ inch thick, dredge these pieces in seasoned flour, and fry in hot fat until they are a golden brown.

Boiled Green Breadfruit makes an excellent starchy vegetable for those who have learned to like this South Sea Island fruit. Peel and dice the raw green breadfruit, just cover with water and boil for 1 hour, then drain. Add butter, salt, and a little black pepper, and cook uncovered a few minutes to dry it out a bit; serve steaming hot.

A short while after arriving in the Islands, I learned to enjoy the Hawaiian national dish, poi. Poi, as usually served in Hawaii, is a half-sour, partly fermented goo made of cooked and pounded taro root, and it looks like bluish-gray wallpaper paste. Few like it at the first trial, but the taste grows on one, and after a few samplings the problem of learning to like it is replaced by the one of getting enough of it. It is loaded with B vitamins and is highly valued by doctors and dietitians who unanimously recommend it as the first semisolid food to be given to Island babies of all races. Poi had a regular place in my diet during my twelve years' residence in the Islands, and the only reason I have not continued to eat it is that it is unprocurable where I now live.

After launching my beachcombing career I cast around to see if I couldn't make my own poi, for I had a conscientious objection to purchased products. However, the ground around my tropical shack was unsuitable for taro, which grows in flooded fields, and the only wild taro in the Islands is in the remnants of the old taro fields along the streams up in the wild valleys where the former Hawaiian population has died off or moved away since the coming of the white man. I tried making poi of this taro, and it tasted good enough, but it burned and prickled my throat unmercifully because of the minute crystals of calcium oxalate buried in the flesh, which characterize not only taro but many other members of the arum family. The ancient Hawaiians removed this characteristic by aging their poi for long periods, but I don't like my poi quite so old and sour. This objectionable feature has been completely bred out of the taro that is raised in the Islands today, but the wild stuff from the mountain valleys still has it with a vengeance. So I reluctantly continued to purchase the poi I needed, only partly salving my conscience by bartering Indian almonds and fresh fish for it, instead of using money.

I knew that the Tahitians and Marquesans made poi of breadfruit, so I started experimenting with this material, but my first few trials yielded some pretty awful stuff. Finally I learned to make palatable Breadfruit Poi, but only by combining it with a little of the purchased product made of taro by the professionals. I used breadfruit that were ripe but not too soft, and the first step was to cover the fruit with water and boil it for about 1½ hours. It was then drained, cooled, pared, cut into convenient chunks, and ground in a meat grinder. This ground breadfruit was further pounded and worked with a wooden pestle until it became a smooth, thick mass. Then I mixed a little day-old taro poi with water until it was a very thin paste, and I gradually added this thin poi to the breadfruit while kneading and working it with my hands. I didn't add enough of this thin taro poi paste to dilute the breadfruit poi down to eating consistency at this stage, but left it quite thick. When it seemed smooth and well blended, I covered the bowl and allowed it to ripen at room temperature for a day. Then I added water and kneaded and stirred the poi again, until it was as thin as I wanted it. Hawaiians judge the consistency of poi by the number of fingers it takes to scoop up a decent mouthful; therefore one-finger poi is quite thick, and three-finger poi is very thin. I usually compromised and made mine of about two-finger consistency.

At this point I would strain the poi through a piece of muslin to remove any stray fibers or lumps, and then it was ready to eat. This thinned poi could be kept in the refrigerator for about a week, and up to a certain point, it improved with age. In flavor it was quite mild when new and became very sour when it was about a week old.

I was not the only one who learned to appreciate breadfruit poi, for Jim and Falani, as well as Hugo and his little family, not only learned to tolerate this new taste, but actually came to prefer it to all-taro poi.

Breadfruit is a good source of calcium, and, especially when eaten as poi, it is a very wholesome food indeed, contributing significant quantities of ascorbic acid and thiamine. Although it will never furnish either bread or fruit, the breadfruit will find an important place in the cuisine of anyone who is doing an artistic job of beachcombing.

PINEAPPLES

Pineapples are big business in Hawaii, and the entire industry, from setting the plants in the field to pasting the labels on the cans, is as mechanized as the Ford Plant. Hawaiian pineapples are the best in the world, and they are constantly being improved through an extensive program of research and plant breeding. A trip to Hawaii without enjoying the pineapples would be like failing to enjoy the climate, and truly, a prime pineapple that has been thoroughly field-ripened can furnish a gustatory thrill that is seldom equaled.

However, all these perfect pineapples are owned by huge companies, and how is the beachcomber to secure a supply of this fine fruit without buying them at the market like any ordinary householder? Woe unto the light-fingered adventurer who gets caught lifting any of the beautiful pineapples that grow in fields so temptingly near the roadside, for Hawaiian laws favor plantation owners rather than beachcombers, and pineapple purloining is heavily penalized.

There are wild pineapples in Hawaii, but they are a far cry from the huge, uniform fruit that is almost mechanically mass-produced for the canning industry. Nevertheless, like strawberries in our own country, these variable little wild fruits are often sweeter and more fragrant than those produced by the combined skill of all the personnel of a mighty industry. I have greatly enjoyed them on the Big Island—Hawaii—and on Molokai, but I was never able to locate wild pineapples on Oahu, which was my beachcombing headquarters.

I can tell you how I finally gained access to a dependable supply of pineapples, but I'm afraid my methods might not work for all of those who might want to follow my footsteps in a beachcombing adventure. By chance and not by design I became acquainted with a geneticist who worked as a plant breeder for the Pineapple Research Institute, and by design and not by chance I developed that friendship. The pineapple industry of Hawaii is so vast that if a pineapple containing only a fraction of one percent more sugar, or an immeasurably small amount less acid, could be developed, it would save hundreds of tons of sugar in the canning process in the course of a year. Therefore, the industry welcomes even the most minor improvement that can be made by plant breeding. My friend's job was no less than to produce a tailor-made pineapple of exactly the right size and shape to be handled by automated machinery and having all the qualities desired by the industry and finally the housewife. He worked toward this goal by hybridization and selection, and many of the plants in his experimental plot had very fancy pedigrees.

Size and form can be measured, sugar and acid content can be determined by chemical tests, but *flavor* is far more ethereal and much harder to pin down. There is no test or machine that can determine whether a pineapple will be judged good, bad, or indifferent by the ultimate consumer, so this is one job that still must be performed by that most complicated machine of all, *Homo sapiens*.

When my friend discovered that I had an appreciation of fine flavors and some ability to discriminate between them, he began plying me with pineapples and soliciting my judgment on their worth. As payment for thus aiding the industry, he kept me supplied with all the fancy pineapples from his experimental plots that I could use. Imagine receiving compensation for tasting pedigreed pineapples with some of the most delicious flavors that the combined efforts of science and nature have yet been able to produce!

If a beachcomber has access to some ground, he could raise his own pineapples, but it is a pretty specialized crop for a home gardener, and the fruit won't be ripe next month. If suckers from established plants are set out, they will, under ideal conditions, produce the first crop of ripe fruit in about 18 months, and this means mulching, fertilizing, spraying, and closely tending the plants for all this time. I planted a few of the spiny crowns from choice fruit shortly after finishing my thatched hut, and though I lavished many hours of loving care on them, and sprayed them regularly with iron sulphate to keep them bright and green, I still hadn't picked a single fruit from them when I moved to Maui more than two years later, although when I left, there were several good-sized green ones that showed promise.

On Maui, I found that the chief pineapple company supplemented the yield from their own huge plantations with fruit raised by small farmers under contract, so I immediately sought out one of these small farmers and made friends with him. After the first crop of pineapples is harvested, the plants are cut back to two suckers, which produce the next crop. This and succeeding crops from the same plants are known as ratoon crops, and on good fields as many as four ratoon crops can sometimes be harvested before the plants are plowed under. However, as the plant grows older, it tends to produce small, unmarketable pineapples, and it was this undersized fruit in which I was interested, for these little pineapples are wonderfully sweet and flavorsome when fully ripened in the field. My new friend took me to a small field on his place that had been abandoned by the pineapple company the year before. It was overgrown with grass and weeds, but among this wild growth the old pineapple plants were bearing a sparse crop of small but very sweet and luscious fruit. He gave me *carte blanche* to help myself to all I wanted, so once again I fairly reveled in pineapples.

The pineapple, both canned and fresh, has long been a familiar item on our grocers' shelves, so Northern cooks and housewives are familiar with its use. Every standard cookbook gives numbers of ways to use this delicious fruit, so I will not clutter up these pages with conventional pineapple recipes, but will rather concentrate on trying to give you information that might be difficult to obtain elsewhere.

The pineapple differs from most other fruit in that it contains no starch when it is green. Rather, the plant has a large starchy root, and it is this root starch that is converted into sugar and pumped into the ripened fruit. For this reason, the pineapple never gets any sweeter after being picked, no matter how long it is ripened. This is why even the best-looking fruit in our Northern markets is apt to be of poor quality. To be firm enough to withstand long shipping, pineapples simply have to be picked before they are ripe enough to be at their best.

Selecting a pineapple that will prove sweet and juicy when tasted is a skill which requires practice. You will meet many self-styled experts in the Islands who will tell you foolproof ways to pick out the best pineapples. Some pull a leaf from the crown on top of the fruit and judge its ripeness by how easily the leaf comes away. Others thump the pine and listen to the sound, while others look at the color, or at the state of the withered blossoms that still adhere to each section of the fruit. The only thing all these experts seem to have in common is that all of them sometimes select hard, sour fruit that has somehow passed their test for ripeness. Color is a poor indicator, for from the same plant one may pick one pine with a beautiful golden color and have it turn out to be too green to be good, and another with a greenish outside that will be ripe and perfect. The fragrance of the ripe pineapple would be a good recognition feature, except that out in the field one's olfactory organs are so bombarded with the aroma of ripe pineapples that it is difficult to distinguish the smell of any one fruit. I'm a thumper. If one thumps a green pineapple, the finger easily rebounds, and the sound is a sharp *pink-pink-pink*, but if the fruit is ripe and juicy, the finger lands solidly on it with a *thud-thud-thud* sound. I've picked some wonderful pineapples using this method of selection, but I must admit that I've also carried home some hard, sour ones.

One of the most delightful ways to serve fresh pineapple is in the shell, or luau-style, as it is called in Hawaii. Preparing this decorative dish is really little more work than fixing pineapple any other way, and it looks very smart. Cut a thick slice from the stem end of the pine, squarely across the fruit so the pineapple will sit perfectly upright on a plate. Now cut straight across the top end of the pineapple just where it starts to narrow, that is, just below its shoulders. If your pineapple is the best shape for serving in this fashion, the center part that is left will be an almost perfect cylinder. Run a very sharp, thin knife endwise through this cylinder, near the skin, cut right around the pineapple about ½ inch from the skin, and slip the juicy cylinder of peeled pineapple from inside the shell. Unless you have left a very thick rind, the outside of the peeled part of the pineapple will be dotted with little eyes. Study these eyes for a moment, and you will see that they are spirally arranged in rows running diagonally from top to bottom. Once you have seen the pattern, it is an easy matter to make a few V-shaped cuts that will remove these eyes a whole row at a time. Now, cut the pineapple into a number of wedge-shaped pieces, and return to the hollow rind. Set it upright on a plate and replace the crown, trimming the little leaves at the top to remove the points and to make a shapely handle with which to lift it off when you are forking out a luscious wedge for yourself or a guest. When pineapples were plentiful I usually kept a luau-style pineapple chilling in the refrigerator at all times, to have a treat to offer to unexpected guests. If no guests showed up, so much the better; I could eat it all myself. This is not only a nice way to serve pineapple at parties and luaus, but it gives a festive air to between-meal snacks, coffee breaks, and afternoon teas. Imagine—a beachcomber serving afternoon tea! How square can you get?

While I was beachcombing I was the proud owner of an electrical vegetable juicer that would get some kind of liquid out of almost anything. It worked by first grating the fruit or vegetable fine and then by centrifugal force hurling the juice out of a perforated basket that turned at high speeds. It was a handy gadget, but it isn't an absolutely essential piece of beachcombing equipment. The juice flows easily from a pineapple in prime ripeness, and one only has to chop it fine and squeeze out the juice through two thicknesses of cheesecloth. When I give someone a recipe for tropical punch and come to pineapple juice, nine times out of ten they will say, "Oh, I'll use canned pineapple juice for that. It's so handy."

It is handy, but it isn't nearly as good as the sweet juice freshly squeezed from the living ripe fruit. In all my recipes that call for pineapple juice, use fresh juice from fully ripened fruit, if you would enjoy them at their best.

Pineapple-Crab Salad was one of my favorite lunches while in the Islands. In fact, it was such a favorite that I often ate it for dinner, too. The huge Samoan crabs are in season the year round in Hawaii, and getting an ample supply of them is simply a matter of a little work and a great familiarity with their haunts. Boil and cool a good-sized Samoan crab; then crack it and pick out the meat. This should yield ½ cup or more of crab meat. Mix this with 1 cup of diced pineapple from a sweet, ripe fruit, and dump it over ½ avocado that has been seeded and peeled. Now take 3 tablespoons of mayonnaise, 1 tablespoon of guava catsup, and 1 teaspoon of Worcestershire sauce, mix them all together, pour over the salad and then dive in.

Chutney can be made of pineapples that has a flavor that rivals, if it does not actually surpass, that of mango chutney. To 4 cups coarsely diced fresh pineapple add 1 cup vinegar, 1 cup brown sugar, 1 level tablespoon salt, 2 tablespoons finely chopped candied gingerroot, 2 cloves garlic chopped fine, two small pickled red peppers chopped fine; stir well, and allow it to stand until the next day. Then boil slowly until pineapple is tender, add ½ cup slivered almonds, and cook until the mixture thickens to the desired consistency. Pour into hot sterilized jars and seal. I once made this Pineapple Chutney using pineapples I had received as a gift, palm vinegar, palm sugar, wild ginger, and wild peppers, and substituted foraged macadamia nuts for the almonds. It was preserved in baby-food jars given me by a neighbor. The flavor of the resulting chutney was superb, but even more important, it gave a spiritual satisfaction that no product made of purchased materials could ever yield.

At another time I made some Pineapple-Orange-Honey Marmalade that gave the same kind of satisfaction. This was on Maui, and a friend of mine, who lived in the Kula District, about 4000 feet up on the slopes of Haleakala, asked me to help him remove a swarm of bees that had made a home between the walls of an outbuilding on his place. On a December day I arrived there at daybreak dressed in heavy clothes over which I wore my boating foul-weather gear tied at waist, wrists and ankles. With heavy gloves and a net over a big hat, I was bee-proofed. At that altitude it was so cold at dawn that these clothes felt good, and that cold also numbed the bees until they could hardly fly. It was such a simple matter to remove some boards from the outside of the double wall that I was able to fill a washtub with fine comb honey.

On the way home I stopped to pick some pineapple, and found a wild orange tree and loaded up with those. Halting at a little stream, I found some ginger growing on its banks, not the wild flowering ginger that is common in Hawaii, but the real spice ginger. I dug some roots. On reaching home, I peeled 6 oranges, boiled the rinds through three waters, and cooked them in the last water until tender. Then I scraped the pulp from inside the rinds with a spoon, cut the rinds into fine slivers, and removed the membranes from the sections of the six oranges. This I combined with the slivered rinds, then added 10 cups of diced fresh pineapple, ¼ cup of grated fresh gingerroot and 3 cups of strained honey. Although I cooked it until the pineapple was tender, there was still too much watery juice. I solved this by draining off the juice and boiling it down separately until it was a thick syrup, then recombining it with the fruit and heating the whole to the boiling point before pouring it into small sterilized jars, which were then tightly sealed. It was delicious, and the fact that I knew the origin of every ingredient, right back to where Mother Nature had produced them, gave a meaning to this condiment that other marmalades simply don't possess.

MANGOES BY THE BUSHEL

The mango was introduced into Hawaii early in the 19th century and has found a congenial home there, being widely naturalized along roadsides and up in the deserted valleys, and it has become the favorite fruit of Hawaiian children. Although there is considerable variation in the quality of the fruit produced by these feral mangoes, the wild trees produce surprisingly good fruit, on the whole, considering that they are all seedlings. As a usual thing, I prefer the flavor of the seedling Hawaiian mango to that of the cultivated, grafted varieties such as the Hayden and the Pirie.

These seedlings make very large trees, and the fruit varies in size from *maninis* about two inches long, that are mostly seed, to big meaty mangoes more than six inches long and three inches wide and rivaling the finest grafted fruit in quality. The color of the ripe fruit varies from yellowish green through yellow, orange, and red, often with spots of a contrasting color. The flesh of a ripe mango may be light-yellow to deep-orange and closely resembles that of a peach in color and texture, but don't expect it to resemble a peach in flavor. Ripe mangoes are sweet and good, and few mainlanders have any trouble learning to like them, but they are not peaches. Some people detect a taste faintly reminiscent of turpentine in the mango, but this is found only in fruit from certain trees; believe it or not, one can learn to appreciate this flavor, and then one misses it when eating mangoes in which it is absent.

Chronic laziness would be the only possible excuse for a beachcomber not to have all the fresh mangoes he could use while they are in season, and all the canned mango slices, chutney, and mango sauce he could eat at other times of the year. Seedling mango trees on the leeward or dry sides of the various Islands usually ripen their fruit in

April, May, or June, and about the time the last of these are gone, the trees on the wet, windward sides take over and continue the season until about the beginning of October. Once I found a mango tree hidden far up in one of the deserted valleys that was loaded with fine ripe fruit in February. I was jubilant, thinking I had discovered a tree that would always start the season of ripe mangoes two months early. I carefully noted the date on which I had first picked this early fruit, and next year when that date rolled around I made my way up that valley with my mouth all set for juicy, ripe mangoes, only to find the tree covered with tiny, green fruit no larger than that on the trees around it. It was just another case of a tree being confused by the eternal spring that is Hawaii and putting on its fruit out of its usual season.

Later, a Filipino told me that in his home islands they sometimes built a fire under a mango tree at a certain time of the year and allowed the smoke to drift through the foliage, and this tended to force the tree to put on an extra early crop of fruit. He was very vague about details and times, so I never tried this technique. Here is an interesting experiment for some future beachcomber to try. If it worked, it could be very profitable, for mangoes would command good prices if they could be brought to market before it becomes glutted with this common fruit.

The dead-ripe mangoes that fall from the trees can be used for sieved pulp to make mango-ade, frozen desserts, shortcakes, or chiffon pies, but to get this fruit in the very best stage for most mango dishes, it must be plucked from the tree some time before it is ready to fall. A long slender bamboo pole with a wire hook on the end of it will let you pull the mango loose, and a little net fastened below the hook will catch the mango you choose and prevent a bruising drop to the ground. This device will allow you to select the very best mangoes from the tree and, while lowering each mango individually takes time, what is time to a beachcomber? Unlike the pineapple, the mango can be further ripened after being picked, if it is not plucked when too immature.

Fresh mangoes, ripe but still firm, are an excellent dessert fruit, either alone or in combination with papayas or pineapples, and they blend beautifully into fruit cocktails and salads. They also make delicious jams, marmalades, pies, upside-down cakes, gelatin desserts and brown betties. I'll give you a sampling of recipes I have found good, then leave you and the mango alone in the kitchen with your own culinary ingenuity. Just to inject a little order into this section, let's start with uses of the green fruit and work up to a soft ripeness.

Mango Chutney is a familiar item on fancy grocery shelves and at gourmet shops. My own recipe for this universally appreciated condiment went through a sort of circular evolution, becoming more and more complex until I noticed that I was picking out the mango slices and shoving the other ingredients to the side of my plate. After that I began trying to see how much excess garbage I could eliminate and finally came up with a comparatively simple recipe that yields *mango* chutney, and not a mysterious mixture of dried and preserved fruits through which one must diligently search to find a single piece of mango.

Mangoes that are full-sized, but still green and hard, make the best chutney. Peel the mangoes and slice the fruit from the seed. Use large slices for chutney and small slices to make Green Mango Sauce according to the recipe that follows this one. To 16 cups of the large slices add 2 cups of vinegar, 7 cups of sugar, ¼ cup of thinly sliced green gingerroot, 6 little wild red peppers with the seeds removed, 3 cloves of garlic, two large onions chopped fine, and a heaping teaspoon of salt. Mix everything together and allow it to stand for 24 hours, then cook it for about an hour, or until the juice gets nice and thick. Pour into half-pint jars and seal with two-piece dome lids. This recipe makes about 16 jars of chutney in which the mango flavor predominates, and it is an excellent condiment with beef, pork, or lamb.

For Green Mango Sauce, cook 12 cups of green mango slices with 3 cups of water until they are soft, then add 4 cups of sugar, and cook 5 minutes more. Pour boiling hot into hot, sterilized jars and seal with sterilized, two-piece lids. That's all there is to it. Green mango sauce is used exactly as you would use apple sauce; for instance, it is *the* dish to serve with wild pork from the mountains.

Ripe Mango Sauce is made exactly like the above, except that firm-ripe mangoes are used instead of green ones. Ripe mango sauce is better than the green as a dessert fruit, and a bowl of this brightly colored sauce with a swirl of whipped coconut cream to top it off is a dessert I would be proud to serve to even the most discriminating gourmet.

Canned Mango Slices are best made of firm-ripe fruit. Peel the mangoes and slice them from the seeds. Use the large slices for canning, and the small ones for ripe mango sauce. Make a syrup of equal parts, water and sugar, and when this syrup is boiling, drop the mango slices into it and cook for about 15 minutes until the edges are translucent. Pack in hot, sterilized jars, cover with boiling syrup, and seal immediately. Use canned mango slices in any way you would use canned peaches. They are excellent as a dessert, with or without whipped cream, and they make wonderful upside-down cake.

Mango-ade is best made of the soft ripe pulp of windfall mangoes. Press this pulp through a sieve to mash it thoroughly and to remove any fiber. To one cup of sieved pulp add ¼ cup of sugar, the juice of 1 orange and a little of the grated peel, the juice of 1 lemon, and two cups of water. Shake or stir until the sugar is completely dissolved, and serve over cracked ice.

Mango Chiffon Pie uses this same kind of sieved pulp from windfall mangoes. Mix 1 envelope unflavored gelatin with ½ cup sugar, then add 1 cup sieved ripe mango pulp and four egg yolks slightly beaten. Mix well and dump into the top of a double boiler, stirring until the mixture thickens. Add 2 teaspoons of lemon juice and chill the mixture until it mounds slightly when spooned. This will take the better part of an hour, so you will have plenty of time to make a graham-cracker crust (see index). When the crust is ready, beat the whites of the four eggs until they form soft peaks, then, slowly adding ¼ cup of sugar, beat them until they form very stiff peaks. Fold the thickening mango mixture into the egg whites and dump the whole into the crust. Chill until firm, and you will find this pie light and fluffy with a wonderful melting flavor.

Mango Shortcake is made by making biscuit bases (as described in the section on papayas), heaping them with sieved ripe mango pulp, and topping it off with some whipped coconut cream.

To make a Mango Mousse, mix 1 envelope unflavored gelatin with ½ cup sugar and then dissolve in ¾ cup of boiling water. Cool, then stir in 1 cup of sieved ripe pulp, the juice of 1 lime, and a pinch of salt. Put this mixture in a refrigerator tray and freeze it until it is mushy. Whip a pint of cream—cow's cream this time, not coconut—until it is soft and fluffy, fold in the half-frozen mango mixture, heap it all in an ice tray, and freeze from 4 to 6 hours.

Surely I have said enough so you will not ignore those mangoes growing by the roadside in most tropical lands. The beachcomber who refuses to learn to like this fruit is going to miss one of the best features of the tropical life.

11. To Tickle Your Appetite

IN any tropical land suitable for beachcombing you will find many more minor but delicious fruits growing wild, or in a semiculti-vated state as garden or dooryard plants, than I have covered in this book. Most of these are never brought to market, so the knowledge-able beachcomber, with time and energy to spend in ways that yield no cash profit, can often enjoy delicacies that other, more affluent, visitors to the area never even hear about. These occasional fruits will probably never make up any major portion of the beachcomber's diet, but they can add many a graceful touch to tropical living. Even if the rich tourist could secure these rare fruits in exchange for money, he could never savor their taste in full. The final product that appears on the beachcomber's table is compounded of the joys of the chase, which were exercised in searching for and gathering the materials, and the magic of combining these exotic ingredients into beautiful and tasty dishes, as well as the intrinsic flavors to be found in the fruits themselves.

The few fruits of this class that are presented in this chapter are but a small sampling of the many kinds that could be used by any beachcomber who will take the trouble to learn about them and find the patience to seek them out. And right here is a convenient place to hold forth on the limitations of this book. While it is my hope that this work can contribute to your enjoyment of the tropics, it is far from being an exhaustive treatise on the products and possibilities offered by these warm and fruitful lands. In selecting the material for inclusion in this book I was always bothered by the fact that space limitations seemed to be forcing me to exclude much more than I was putting in. One might, with charity, call this a textbook on tropical living, but it is strictly on an undergraduate level, leading at most to a B.B. or Bachelor of Beachcombing. The equivalent of a doctorate in this subject will require open-eyed attention to all that nature produces in your section, a willingness to experiment that is not dampened by occasional negative results, and a calm spirit that does not consider time wasted that is employed in merely looking at things and wondering about them. Here are a few minor tropical goodies that I have looked at, wondered about, and learned to enjoy, which can be the grace-notes of really talented beachcombing.

A PASSION FOR PASSION FRUIT
Passiflora species

Passion fruit did not get its name from what you are thinking about, and it won't do a thing for you along those lines. Properly, it should be called "passion *flower*" as the botanical designation for the genus indicates. In most countries where it is grown it is known by its Spanish name *granadilla*, meaning "little pomegranate," but I have never heard it called granadilla in Hawaii. There it is called either passion fruit or *lilikoi*, its Hawaiian name. Originally, the *Passiflorae* were natives of tropical America, and when the early Spanish priests first saw their beautiful flowers they professed to see in them symbols of Our Lord's Passion, hence the name.

The passion fruit that is preferred in Hawaii is the *Passiflora edulis*, which has both purple and yellow varieties, the purple being more common. It is easily propagated by seeds or rooted cuttings and is planted along fences and around dooryards as an ornamental vine; it is also found as a naturalized wild plant in many parts of the Islands. There were a number of passion vines growing on the grounds I tended as rent on my thatched hut, and these furnished me with all the fruit I could use from July until Christmas each year. After we moved to Maui, my wife and I found areas on the lower slopes of Haleakala where we could gather all the fruit we could use from the wild passion vines growing on a few square rods of ground, and we used a great many of them. I can easily eat a dozen *lilikoi* for break-fast, but then, I am a pig in the presence of passion fruit.

The *lilikoi* is an unpretentious fruit about the size and shape of a large egg. The brittle shell encloses numerous small seeds, each sur-rounded by a globule of juicy yellow pulp that is the edible part of the passion fruit. There is little difference in flavor between the yellow and purple varieties except that the yellow kind contains more acid, and therefore more sugar must be added to make it palatable. When the fruit is perfectly ripe, the shell becomes dry and wrinkled, but don't let this repel you, for the pulp inside around the seeds will still be fresh and juicy.

Many people like to eat their passion fruit straight from the shell, but I prefer mine with the seeds removed. When the fruits are cut in half the pulp is easily scooped out with a spoon. Pressing it through a colander or coarse sieve yields seedless pulp, or it can be squeezed through a cloth to make clear juice. A bowl of the seedless pulp, with a little sugar added, makes an exciting dessert or breakfast fruit. It has an enticing aroma and an exotic, jungly flavor that is exceedingly pleasant to most palates. Theoretically this seedless pulp will keep perfectly fresh for several weeks in the refrigerator, but it will never last that long if I'm around.

For a pitcherful of as delicious and cooling a fruitade as ever eased a beachcomber through a hot afternoon, mix ½ cup of passion fruit juice with 1 cup of sugar and 4 cups of water. Serve or selfishly con-sume in tall glasses filled with cracked ice. Add passion fruit juice to fruit punches, for it is *the* tropical taste that will lift all such concoc-tions out of the ordinary.

Passionate Ice Cream combines the delicious flavors of coconut and passion fruit. To 2 cups of coconut milk, made according to directions given on page 30, add ⅔ cup of sugar and ½ cup of passion fruit juice and stir until the sugar is dissolved. Freeze in an ice-cream freezer, using 8 parts ice to 1 part coarse salt.

Passion Cake Icing is certain to earn compliments. Cream ½ stick butter with ½ cup powdered sugar until smooth. Add ¼ cup passion fruit pulp and beat until frothy. Then, while still beating, gradually add 2 more cups of powdered sugar, continuing the beating until the mixture is stiff enough to spread smoothly on a cake. Frost the cake

several hours before it is to be served, so it will have the crispy beginning of a crust as it is set before that special guest you wish to please.

Beachcomber Candy again marries the flavors of coconut and passion fruit. Finely shred the meat of one coconut, spread it on a cookie
sheet, and dry it in a slow oven until most of the moisture has evaporated; then cool. This should yield about 2½ cups of dry coconut.
Mix ½ cup of passion fruit pulp with 3 cups of powdered sugar and
beat until the mixture is creamy, then add half of the coconut, 1 cup
of Indian almonds, and 2 more cups of powdered sugar. Wet the
hands and form this mixture into soft balls. Roll the balls in the remainder of the coconut, place them on buttered wax paper, and allow
to harden in a cool place for a day. This recipe makes about 3 pounds
of delicious candy, and when Ogden Nash wrote his "Reflections on
Ice-Breaking," which said, "Candy is dandy but liquor is quicker,"
he obviously had never tried candy made with fresh passion fruit.

The period during which fresh passion fruit can be found extends
over half the year, from midsummer to midwinter, and if one bottles
some Passion Fruit Syrup when the season is at its height, passion
fruit products can be enjoyed the year around. Because of its high
acidity, passion fruit syrup keeps well, and it is easy as one, two, three,
to make. Use 1 cup of passion fruit juice, 2 cups of water, and 3 cups
of sugar. Combine the sugar and water, bring it to a boil, then add
the passion fruit juice, and bottle and seal immediately in hot sterilized bottles or fruit jars. Wrap each jar or bottle individually in
newspaper and store them in a dark closet. Don't try to preserve a
two-year supply of this syrup, for it begins to lose flavor after about
six or eight months. All the recipes given above, and many more that
you can improvise, can be adapted to use passion fruit syrup instead
of the fresh product.

While visiting on the island of Hawaii, I enjoyed eating the sweet
granadilla, there called water lemon, or *liliwai*, its Hawaiian name.
This is the fruit of the *Passiflora ligularis*. It grows wild in many places
on the Big Island, seeming to prefer the jungly rain forests at fairly
high altitudes, where it fruits abundantly. The ripe fruit is a little
larger than the average *lilikoi*, and in color it is orange-yellow with
white spots. The outer shell is quite hard, but the translucent, whitish
pulp surrounding the seeds is soft and so juicy that one wonders

whether to describe it as food or drink. It is sweet-sour in taste, with an attractive aroma and flavor.

Since I was unable to locate a supply of this fruit on Oahu or Maui, and as I had no kitchen available on Hawaii, I never had an opportunity to test its culinary possibilities, but it is easily my favorite *Passiflora* for eating out of hand. I'm sure there are wet mountain-sides on Oahu where this plant would thrive, and someone could do future beachcombers a service by introducing it in these localities.

There is a wild passion fruit that is very common on Oahu, the *Passiflora foetida*. This is a slender vine that actually seems to prefer poor, arid soil near sea level. I have seen this plant climbing over panini cactus and bearing its bright-red, small fruits in great plenty in the arid section where Jim, Falani, and I went shore fishing. Don't be repelled by its unappetizing specific name, which refers to the malodorous, viscid hairs borne on the lacy bracts that support the flower and later enclose the fruit. These fruits are only about an inch in diameter, and the whitish pulp, although small in quantity, is quite palatable. This wild passion fruit can be substituted for lilikoi in any of the recipes mentioned above, but it has less acid and a milder flavor, so one should use more of it.

Nutritionally, passion fruit furnishes some iron and is a fair source of vitamin A and vitamin C. It is high in sugar and citric acid. While one couldn't live on passion fruit, its delightful flavor and refreshing quality can definitely add to the pleasures of the beachcombing life.

THE TAMARIND
(*Tamarindus indica*)

Except for the date, the tamarind is the sweetest of all fruits, being 40 to 45 percent sugar, and yet no one would describe its taste as sweet. The reason for this is that the tamarind is also the sourest of fruits, with an acid content roughly three times that of strong vinegar, and this acidity completely masks its sweetness. Although the acidity dominates the sweetness, it is a delicious sour taste and Hawaiian children who know this fruit eat it straight from the pod with great relish. In the Far East it often replaces vinegar in making chutneys and pickling fish. If it takes a mixture of acidity and sweetness to make a good fruit, then tamarinds must be the best in the world, for they have more of both than any fruit I know.

The tree that bears this strange fruit is a legume, related to our locusts and mesquites, and like them it has decorative pinnate leaves and bears its seed in a beanlike pod. The edible part of the tamarind is a sticky brown pulp that surrounds the seeds inside the brittle, cinnamon-colored pod, which is 3 to 7 inches long. This fruit is highly prized by the East Indians and Arabs, who feel that they cannot stay in good health without eating tamarinds. In a book on Eastern herbal medicine I found listed over 50 medicinal uses of this fruit. It makes one wonder how we ever survived without it.

The tamarind was introduced into the Hawaiian Islands in the 18th century and was a favorite fruit of the early settlers, but now it is valued chiefly as an ornamental. In this modern, westernized, affluent society, the tamarind is neglected except by a few street urchins who have learned what a prize lies inside that brittle brown shell. But the fact that the overcivilized inhabitants of present-day Hawaii ignore the tamarind is no reason why you should do so. The fruit on wayside trees goes unclaimed and can be gathered in abundance by any who appreciate its piquant flavor. Tamarinds can add interest and liveliness to the meals of the beachcomber wise enough to take advantage of this free bounty.

Tamarinds ripen during the summer and fall, but the fruit contains so much sugar and acid that it is easily preserved in a nearly fresh state throughout the year. I stored my tamarinds in a rectangular, covered glass dish by first pressing in a layer of the pulp, then sprinkling it with sugar, then adding another layer of pulp and more sugar, and so on until the dish was almost full. Then I made a syrup of 2 cups of sugar and 1 cup of water and poured this over the fruit. The dish was merely covered, not sealed, and when I used the last of the tamarinds, months later, there was no sign of spoilage. I used them as a sort of sweet-sour condiment to eat with meat, fish, or vegetables, and found they really added piquancy to an otherwise uninteresting meal.

Don't overeat tamarinds until you find how they affect you, for they have a decidedly laxative effect on some people, if more than an ounce or two is eaten at one time. However, when you need a laxative, there could hardly be a safer or more pleasant medicine to take than tamarinds.

I also made a Tamarind Syrup that I used as a base for refreshing cold drinks any time of the year, particularly the tropical fruit punches with which I was so fond of experimenting. I boiled 1 cup of tamarind pulp with 3 cups of water and 3 cups of sugar for about 20 minutes, then pressed it through a colander. This syrup was then reheated to the boiling point and sealed in hot, sterile jars. To make a delicious Tamarindade it was only necessary to add ¼ cup of this tamarind syrup to 1 cup of water and pour it over cracked ice in a tall glass.

The tamarind, like other fruits described in this section, is not essential to survival and will never be a major item in your diet. It is just another of those little extras without which the beachcombing life cannot be lived at its most gracious level.

A BRIGHT AND BEAUTIFUL WILD FRUIT

The *ohia-ai*, or mountain apple (*Eugenia malaccensis*), must have been a favorite fruit of the ancient Polynesians, for they carried the seeds with them on their far-flung migrations and introduced it into Hawaii as well as into many other island groups. Although the mountain apple seems somewhat particular about the location in which it will grow, it found a congenial home in the lower mountain valleys of Hawaii and was a common wild fruit in the Islands long before the coming of the white man. On the floors of these fertile valleys it sometimes forms pure stands many acres in extent, the trees reaching 50 to 60 feet in height.

Like so many of the tropical fruits we have discussed, the ohia-ai, with its thick, shiny, dark-green leaves, is such a beautiful tree that it really has no need to bear its annual crop of attractive fruit in order to justify its existence. But it is the nature of Nature in the tropics to be bountiful as well as beautiful. Handsome at any time of the year, the ohia-ai becomes breathtakingly beautiful when it flowers in late spring or early summer. Its showy red flowers are little more than streaming clusters of scarlet stamens, and they contrast charmingly with the rich foliage. Spreading and drooping downward, these scarlet threads seem to fill the shady interior of the tree with a delicate red haze.

The fruit, also, is highly decorative, being a blocky, oval shape 2 to 3 inches long, the color varying from scarlet through pink to some that are almost pure, waxy white. All have a polished, almost artificial appearance, striking one as too pretty to be true. The skin is tender,

and the flesh is crisp, juicy and pleasant, but the flavor is not particularly rich or distinctive in character. It is the kind of fruit that
everyone will eat but about which no one will be wildly enthusiastic.
This lack of distinctive flavor makes the mountain apple a poor fruit
for cooking, but it is very refreshing to eat out of hand, and I consumed a great many of them during the late summer and fall when
they were in season.

THE JAVA PLUM
(*Eugenia cuminii*)

A relative of the mountain apple that is very common in the Islands
is the Java plum, which is also sometimes called the jambolan. In
late summer and fall this common wayside tree bears abundant crops
of purple fruit about the size and shape of an olive. Most of this fruit
drops to the ground unclaimed, creating a messy condition that does
little to recommend this tree to those who value fastidiousness above
fruit. Since birds have scattered Java plum seeds far and wide,
and since there is little competition for the plums, the enterprising
beachcomber will have no trouble securing all of this fruit he can
use. There are at least two varieties of Java plum in the Islands, one
white-fleshed, one purple-fleshed. I care very little for the Java plum
as a fruit to eat fresh, finding it too astringent to be palatable, but the
Hawaiian children enjoy them, and you often see brown-skinned
youngsters swinging in these trees, coloring their faces and hands an
indelible purple as they stuff themselves with plums.

I tried Java plums in pies, tarts, and jam, but found them all too
astringent. However, the bright jelly made from this fruit is fine.
The purple-fleshed variety contains little or no pectin, but the white-
fleshed kind is so pectin-rich that one must be very careful not to
get a jelly from it that is too stiff and tough. The obvious solution
to this is to combine the two kinds to get an excellent Java Plum Jelly.

Use 4 cups of purple-fleshed to 6 cups of white-fleshed plums, add
2 cups of water, and boil for about 25 minutes until the fruit is soft.
Strain through a jelly bag or two thicknesses of cheesecloth, and allow
the juice to sit overnight. Next day, carefully strain off only the clear
juice; there should be just 4 cups of it. To this add 3 cups of sugar
and boil until you get a successful jelly test. Pour into jelly glasses and
cover with melted paraffin or use straight-sided, half-pint jars and seal

with sterilized, two-piece lids. The plums were free and the sugar inexpensive, so I made quite a bit of this jelly during the Java plum season and gave it away at Christmas.

CITRUS FRUITS

I have already mentioned limes and lemons in many of the recipes given. The limes I used were mostly from a tree in my landlord's house grounds, but when they failed to supply all I wanted, I knew where there were a dozen or more lime trees growing in a gulch out near Pearl Harbor, in a fairly arid section of the Island. I never learned whether these were true wild seedlings or grafted trees that had been abandoned. All I know is that they bore excellent crops of very good, though small, limes, and that among that many trees there were always as many ripe limes as I needed.

The Hawaiian lemon I like best doesn't resemble anything you'd be likely to call a lemon. It's a rough, green thing about the size of an orange, but much more misshapen. These strange-looking fruits are very rich in citric acid and good lemon flavor, but alas, they haven't the uniform size, shape, and gas-induced color of California lemons, so they often go begging. I have actually seen an otherwise intelligent man rake up the really excellent natural lemons that had fallen from the trees in his yard and throw them in the trash can, while paying good money for the gas-ripened, graded, and stamped variety at a supermarket. You can bet that I immediately offered to relieve this man of the burden of having to collect and dispose of this "trash," and these trees, four in number, furnished me with all the lemons I could use during my beachcombing days, except for a month or two in the spring when they were out of season.

At one time, in the early days, Hawaii shipped oranges to California, but now the traffic is all in the other direction. Captain Vancouver presented some young orange trees to the natives in 1792, and from these a seedling variety was developed that comes fairly true. The Hawaiian orange has a rather tough skin and is somewhat seedy, but it also has a bright-colored, juicy flesh with a spicy flavor that is unequaled by any imported fruit. I was able to locate trees bearing these good oranges back in the abandoned valleys on Oahu, Maui, and Hawaii, and these "wild," or feral, trees furnished me with all the oranges I could use during October, November, and December of each year.

I used this native fruit in any recipe that called for oranges, ate them out of hand, and used a great many of them to make orange juice. The only advice I have about preserving orange juice is "Don't." If you would enjoy orange juice at its very best, drink it within ten minutes of the time you squeeze it from the fruit. It develops an un-interesting flavor on standing, so the only way to store orange juice is in the orange. Fresh-frozen orange juice is much better than the canned product, but it is still a far cry from newly made juice from fresh, tree-ripened fruit. I had so many kinds of vitamin-rich fruits and juices that I easily did without oranges when the local variety was out of season, and therefore I appreciated the first ripe fruit of the year with a zest that can only be engendered by abstinence.

Another valuable citrus fruit the beachcomber may sometimes find is the shaddock, or pomelo, which resembles an outsize grapefruit, but when you peel it you will find that its generous size is mostly thick, pulpy rind, leaving an edible part actually smaller than that of the average grapefruit. The peeled pomelo is easily divided into sections, and while somewhat drier than the grapefruit, it is pleasantly palatable. I often kept a plate of pomelo sections in my refrigerator and enjoyed them in salads or as between-meal snacks and even offered them to my most important guests with no apologies.

My favorite Marmalade combines the native lemons, oranges, and pomelos that cost only the labor of picking and carrying them home. Remove the peels from 2 oranges, 2 lemons, and 1 pomelo, and after scraping most of the white pulp from inside these peels, cut them very fine with a sharp knife or kitchen shears. Cover the peels with 3 cups of boiling water, add ⅛ teaspoon of soda, and boil for 20 min-utes; then drain. Rinse them twice with boiling water, allowing them to sit in the water a minute or two each time before draining. Every-one knows that the peels of citrus fruit have a good flavor, but there's rather too much of it, and this hot-water treatment is designed to weaken it and bring it within palatable limits. I hope you didn't eat the fruit from which we removed the peels, or throw it out, for we will want it in the marmalade. Remove the seeds from this fruit and chop it fine, then mix it with the peels and add 1 cup of orange juice and ½ cup of lemon juice and simmer all together for 10 minutes.

Stir in one package of commercial pectin, bring to a boil again, and add 6½ cups of sugar, all at once. Over a high flame, stir and cook until it comes to a boil; then let it roll for about one minute. Pour immediately into sterilized half-pint jars and seal. This marmalade is tart, with a delicious hint of bitter, and none of the cloying sweetness so common in commercial products.

All about the Islands, near the past or present haunts of men, one sees small seedling tangerines, locally called "Chinese oranges" (although I seriously doubt that this small tree has anything to do with China, the Chinese, or even Chinese-Hawaiians). These shrub-like trees bear blooms, green fruit, and ripe fruit all at the same time, so some ripe fruit can be found on them most of the year. For the most part they are entirely ignored, leaving them eminently available to the beachcomber who will learn to know a good thing when he sees it. The oranges this tree bears are tiny, an inch to an inch and a half across, sometimes even smaller. They are vivid orange when ripe, and offer a juice and flesh with an orange flavor that is, however, sour as a lemon. Their thin skin peels off as easily as that on a tangerine, but inside you find their one flaw to my mind—they are extremely seedy.

I often made a tart and sprightly orangeade from these plentiful fruits, and Jim considered them the greatest for mixing with arrack or okolehau to make a sort of tropical screwdriver. I substituted Chinese-orange juice for lemon juice in many a recipe and frequently found the product improved.

My Chinese-Orange Chiffon Pie helped to establish my reputation as a tropical cook. Thoroughly mix 1 tablespoon unflavored gelatin, ½ cup sugar, and ½ teaspoon salt. Beat together 4 egg yolks and 1 cup Chinese-orange juice. Dump the egg-and-juice mixture into the gelatin-sugar and cook and stir until it just comes to a boil. Cool, and then chill until the mixture mounds slightly when dropped from a spoon. This will take about an hour, so you'll have plenty of time to make a graham-cracker crust (see index). When the gelatin mixture begins to thicken, beat the 4 egg whites until they form soft peaks, then gradually add ¼ cup of sugar and beat to very stiff peaks. Fold the gelatin-orange mixture into the egg whites, and if you want to be spectacularly impressive, whip a cup of heavy cream and fold that in, too. Pile the filling into the graham-cracker crust and chill until firm.

It will be a mile high, light and fluffy, with a flavor like heaven itself.

I also preserved these tiny oranges whole and served them as dessert, especially if my guests happened to be Chinese. Gather the little oranges when barely ripe and soak them through five successive changes of boiling water, leaving them about 10 minutes in each bath. Measure the fruit, and to each cup of miniature oranges add 1 cup of sugar and 1 cup of water. Set over the lowest heat possible and simmer very, very slowly for several hours. When they become heavy and translucent and the syrup is quite thick, pour into jars, cover with boiling syrup from the kettle, and seal. If you are serving them to finicky guests, it is probably better to cut each one in half and remove the seeds, but I usually allowed my guests to pick out their own seeds or eat them seeds and all, just as they preferred.

Among the fruits that contributed to the joy of beachcombing were a few old friends like the mulberry, blackberry, and ground cherry. The Hawaiian mulberry is the Asiatic or black mulberry (*Morus nigra*), which is also common in our own Southland. In the Islands this fruit has spontaneously developed a seedless, or almost seedless, variety, which is a great improvement. I was able to locate plenty of trees with unclaimed fruit on both Oahu and Maui, and found them excellent.

The ground cherry of the Islands, called *poha* by the Hawaiians, is the *Physalis peruviana* of the botanists, and as its specific name suggests, it originated in South America. However, it closely resembles, in appearance, flavor, and use, the wild ground cherries found throughout the eastern half of the United States, which are northern species of *Physalis*. The Hawaiians are very fond of preserves and jam made of this fruit, and I share their enthusiasm, but I also find it delicious as a fresh fruit, blending tastefully into both salads and desserts.

The blackberry was introduced from mainland United States sometime before the turn of the century, and in some sections it has gone native with a vengeance, threatening to become a pest. However, it is a pest only to the landowners, and not to me or any other beachcomber who appreciates the abundant crops of delicious fruit it bears every summer. I have enjoyed blackberries since childhood, and their flavor when eaten fresh from the bush in high-altitude sections of Hawaii was like a visit by an old friend from home. I have picked them by the pailful in the mountains of western Oahu, in the Olinda section of Maui on the slopes of Haleakala, and near Kilauea on the island of Hawaii. I have detailed the uses of mulberries, blackberries, and ground cherries in a previous book [1] and will not repeat them here, but the beachcomber who overlooks these three excellent fruits is missing out on some very good food.

Another berry that deserves the attention of the beachcomber is the *Rubus rosaefolius*, or red thimbleberry, which thrives on all the main Islands. This remarkable berry bears its fruit throughout the year, and one often glimpses its red brightness peeking through the leaves near the roadsides, fairly beckoning the beachcomber to go a-berrying. There are those who complain that this berry lacks flavor, but I find its piquant, subacid taste very satisfying. Picking and eating the berry directly from the bush furnished me with many a pleasant pause as I drove on Island roads in my Jeep. I frequently carried some home, where, sweetened with honey and smothered in thick coconut cream, they were a pure delight.

Hawaii has an indigenous raspberry, the *Rubus hawaiiensis*, which is a very frustrating plant. On the northwest slope of Haleakala, on Maui, these berries are very common, and in that area I have seen gorgeous raspberries, two inches long and nearly as wide, but alas, most of them are too bitter to be considered good by even the most tolerant taster. Here and there one finds a plant with fruit that is almost edible, so I'm sure this *Rubus* offers a great opportunity to some patient plant breeder, for there certainly is no larger or more beautiful raspberry in the world, if only a present-day Burbank can persuade it to bear better-flavored fruit.

Hawaii has date palms, but the fruit is apt to be disappointing, as most of them are seedlings that were planted as ornamentals. However, even the finest varieties of dates originated as selected seedlings, so the beachcomber with a true forager's eye can discover palms bearing good dates. I located several such palms on Oahu and a single very heavy-cropping specimen on Maui, and these were able to furnish me with all the dates I could use. When the first dates on a bunch began to ripen, I would cut the whole bunch, pack it into a tightly-closed box and let it sit a week in my warm attic. This would

[1] *Stalking the Wild Asparagus*, David McKay, 1962.

ripen the fruit beautifully. I ate fresh dates, used them in cooking, and dried them for out-of-season use.

Hawaii is rich with countless other fruits that tempt a forager's palate. The exotic litchis, whose ancestors came from far Cathay, were a pure joy as they matured in my yard. I ate them from the tree during the short season they were ripe, dried many of them to make the "litchi nuts" so familiar to diners in Chinese restaurants, and canned some in sugar syrup to make one of the finest of all preserved fruits. There were the roselles, Surinam cherries, and carissas, from which I made tart sauces to eat with meats. I could grow ecstatic about the cherimoyas I discovered in the Kula district of Maui, which I thought the most delicious fruit I had ever tasted. There were the loquats from the same district that had a sweet-sour piquancy reminiscent of Northern fruits. All these, and many more, are good food, and the beachcomber should claim them all as his own.

12. Some Old Friends

SHORTLY after I started beachcombing, I met a man who said that he wanted to live the same way I was living, but would never try it in Hawaii because the Islands had no fruit growing on them. I was astounded at such a statement and started naming mangoes, papayas, bananas, guavas, and breadfruit as only a few of excellent fruits that grew in abundance there. He angrily retorted, "Do you expect me to eat that stuff? Where are the apples, peaches, pears, and plums?"

I had a good laugh and reflected that if this man continued his search for a South Sea island that grew Northern fruits he would at least become very well traveled. Later I discovered that his request wasn't so unreasonable, after all. The fruits he craved are borne on deciduous trees that not only will tolerate frost but absolutely require frost in order to fruit properly. Therefore, they are never found in tropical lowlands. However, the Hawaiian Islands are near the northern edge of the tropics, and at higher elevations the seasons are fairly well marked. On my first hunting trip to Maui I stayed with some Portuguese friends who lived on the slopes of Haleakala at an altitude of nearly 5,000 feet. Here grew no coconuts, avocadoes, breadfruit, or other tender, tropical plants, for there were occasional frosts every winter. What my host did have was a treeful of some of the most delicious peaches I ever tasted, ripened to perfection in the month of May.

A forest ranger tipped me off about the "wild" apple orchard on Maui. In an isolated high section that had winter frosts, the Forest Service had planted a number of apple trees, and these had thrived and had now started bearing fruit. A friend and I combined a pig hunt with an apple harvest and came home with a fat young pig slung between us and our knapsacks full of ripe apples. These apples were not really of first quality, but some pork chops with fried apple rings tasted like a visit to my childhood home. I know a Polynesian would have considered these undersized, misshapen, sour fruits inedible, but a dish of plain applesauce made from this imperfect fruit was a pleasant, nostalgic experience to my Northern-trained taste buds, long deprived of such fare.

On the island of Kauai great numbers of really excellent plums have been planted in the mountains, and stalking these half-wild plums became such a popular sport that it had to be regulated. Now one must buy a plum-hunting license, there are daily bag limits, and during the plum-hunting season a ranger checks the foragers in and out of the plum area to see that no one gets more than his share.

So many plants have been introduced into Hawaii that one now meets old floral friends from other parts of the world in the most unexpected places. Once I was hunting goats high on the slopes of Haleakala above Koolau. I walked in before daylight, and before sun-up I saw a herd of goats. Unfortunately, they also saw me. I tried every stalking trick I knew, but always the goats outguessed me, and I never came within shooting range. This was all uphill work, and I was getting very tired and exceedingly hungry. Finally, several hours later, I saw the goats cross into the National Park, where I was not allowed to follow with a gun.

I sat down to rest at the edge of a little wet meadow in the bottom of a narrow valley, and because the sun had not yet penetrated into this canyon it was quite cold at this altitude, so I built a little campfire. While sitting there I noticed a cluster of plants growing in the wet meadow that I did not recognize. They bore great numbers of yellow, tomato-like fruits or seedballs, but since the plants were obviously members of the nightshade family, I was not about to try eating any of that fruit, for this family contains many poisonous species, as well as many fine food plants. I decided to dig one up, roots and all, and take it home and see if I could get someone to identify it.

I started scratching in the loose, volcanic soil at the base of the plant, and I turned up a tuber, round, firm and about the size of a plum. I cut into this tuber with my knife and found it crisp, juicy, and fiberless. I smelled a cut end and recognition flooded in, leaving me feeling as embarrassed as one who fails to recognize an old friend. It was the ordinary potato, a plant I had known all my life. I had failed to recognize it because I had never expected to see it in this outlandish place. I quickly scratched up enough small tubers to fill my canteen cup, covered them with water from the canteen, and half an hour later I was enjoying a meal of boiled potatoes.

Later, I learned that potatoes had been raised in these high meadows during the 19th century, when they could be sold at fancy prices to the whaling ships that put in to these islands in search of fresh supplies of food. When this enterprise died, the potato escaped from cultivation and became naturalized. The ones I gathered were true wild plants, many generations removed from their domestic ancestors. They reverted to what must have been the original wild type, bearing small but perfectly edible tubers and heavy crops of yellow seedballs about the size of marbles. After that discovery I often combined a goat hunt with a potato harvest.

Sweet potatoes were cultivated by the Hawaiians long before the white man appeared on the scene, and these, too, sometimes go wild and actually run away from the garden or field where they were originally planted. The plant is a long, trailing vine, and if the outer, growing end of this vine finds a suitable patch of soil, it will put down roots, produce a few sweet potatoes, and start new vines reaching out for new locations. I remember one such row of wild sweet potatoes that kept me supplied for three years. The best potatoes are found near the new, growing end of the series of vines. At the end of three years I was still gathering good potatoes from what was no more than new growth of the same sweet potato vine, but I was gathering them several hundred yards from where I had started the harvest three years before. These sweet potatoes were excellent boiled, baked, or fried. My favorite way of preparing them was to peel and grate a casserole full of sweet potato, cover it with thick coconut cream and bake in the oven until it was a gooey, delicious mass.

When I first moved into my thatched hut, there was a net-wire fence along one side of the property. One sunny, 50-foot section of this fence was entirely covered with one bean vine, the main stem as large as my arm. It was not very ornamental, in fact, it was somewhat bedraggled, and I planned to replace it with some better plant. Before I got to it in my general clean-up of the grounds, I noticed that it was putting on bright new growth and a great crop of blossoms. I let it go, and in a few weeks I was gathering all the fine lima beans I could use from this one vine. It bore abundantly for a month or two, then rested awhile, then started bearing again. It behaved as a perennial in the tropics, and all the time I lived there it gave me several crops of beans a year, apparently with no time or season, just putting on blooms and beans whenever it felt like it.

Cowpeas behave the same way in tropical Hawaii. They originally were planted in soil-enriching programs, to turn under as green manure, and now have gone wild around the edges of cultivated fields. I knew of several of these huge spreading vines, growing over brush piles or rock piles. One or another of them would be bearing whenever I had a hankering for some snap peas. These long, pencil-like pods could be snapped into short lengths, and when cooked and served like green beans they were delicious.

When I was a boy in Texas, I used to love to chew on joints of sugarcane. Although sugarcane did not grow in the section where I lived, it was often sold in the markets, or even by peddlers along the streets, so cane was an old friend. At first I was greatly disappointed in Hawaiian sugarcane. The kinds grown on the sugar plantations had a tough rind and very hard pith that was almost impossible to chew, and the flavor wasn't nearly as good as that I remembered from childhood. Then a Hawaiian gave me a stalk of cane from his garden that took me right back to my boyhood. It was thin-skinned, soft, and easy to chew, and the flavor was delicious. He called this kind *ko kinikini*, and said it was one of the best kinds the old-time Hawaiians raised for eating. It was smaller than plantation cane, and the stalk was striped with purple. I have been unable to find this cane listed among the Hawaiian varieties as recorded by ethnobotanists, and I suspect that at least the name is modern, for *ko kinikini* would translate "ten-cent cane." I planted joints of this cane, not only on my landlord's place, but in many other places, without inquiring who owned the land. Whenever I went foraging or hunting, I was likely to have a few joints of this cane in my knapsack, for its sweet juice served as both food and drink. After I ate it, wherever I was, I would cut out the nodes out of the remaining joints and plant them. I know many of these sprouted and grew, for I gathered full-grown stalks of this "wild" cane before I left the Islands, and I'll bet that some I planted is growing today.

Another old friend that I unexpectedly met on Maui was a wild grape. I had decided to hike through a roadless section, just to see what could be found, and came on several grapevines running over surrounding brush and bearing grape clusters that had just reached a perfect stage of ripeness. They closely resembled the fox grapes of Eastern United States, and when I tasted one I could instantly detect the "foxy" flavor. This was as surprising as finding a coconut palm in New England, but I will accept any good gift that nature offers, no matter how incongruous, so I carried home all the ripe clusters I could find. I made several later visits to this hidden vineyard, and gleaned all the late-ripening grapes it produced that year. On my last trip in the year I drastically pruned the vines, and set out the prunings, cut to two or three joints long. I marked on my foraging calendar the day that I first found the ripe grapes, and the next year I was back on the same day. The grapes on the pruned vines were larger and better than they had been the year before, and some of the cuttings had taken root and were starting to grow.

I never did discover how a wild grape indigenous to the temperate zone came to be growing on a tropical island, for I never wanted to ask questions that might lead someone to my wild vineyard, to plunder the grapes. However, I did see some similar local grapes for sale at a small market and asked about them. I found that they actually were a seedling improvement of the Eastern fox grape, called the Isabella Grape, which had been introduced into the Islands, and for some paradoxical reason succeeded very well there.

In the section on seafood cookery, when I wrote of garnishing dishes with cherry tomatoes, parsley, and watercress, I'm sure some readers thought "Aha! Here is this beachcomber pretending to live on wild produce, but buying expensive greens and garnishes." Not guilty. Cherry tomatoes grow wild in Hawaii, springing up in the most unlikely places, bearing copious crops of their bright little fruit for months, then disappearing or dying out in that location, forcing one to keep seeking new sources of supply. Parsley, the uncurled kind, grows wild in many high-altitude sections of Hawaii, and I not only enjoyed this wild parsley fresh, I dried quantities of it for flavoring soups, stews, and salads. Watercress can be found along many rural and mountain streams, and I always knew where I could go and gather a supply of fresh watercress without having to pay for it. All these plants have been introduced into Hawaii, but they have gone thoroughly wild.

I could go on and on, about purslane and amaranth and many other familiar "weeds" that make excellent cooked vegetables or salads, but this sampling is enough to show that there are ample gustatory rewards for anyone who will approach nature with open eyes, an open mind, and an open and receptive spirit.

13. Climate, Cactus and the Cup That Cheers

I OFTEN meet people who are fascinated by the idea of living on a tropical island, but are afraid to try it because they fear that they could never endure the climate. I've mentioned the early classic books about castaways on tropical islands written by men who never left Europe. Of all their errors, none seems to have made a deeper impression than their lurid descriptions of the tropical rainy season. Apparently, years ago, returning travelers described the tropical year as divided into wet and dry seasons instead of summer and winter. The gifted imaginations of the early romancers transformed these tropical rainy seasons into almost unbearable times of storms, winds, floods, and rains, beating down so heavily and continuously that they made Noah's deluge seem like a summer shower. For months on end, their protagonists huddled in crude shelters and suffered like early Christians. The influence of these exaggerated stories is still evident, for when I speak of the joys of a tropical island, some untraveled listener is sure to ask, "But how about that terrible rainy season when you can't go outside for months at a time?"

This literary rainy season interests me. Did these writers really believe that they were giving an accurate description of the climate of most tropical islands? These men all grew up in rather trying climates, and it must have been hard for them to imagine weather all that much better than the sort through which they suffered annually. Or perhaps, after giving their castaways convenient wrecks to plunder and a great abundance of fruit, nuts, vegetables, and wild game for their sustenance, they thought it only fair to saddle them with at least one major handicap. I think it went even deeper than that. These men lived in a culture where such sayings as "You must take the bitter with the sweet" and "Into each life some rain must fall" were common, and I'm sure they all firmly believed that every silver lining must have a cloud. And so they gave their castaways clouds, thick, heavy, and black, from which incessant rain poured for a big part of the year. I suspect these old-time Calvinists thought that a climate that did not have at least the moral equivalent of an English winter was, if not impossible, at least very reprehensible.

The truth is that small tropical islands, when located far from any weather-modifying mass of continental land, enjoy some of the finest climates to be found on this globe. They usually have more or less well-defined wetter and drier seasons, but the wet seasons have no resemblance to that awful, confining period described by the early writers. On most oceanic tropical islands, one could, during the wettest month of the year, enjoy more sunshine than one would be apt to see during an entire English summer.

In the popular imagination, the landscape of a South Sea island is a lush, green paradise of waving palms, banana plants, and bamboo forests. This is a pretty accurate picture of the well-watered, windward valleys of the Hawaiian Islands, but it doesn't prepare one for the arid deserts of the leeward slopes. Local people brag that the climate is so perfect that the Hawaiians do not even have a word for weather in their language, but this is very misleading. Hawaiian has no word that translates "weather," simply because the Polynesian can see no need for a term so broadly inclusive that it embraces floods and droughts, cold spells and heat waves, high winds and flat calms, but he has plenty of terms for specific kinds of weather.

The word "weather" implies variation, and Hawaii actually has weather, although it is more spatial than temporal; that is, it varies more from place to place than it does from time to time and is therefore probably better defined as a number of micro-climates than as weather. Although one spot on Kaui lays claim to being the wettest spot on earth, the rainfall on the windward slopes of all the high mountains is tremendous. There is a 100-inch rain gauge on the slopes of Haleakala volcano on Maui in a district where the rain is almost constant. The accumulated rainfall at this location is measured only once per month, and one time when the recorder made his monthly visit he found the rain gauge overflowing. More than 100 inches of rain in 30 days! And yet, within fifteen miles, as the mynah bird flies, of this ever-filling rain gauge are areas dryer than the Sahara, with less than 2 inches of rainfall per year.

It is hard for a stranger to believe that such great variety of climates can be found on an island so small that it can be circled by automobile in a few hours. This is explained by the fact that Hawaii lies in an area where the wind blows from only one direction most of the time. I once heard a *malahini* (newcomer) ask a *kamaaina* (old-timer) why the wind always blew from the northeast. The answer was, "So the boats in the San Francisco-Honolulu Yacht Race can make a quick passage."

There is a better explanation. The equatorial sun beating down on a central belt about the earth warms the air, causing it to rise and create a partial vacuum, which the cooler air from nearer the poles rushes in to fill. If this were the only force in action, the trade winds would blow straight along the longitudinal lines from the poles toward the equator, but the earth is also rotating and its surface at the equator is rushing eastward at the rate of 1000 nautical miles per hour, relative to the sun. Generally speaking, the air envelope about us rotates with the earth, but there is a slight lag, giving the air a seeming motion from east to west relative to the earth's surface, especially near the equator where the surface velocity of the earth, because of rotation, is highest. These two forces acting on the air according to Newton's Second Law result in the northeast trades in the northern hemisphere and the southeast trades in the southern hemisphere.

The northeast trade wind sometimes blows steadily for months on end in Hawaii with little variation in either direction or velocity. Having crossed thousands of miles of very wet ocean, these winds are saturated when they strike the high mountains of Hawaii Nei. The mountains bend the trade winds upward, and, as they rise into cooler altitudes, they can no longer carry so large a burden of moisture, so they deposit it on the mountain slopes in unbelievable quantities. By the time these winds pass over the summits they have been wrung dry and have no moisture left to contribute to the leeward slopes, which remain bare and dry in remarkable contrast to the sodden rain-jungles of the windward slopes.

The island of Kaaholawe lies a few miles off the southern coast of Maui. It has an area of 48 square miles, and its mountains rise to about 1500 feet. It would be an ideal beachcomber's tropical island except for one thing. Lying directly southwest of 10,000-foot Haleakala volcano and wholly within its "rain shadow," Kaaholawe gets very little rain. It receives the trade winds only after massive Haleakala has robbed them of their moisture, and so Kaaholawe remains a true "desert island" in two senses, being both arid and uninhabited, with limited flora consisting mainly of desert plants.

Of course this explanation of Hawaiian weather is too simple, and there are many "wild variables" that modify this neat picture. Honolulu has considerable rainfall, although it lies on the leeward side of the Koolau Range. These mountains are not very high, and the rain is released near their summit, but it doesn't all fall there. The steep windward faces of these abrupt mountains bend the trade wind upward, and this upward-blowing wind is so strong that it picks up the raindrops and carries them for several miles to be deposited on Honolulu, where they often fall from a perfectly clear sky. These showers of "liquid sunshine" make this section of Oahu riotous with rainbows flaunting their colors all over the landscape. These showers from a clear sky do not cease at sunset, nor do the rainbows necessarily disappear at the fall of darkness. When the moon is full, one often sees lunar rainbows, pale counterparts of their gaudy daytime sisters, but standing out plainly against the night sky, nevertheless.

Another feature that mars the neat picture I have drawn is *kona* weather. Sometimes a low-pressure area to the north of the Islands will cause the trade winds to die, and the land will swelter under a hot, flat calm. These are trying periods and the only times one really suffers from the heat in Hawaii, where it is usually pleasantly cool. Sometimes these low-pressure areas are powerful enough to reverse the normal flow of the wind, and then the dry sides of the Islands get a drenching. Some of these *kona* storms bring dangerously high winds, and then the heavy rains that fall on the normally dry parts of Hawaii may cause serious flooding and erosion.

A common error is to suppose that *kona* weather is so named because this kind of weather is prevalent on the Kona Coast of the
island of Hawaii, but this is a vile slander against a delightful climate.
Kona means "south," and when applied to weather, it has no refer-
ence to the Kona District, which lies along the southwest coast of
Hawaii and has wonderful weather.

The pleasant climate of Kona needs explaining, for here is another
factor that messes up my pretty picture of Island weather. Kona lies
to leeward of the highest mountains in the state, and according to
the scheme I have presented it should be dry and barren, whereas, in
fact, it is well-watered, fertile, and very tropical.

Hawaii is no small body of land, as are the other islands in this
group. This one island is considerably larger than Delaware and
Rhode Island combined, and rises to an altitude much higher than
New Hampshire and Vermont would be if they were stacked one on
top of the other. This huge land mass, which has a different rate of
heating and cooling from that of the surrounding sea, is able to
modify the climate by creating land and sea breezes like those along
continental coasts. The sea breezes bring rain that Kona could never
get from the trades, and keep this stretch of coast beautiful and fruitful, making it a very pleasant place to visit and an even better place
to live.

The section where Jim lived, on the windward side of Oahu, had
an almost perfect climate. The plentiful rain fell mostly at night in
intermittent showers, making the land cool and green and leaving
most of the days bright and sunny. There were times when the clouds
would pile up from the ocean horizon to the tops of the mountains
and it would rain for several days, but these occasions were rare.

The "weather by district" that characterizes Hawaiian climate is
a handy feature of Island living. I remember times when we actually
set off in the rain to go camping and fishing, for we knew that the
section toward which we were headed would be dry and sunny by the
time we got there. Whether we were going on a picnic, a hunting
trip, or a foraging expedition, we could almost always drive to some
part of the Island where the proper weather for the project could be
found, and even predicted.

The first time I laid eyes on one of the dry, desert sections of Hawaii
I was struck, not by its strangeness, but by its utter familiarity. The

weathered lava rocks, the scanty grass burned dry by drought, and the prickly-pear cactus growing so profusely—these were all old acquaintances. I could have very easily imagined myself back in the poorer parts of New Mexico, where I spent much of my boyhood. Even the few trees about, called *kiawes* by the Hawaiians, were only a slightly different species of the mesquite so familiar in our own Southwest.

One might think that the arid areas offer little to the foraging beachcomber, but that would be an error, for you would be overlooking an excellent wild fruit and a very good vegetable, both produced by the prickly-pear cactus, or *panini*, as it is called by the Hawaiians. This is the same fruit that is called "tuna" in Mexico, where it is a very important item in the diet of the poor people who dwell on the dry Mexican plateau.

The two common kinds of *panini* in Hawaii, the red and the white, are much alike except for the color and quality of the ripe fruit. Both are species of the genus *Opuntia*, and they grow in the familiar prickly-pear form, having flattened, oval, leaflike stems, and building up by growing one thick, spiny "leaf" upon another, and they commonly reach a height of 10 feet with a spread of a yard or two. The showy blossoms that appear atop immature fruits along the upper edges of the "leaves" are large, yellow, and beautiful. The fruit ripens abundantly, and the beachcomber can be sure of all the paninis he can use, both white and red, from midsummer until late autumn.

Both kinds produce fruit from 3 to 4 inches long by 1½ to 2 inches in diameter. Scattered over the outside skin of the fruit are little tufts of fine, hairlike stickers that come off in any hand that touches them and can be very bothersome if they get into the lips or tongue from eating paninis that have been improperly gathered or awkwardly peeled. Fear of these vindictive little bristles needlessly prevents many people from enjoying this fine fruit, for the tiny harpoons can be circumvented if the panini is handled skillfully.

The panini plant must be approached with respect, for each "leaf" bears many clusters of vicious spines up to 1½ inches long, very hard and amazingly sharp. The circumspection necessary in the presence of prickly pear is almost instinctive with me, for as I have mentioned, this plant was very common in the section where I grew up. We used to clip off the largest and toughest spines and use them as phonograph

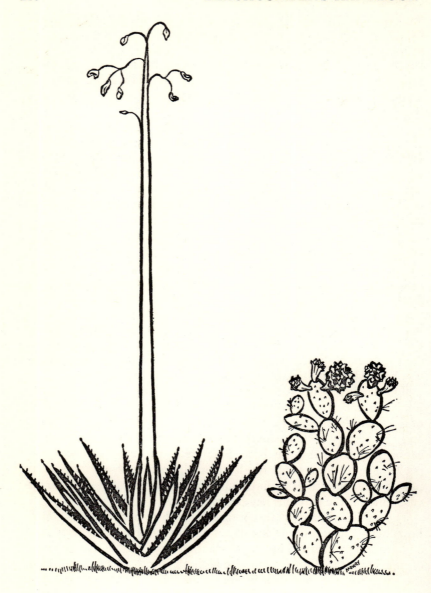

needles to play the hand-wound diaphragm "talking machines" of that day, and they produced a softer, truer tone and caused less wear on the records than did the commercial steel needles. This plant also deserves credit for developing me into a fair bronc rider when I was a lad, for I have often managed to stay on the back of a bucking range animal simply because there was no place to land except in a clump of this spiny horror.

I had probably eaten several tons of prickly pears before I ever saw those of Hawaii, but it was only after taking up beachcombing as a way of life and becoming dependent on wild fruits for a big part of my daily diet that I perfected the method of gathering and preparing this food. I would gather a handful of stiff grass or weeds to serve as a whisk broom and simply sweep the deciduous clumps of bristles from the ripe fruit while it was still on the plant. Then, wearing a pair of heavy leather gloves that were reserved for this task alone, I would cut the paninis from the plant and rub each one with an old burlap bag before dropping it into the pail. This may sound like a complicated procedure, but it is all very quickly done and the pail fills rapidly. On arriving home, I washed the fruit under running water to remove any loose bristles that might be adhering to the skin, and then it was safe to handle with bare hands. Both the blossom end and the stem end were sliced off with a sharp knife, and the skin was slit along one side from end to end. Starting at this slit, I would fold back the skin and remove it by turning it inside out, allowing the peeled fruit to drop into a bowl, untouched by human hands and guaranteed free of stickers. This whole process is handily done after the technique is acquired, and in 10 minutes I could easily clean and peel as many paninis as I could eat in a week.

The red panini has a dark-purplish skin, and the pulp inside is a deep scarlet. I once thought this an excellent fresh fruit, but that was before I had tasted a Hawaiian white panini. The white panini really has a light-yellow skin when ripe; the peeled fruit is a greenish amber color; and the flavor is so superior to that of the red panini that it makes the latter fruit taste like nothing at all by comparison. The flavor of the white panini was best described by a schoolteacher to whom I had just served a prime fruit, crisp and ice cold. She took a bite and then said, "Why, it tastes like a good, sweet watermelon, only more so."

Some people are bothered by the numerous seeds imbedded in the panini pulp, but I never allowed them to interfere with my enjoyment of this fruit. I would avoid biting down hard on these seeds and chew the fruit softly, savoring its sweet pulp and juice, then swallow it seeds and all. I never felt better in my life than during the panini season when I was consuming from three to a dozen of these fruits per day. The whole fruit, including the seeds, has a smooth demulcent quality that makes it slide soothingly down your throat. This mucilaginous smoothness seems to persist even into the stomach, for these fruits always have had a soothing effect on me.

I have tried, with only moderate success, to use the panini as a cooked fruit. Both the white and red kinds, when stewed in the skins, then strained to remove the skins and seeds, are edible, but they are nothing to wire home about. When the peeled fruit is diced, then put through a food mill or ricer to remove the seeds, one gets a sweet pulp that can be combined with whipped coconut cream and frozen into a rich Panini Ice right in your refrigerator tray. Some of my friends thought this concoction very delicious, but I preferred ices made with guavas or mangoes, so I seldom bothered with it. This same pulp makes a pretty good Jellied Panini Dessert when stirred into lemon-flavored gelatin when red paninis are used and lime-flavored when you have pulp from white ones.

I also made a fair Panini Jam from this pulp. To 5 cups of red pulp add the juice of 2 lemons and 1 package of powdered pectin. Bring to a boil and add 7 cups of sugar. Bring back to a boil and boil hard for 1 minute, then pour into jelly glasses or half-pint jars and seal. When you use the pulp from white paninis, substitute the juice of 3 limes for the lemons and add only 6 cups of sugar. Otherwise, the procedure is the same. This jam would certainly be worthwhile if the panini were the only fruit one had, but I was so surrounded with delicious tropical fruits that made better jam that I soon abandoned these experiments. The best way I know to use white paninis is to eat them crisp and cold, straight from the refrigerator, and there are few fruits that make better appetizers, desserts, or between-meal snacks.

The new growth of both the white and the red panini, the flattened young stems usually called "leaves" by non-botanical cactus lovers, make a very good vegetable if gathered when about half-grown. The spines on this tender new growth are not as hard and sharp as they are on the older parts of the plant, but they are still bothersome, so I gathered these young "leaves" by grasping each one with a pair of kitchen tongs and slicing through its base with a sharp knife. When I gathered as many as I wanted, I disarmed them by passing each "leaf" through an open flame until at least the points of the spines and bristles were singed away. Then, using a very sharp knife, I peeled each piece, being very careful not to let the outside of the skin touch the inner flesh which I intended to eat. This left me with irregular disks of tender, mucilaginous vegetable which was very good boiled and buttered, or dredged in seasoned flour and fried.

The Mexicans are very fond of this vegetable, and one sometimes sees Indian women boiling it over little fires on street corners or along roadsides and selling it to passersby for a few centavos per piece. This is one vegetable the Mexicans like well enough to refrain from smothering it with chili peppers or disguising it with garlic, and that speaks well for it, for most Mexicans have very little restraint when it comes to hot seasonings. I think peeled panini "leaves," either boiled or fried, make one of the most palatable vegetables that can be foraged from the wild.

After discovering how much better the white panini was as fresh fruit, I didn't entirely desert the red kind. In fact, through the year, Jim and I would gather many more red paninis than white ones, for we began using them to make red wine, or *swipes*, as it is called in local pidgin idiom. We had tasted some Puerto Rican panini swipes and had liked it, but when we decided to try our hand at making it, we had to work out a recipe by trial and error.

In the beginning it was mostly error, and the first three batches of panini wine we made were frankly undrinkable. Even Jim couldn't stomach this slimy slop, but, processed, it did make some very passable brandy.

Finally I tried adapting an old elderberry wine recipe to paninis and, almost by accident, we learned to make a better vintage. I sliced three pecks of paninis into a huge pot, just covered them with boiling water, and put them over a fire to simmer for 30 minutes. This caused the juice to flow freely and eliminated the wild ferments. Then I strained the juice through a sugar bag into a large crock. There was just 5 gallons of juice, so I added 10 pounds of sugar, and next morning, when it had cooled, I spread a cake of soft yeast on a toasted slice of rye bread and floated it on top of the juice.

It fermented and foamed furiously for about a week, then settled down and cleared up. We siphoned it into gallon jugs and stopped them with wads of cotton and capped them loosely. We sampled it after three weeks and found it had a half-sweet, half-dry, sprightly, fruity flavor. Of course, it was still too new and somewhat "burpy," but I was afraid further fermentation would destroy this pleasant flavor, so we racked off three gallons of it and to this quantity we added two quarts of a panini brandy Jim had made. This raised the alcoholic content high enough to prevent any further fermentation, so after allowing this fortified wine to sit another week in the jug for the brandy and wine to blend, or "marry" as the vintners say, we bottled it and corked it tightly. The remainder of that batch of wine, being unfortified, went on to develop into a sour, flat, ill-tasting brew that was unfit for anything except converting into brandy.

Thus we learned to make good wine of paninis, and since the raw material was plentiful, we made quite a lot of it. After one year it was delicious, and after two years it was even better. It had a beautiful, bright, clear color, and the demulcent quality found in the raw fruit carried over into the wine, making it smooth and pleasant. I discovered that a very small swallow would temporarily relieve a cough due to a cold or to heavy smoking, so this wine served as a medicine as well as a beverage.

Panini swipes and cactus brandy were not the only potables we manufactured. The hard liquor that we made in greatest quantities was an indigenous Hawaiian tipple called *okolehau*.

Okolehau is a very potent liquor distilled from a fermented mash of *ti* root. The word *ti* is spelled *ki* in modern Hawaiian, which has no *t* in its alphabet, but it is ordinarily pronounced like the English word "tea" said very shortly and quickly, although the firewater derived from this plant is a far cry from English tea both in taste and in violent effects. The word is properly used only for the root of this plant, while both the whole plant and the leaves were formerly called *la'i,* but today one hears even Hawaiians speaking of "ti plants" and "ti leaves." Its botanical designation is *Taetsia fruticosa,* a member of the lily family, and it grows abundantly in all the Islands, probably introduced by the earliest Polynesians to settle there.

The la'i usually grows as a simple, unbranched plant, 3 to 10 feet high, arising from a thickened root. The stem is yellowish, and at its summit is a spirally arranged cluster of shiny green leaves borne on grooved stalks and having pointed-oval blades up to 3 feet long by 1 foot wide. The flower is not particularly attractive, but because of the plant's variability, several ornamental kinds, with varicolored leaves of many hues, have been developed and are commonly planted in tropical gardens around the world.

The la'i or ti leaf was very important in the Hawaiian culture a generation or two ago, and it still finds a multitude of uses, serving the Islander in any capacity where we would use paper bags or wrapping paper. The ti leaf is indispensable for wrapping food to be cooked in the imu or underground oven, and I have recommended it in the section on fish cookery for making laulaus. The whole plant was sacred to Lono, who was the very finest of the ancient Hawaiian gods, being a deity who loved and cared for his people, and the enclosures sacred to his worship were thatched with la'i. The great clusters of slippery leaves were used by the sun-kissed children of the tropics in a snowless version of sledding. One can still sometimes see Hawaiian children sliding down grassy slopes seated on clusters of ti leaves with the stems of the plant projecting between their legs and being held in front. I've even tried this ti leaf sliding myself and it is great fun if the slope is grassy enough to be smooth and steep enough to give a fast ride.

The happiest use of ti leaves is in making the *pau*, or grass skirt, which was formerly the common dress of women and is still often worn for hula dancing or pageants, especially when performed by children. I think this green natural skirt far more fitting than the cellophane "grass skirt" affected by some modern hula dancers. The la'i pau is made by braiding the leafstalks together to form a belt and shredding the leaves with the thumbnail. Though it is worn low on the hips, it still only reaches halfway to the knees and it is a very pretty and most provocative garment when worn by a barely nubile little charmer.

In days when the pau was a common dress, it was worn only until it wilted, shrank, or became soiled; then it was discarded, and a new one was made on the spot from the plentiful material that grew all about. Making a new ti leaf skirt was little more work than modern women expend on washing and ironing their soiled summer clothes, and any little girl could have a new dress whenever she wanted one. I wish the custom of wearing the pau as play clothes could be revived, especially for little girls and young women, for no modern fabric blends so beautifully with brown skin and Island backgrounds as does this saucy little green skirt.

While these large glossy leaves with their abundance of chlorophyll are still on the plant, they are veritable factories of food, which is stored in the thickened root in the form of sugar, instead of as starch, as with most tuberous plants. When the roots are dug, washed, and roasted in an underground oven, they are very sweet, with a flavor reminiscent of molasses candy. Most adults do not relish this gooey confection, and the ancient Hawaiians seldom ate roasted ti root except in times of food shortage, but children love its sticky sweetness, and I'm sure it was better for them than the cheap commercial candy that has replaced it.

Before the coming of the white man, the Hawaiians made a mild alcoholic drink by fermenting roasted ti roots in water. According to one tradition, it was a group of escaped convicts from Botany Bay who taught the natives to convert this comparatively harmless drink into potent okolehau by distillation.

The derivation of the name of this strong Hawaiian whisky is interesting. The Hawaiian word *okole* sometimes referred to rounded buttocks, but it was also applied to the rounded bottoms of the calabashes and wooden bowls used in ancient Hawaiian households, so probably it was more nearly the name of a shape than of a thing. When the whalers first came to the Islands they brought huge rounded kettles that were used for trying whale oil, and since the Hawaiian word for iron is *hau*, these were promptly christened *okolehau*. According to the story mentioned above, the escaped convicts made the first still in the Islands by covering one of these large trying kettles and using a gun barrel for a condenser. The Hawaiians, in conformity with their habit of making every word in their language give maximum service, called both the still and the smoking whisky it produced "okolehau," or "iron buttocks."

Since the materials for okolehau cost nothing but the labor of gathering and preparing them, I felt that making this liquor was a legitimate beachcomber activity, and I moonshined enthusiastically, although I required very little okolehau for my own use. We would gather and roast three bushels of the roots, chop them up with a spade, and mix them thoroughly with enough water to fill a 50-gallon barrel. A half-pound of soft yeast was mixed with some of the liquid and added to the mash. After bubbling and fermenting for 10 to 12 days, it would settle down, and then it was ready to be distilled. Each barrel of mash yielded 6 to 8 gallons of okolehau, or as Jim liked to figure it, 48 to 64 pints, which is a lot of whisky when you think of it. The sugar in ti root is not sucrose, but fruit sugar, so okolehau is really a brandy. Its smoky flavor makes it resemble Irish whisky more than it does cognac, but really it tastes like neither.

I usually kept a few bottles of panini swipes at my shack to serve to guests, and I often mixed wine or stronger liquor in the tropical punches I served at parties, but ordinarily I would fill my own glass with natural juices before serving guests alcoholic drinks. I love to use wine in cooking, and I enjoy serving certain wines with certain foods; I even like to taste wines by the teaspoonful, but natural tropical juices are so much more delicious than fermented spirits that I advise you to stay with them for the most part.

Epilogue

I HEAR a thousand voices asking, "Why isn't he back there now, if beachcombing and Island life are all that pleasant?" "Now" is a relative term that changes each time the clock ticks, and by the time you read these words I may very well be off on another tropical adventure, for the truth is that I have never stopped beachcombing. Other islands in other seas are calling to me, but when I heed that call it will be a going-on and not a going-back.

I have no intention of rebuilding my thatched hut on that same Island and attempting to renew my life there. If there is any lesson I have learned from life, it is that one should never attempt to recapture an experience that is past. The pursuit of happiness may be the inalienable right of all men, but happiness is seldom captured by pursuing it, and almost never recaptured.

Never say, "I have found the road to happiness," for happiness is a gypsy, and the same road does not lead twice to her dwelling place. Say rather, "Happiness walked with me on the road I was taking," for happiness walks on many roads. Welcome her as she falls in step beside you, revel in her companionship, but don't attempt to lay permanent hold of her, for she easily slides from the hands that clutch too tightly. As William Blake put it:

> He who binds to himself a joy
> Does the winged life destroy;
> But he who kisses the joy as it flies
> Lives in eternity's sun rise.

If you find that happiness has given you the slip at some fork in the road that you failed to notice, never run back along the path searching for her where you knew her best. A man who tries to re-create a joy that has had its day is likely to find himself embracing a skeleton.

There is another sense, however, in which happiness, once she has shared our path, never deserts us entirely. I am not speaking of those pleasant daydreams of the past in which all of us occasionally indulge, for that is a phony, substitute happiness with little resemblance to the real article. I'm talking about how past experience affects present activities. While sharing a thatched hut with happiness, I learned a way of life that was not based on the conquest of nature or on making her stand and pay tribute, and that way is with me still. I learned to approach nature with love and cooperation. I learned that a life in harmony with nature is a necessity to me. To battle with nature is to war on myself, for I am part of this great mystery and must learn to play my proper role in it. I came to trust nature, during my Hawaiian sojourn, and the bounty of nature, and this faith has led me from one joyful experience to another, and on each new adventure I have had at least a brief rendezvous with happiness.

My beachcombing past intrudes into my satisfying present-time in many pleasant ways. I still gather the wild fruits, nuts, and vegetables that nature freely offers in all areas, and this wild fare is lovingly transformed into gourmet dishes that feed my wild spirit as well as my body.

Recently a reporter, after enjoying a meal in our home in Pennsylvania, at which every dish was made entirely of wild ingredients, wrote of what he called my "secret smile."

Perhaps he is smiling because he has the insight to nourish his primitive streak and the wisdom to find the South Seas in Pennsylvania.

I am not searching for a replica of the Island where I spent three happy years. I skimmed the cream from that experience when I was the right age to enjoy it to the utmost. I'm a little older now, and I probably couldn't run up a palm tree for coconuts and sweet toddy with the same ease and agility that I once displayed. Scaling crumbly volcanic cliffs for strawberry guavas might now prove more work than play. I am no longer so keen on diving under the sea and trying to outwit the spiny lobster and the wily octopus in their own element. My present attitude is summed up by a bit of doggerel I once heard from a taxi driver:

> How do I know that my youth is spent?
> Because my get-up-and-go has got up and went,
> But I still can grin,
> When I think where it's been.

Of course it is only the youthful, strenuously energetic brand of get-up-and-go that has deserted me. A slower-paced, more sedate article is still available, so I have two grins, one for where my youthful energy was expended, and another for wherever that which I still possess intends to go.

Index